Law and Democracy in the Empire of Force

Law and Democracy in the Empire of Force

EDITED BY

H. Jefferson Powell and James Boyd White

THE UNIVERSITY OF MICHIGAN PRESS

Ann Arbor

Published in the United States of America by
The University of Michigan Press
Manufactured in the United States of America
⊗ Printed on acid-free paper

2012 2011 2010 2009 4 3 2 1

A CIP catalog record for this book is available from the British Library.

Library of Congress Cataloging-in-Publication Data

Law and democracy in the empire of force / edited by H. Jefferson Powell and James Boyd White.
p. cm.
Papers presented at a conference held at the University of Michigan Law School, April 13–14, 2007.
Includes bibliographical references.
ISBN-13: 978-0-472-11684-3 (cloth : alk. paper)
ISBN-10: 0-472-11684-3 (cloth : alk. paper)
1. Law—Congresses. 2. Law—United States—Congresses.
I. White, James Boyd, 1938– II. Powell, Jefferson, 1954–
K555.L388 2009
340—dc22 2008048160

Acknowledgments: Jedediah Purdy's essay appears in a different form in his book, *A Tolerable Anarchy* (Knopf, 2009); Howard Lesnick's essay appears in expanded form as "The Rhetoric of Anti-Relativism in a Culture of Certainty," 55 *Buffalo Law Review* 887 (2007); and an extended version of Jed Rubenfeld's essay appears as "The End of Privacy," 61 *Stanford Law Review* 101 (2008). Necessary permissions have been obtained by the authors.

Contents

Introduction

This book has its origin in a sense that is shared by the editors and the authors of this book, all people of the law, that in the past couple of decades our public world has been changing under our feet faster than we can see or understand it, especially with respect to the fundamental character of law and democracy. The changes we speak of show up in judicial opinions, congressional deliberations, executive-branch legal advice, international relations, national politics, the nature of law practice, law teaching, legal scholarship, in fact in virtually every aspect of our professional lives. In each of these fields our expectations are repeatedly thwarted or upset, often in ways that do not seem good.

But prevalent and persistent as they are, these changes are hard to identify, let alone understand. The response we made to this situation was to come together in a conference at the University of Michigan in April 2007. The idea was not that we would give papers of the usual scholarly kind but that each of us would pause and ask ourselves what, of all the things that might be said, most needs to be said at this moment in our history. We encouraged each other to say whatever was actually on our minds, and to say it directly, in whatever form seemed best. Of course different people saw things differently and spoke differently about them. To reflect and express these differences was indeed one point of the conference as it is of this book as well.

The authors of these essays share no set of premises or conclusions, no common program for action. We disagree among ourselves on many issues, both in our underlying moral commitments and about what changes we would like to see in the world of public and political action. What we do share is a belief in the value of living speech, a kind of discussion and debate that works by the candid expression of the speakers' minds and hearts. It would be a shallow optimism that assumed such discussions would lead inexorably to agreement. But we believe that it is only through such discussion, such speech, that a humane and democratic society can have its life.

Our hope is that in this book these distinct voices, talking openly and authentically about different aspects of the cultural and political transformation in the midst of which we find ourselves, will define a topic of thought and concern of interest to others. At the same time we hope it will demonstrate a way of addressing this topic, through collective conversation—both the conversation reflected in the pages of this book and the conversation we hope to stimulate between this book and its readers, and among its readers as well. We hope, that is, that the reader can read these essays as if he were going to contribute one of his own, and, with such a cast of mind, think about what his own perceptions are of the changes taking place in law and democracy; ask himself how he would speak about them; imagine how he would hope others might respond; and so on.

Each of the essays focuses on a different issue, or set of issues, and each of course expresses the perceptions and judgments of an individual mind and person. As one might expect, many of the essays reflect what is seen as a decline or degeneration in our legal and political culture. But it is also true that each in its own way articulates a way of proceeding on these conditions—a ground of hope, in fact. We hope that the book as a whole does this too.

The phrase in our title, "the empire of force," comes from Simone Weil's famous essay on the *Iliad,* where she uses it to mean not only brute force of the kind sometimes employed by policemen and soldiers but, more deeply, the ways of thinking and talking and imagining that make that sort of brute force possible: propaganda, advertising, politics by buzzword and cliché, and so on. In this essay she does not give these words any fixed conceptual meaning but uses them to point to the forces, both internal and external, that move us to deny the full humanity of other people and to trivialize or devalue their experience.

We have used the phrase in a similarly open way, both in our invitation to the conference and in the title to this book, not with the idea that it had an established meaning or with the aim that these essays would collectively achieve such a definition. Rather, we used it first as a way of asking a question of the speakers at the conference, and use it now as a way of asking the same question of the reader of this book: Do you have the sense that our world, especially the part of it associated with law and democracy, has become increasingly subject to the forces of dehumanization? If so, how can you—and we—begin to define and think about what those forces are and how they might be exposed and resisted? To do this is especially difficult because these forces are likely to operate not in an obvious way that makes us aware and conscious of them but somehow beneath the surface of our experience, masked by their very familiarity. In asking these questions we are thus trying to draw attention to the fact that evil can be normalized to the point that it is no longer seen; and we are asking each other, and now the reader too, whether that is what is happening in our own lives, especially in our own public culture.

Of course the answer to these questions, in writer or reader, may be "no." This answer can be given either after considerable thought and reflection or as a gesture rejecting the inquiry in the first place. In putting together this book we, and the other authors, are encouraging people not to adopt the course of outright rejection, for we think the questions are serious and important. On the other hand, we acknowledge that many different responses to them can be appropriate and wise, and in speaking for the authors of the book as a whole we do not urge the rightness of any particular perception or judgment. Quite the contrary. We think it a merit of this collection of essays that there are so many differences among them: in definition of issue, in style of thought and expression, in ethical and political orientation, and so forth. They are the matured work of individual minds.

We think that what we most hoped for has come to pass: namely, that the essays have a kind of deep authenticity, expressing what the writers actually think in the language in which they think it. This means that all our key terms—*law, democracy, empire of force* prominent among them—are defined and redefined in these performances, and this is as it should be.

As we suggested earlier, the idea of the book is to place the reader in a position like that of the contributors, asking him or her, What do you perceive to be changing in our world, especially in connection with law and democracy, and what do you think and feel about it? Our hope is that these essays will provide encouragements to thought on these matters; examples of certain kinds of responses, some of which will naturally be more congenial than others to particular readers; and something of an array of possibilities with respect to which the reader can locate his or her own position as it is worked out.

Jedediah Purdy, who teaches law at Duke University, approaches the character of our present political discourse by the analysis of a form that by its nature tends to capture assumptions that are widely shared in the polity, namely the presidential inaugural address. In doing this he articulates features in our discourse that are deeply troubling, especially a kind of thinness and insincerity that makes it hard to use this language for anything deep and important. Yet he sees perhaps surprisingly hopeful possibilities as well.

M. Cathleen Kaveny, who teaches law and theology at the University of Notre Dame, addresses a structural feature of our political discourse, namely, that sometimes it takes the form she calls "prophecy," sometimes "casuistical reasoning." Each of these genres is appropriate to some occasions and inappropriate to others. It is crucial that they be used properly, in ways that do not silence voices that ought to be heard or stifle conversations that ought to take place.

Robin West, who teaches law at Georgetown University, focuses on the ways in which lawyers and judges tend to imagine the Constitution, namely, as a way of creating occasions for the activity of adjudication, which is for them (or us) the primary way in which that document is given meaning. For her this is to erase from consciousness the political process that the Constitution makes possible, in which it can be given meaning in a more direct and vivid way. Indeed, it is to erase the People themselves.

Martin Böhmer, dean of the law school at the Universidad de San Andres in Buenos Aires, asks why it is that Argentina has had such a difficult time establishing a rule of law. His analysis of Argentine culture, including folk songs and high literature as well as political history, suggests an answer deep in the history and psyche of its people; more than that, it suggests how more recent events may promise a better future.

Howard Lesnick, who teaches law at the University of Pennsylvania, addresses a particular move in the public rhetoric of our day, one that occurs when a person dismisses what his opponent says with a label, such as *relativism,* the real function of which is to claim that the speaker need not respond to what his opponent has said on its merits. This move corrupts the process of debate in a way that promotes mindlessness and erases the claims and experiences of others. Lesnick shows how this move can be both understood and resisted.

Joseph Vining, who teaches law at the University of Michigan, analyzes the ways in which legal thought itself has been distorted or deformed by an insistence that it proceed on the premises of social science. These premises tend to erase from the discourse the human person present in law, the human voice, and human hope. Yet Vining claims that even under these conditions law retains a vitality that resists these deformations, upon which we can found realistic hopes both for law itself and for democracy.

Barry Sullivan, formerly dean at Washington and Lee University and now practicing law in Chicago, addresses changes in the genre of the judicial opinion, which is essential to our law, especially to constitutional law. By analyzing two opinions with care, he shows what some of these changes are and suggests how they might be resisted.

Jed Rubenfeld, who teaches law at Yale University, analyzes what he regards as a collapse in the law of the Fourth Amendment: namely, the reduction of what it protects, and protects against, to a language of "privacy." He proposes a different way of thinking about the Fourth Amendment, one that promises to renew its political and legal force as a protector of values essential to democracy.

A. W. Brian Simpson, who teaches law at the University of Michigan, draws upon his experience in the United Kingdom to analyze the new legal form of social control there called Anti-Social Behaviour Orders. These efforts to control loutish behavior in public places erase the protections and limits of traditional common law, introducing into the law a way of thinking that threatens conditions essential to liberty under law and to democracy as well.

John T. Noonan Jr., a judge on the Ninth Circuit Court of Appeals, speaks about the process of adjudication from the inside, as one who himself has to make the crucial decisions. He identifies three common situations in which there is deep tension between the formal role of the judge and his or her conscience. In doing so, he offers a model of public thought that resists the trivialization and dehumanization of the judge, the litigants, and the judicial process itself.

H. Jefferson Powell, who teaches law and theology at Duke University, describes the respect that lawyers and officials in the executive branch were, as a matter of ethics in government, traditionally obliged to show to the constitutional and legal judgments of the other branches. This tradition has recently degenerated into a view that sees the judgments of others, and law itself, simply as a set of obstacles or restraints, not as a source of genuine authority. The question he asks is whether that tradition can be revived, perhaps in a new form.

James Boyd White, professor emeritus of law and English at the University of Michigan, addresses what he sees as three major changes in our world: the acceptance by poor and middle-income people of vast transfers of wealth to the rich; the decline in the quality and character of legal thought, as exhibited both in Supreme Court opinions and in the life of law schools; and the acceptance of torture, faintly disguised as "severe interrogation," as an activity of our government. These three phenomena are in his view connected, and are to be resisted by a fresh understanding of the nature and value of law.

Languages of Politics in America

Jedediah Purdy

How do Americans imagine themselves and their government? What past, what future do they create for themselves, driven by what values and hopes and fears, shaped by what conception of themselves? Such are the questions Jedediah Purdy pursues in this essay. His investigation is necessarily historical, for these questions would be answered differently at different times in our history; it is also in one sense political, for it is often the case that the struggle between parties, or candidates, is about the right way to imagine ourselves.

In his exploration of the transformations that our language of politics has undergone Purdy makes use of many pieces of evidence, but focuses especially upon the form we know as the presidential inaugural address, the moment at which the newly elected president seeks to articulate a vision that will command widespread assent, including among his political opponents. The sequence he traces, from Jefferson and Lincoln through Wilson, Roosevelt, Johnson, Reagan, Clinton, and the two Bushes, defines our present situation as what Purdy calls a tepid consensus, the exhaustion of political language. The question he presents and begins to answer is how our language of politics might properly be given new life, direction, and shape. He begins by sketching our recent history and present situation, topics to which he returns at the end.

It may seem natural to dismiss presidential inaugural addresses as pabulum and vague uplift. One sounds a lot like the next, and none sounds much like the way we talk when we know what we mean to say and trust that the listener can hear it. These presidential speeches feel exhausted, congested, trapped in language that sounds more like a worn-out ceremony than like a living stream of words. This dismissal is not just a cynical mistake: there is a lot of truth in it. It has not always been that way, though. Of course, presidential speeches have always been calculated and in some ways artificial.

They have never used the language of everyday life. But the kind of artificiality they convey today is special, and understanding it is a way to get at the exhaustion of political language in general. It is also a way to see what would have to change for political language to be more alive than it is now—and how difficult that change might be.

The inaugural address falls in a pivotal moment. Now that the energy and animus of the campaign have begun to drain away, the president has to take on a different kind of persuasion: not reinforcing the loyalty of his supporters, but showing voters who lost, who may have spent the campaign season mistrusting and disdaining him, why he deserves a share of their loyalty, too. Presidents have always marked the day as a turn from partisan to national identity, since Jefferson declared at the end of a bitter campaign, "We are all Republicans, we are all Federalists." Moreover, since that first address of Jefferson's, new presidents have treated the inaugural as a time to set out their interpretation of the American constitutional community.

Woodrow Wilson gave this custom a new democratic inflection in 1913, describing himself as interpreter in chief of the electoral tumult that had put him in the White House. Using a new term to describe what he would do in the address, he offered "to interpret the occasion" and argued that the Democratic victory was important beyond the sake of the party, because "the Nation . . . now seeks to use the Democratic Party . . . to interpret a change in its own plans and point of view." This imagery added something essential to the president's role. Earlier presidents had cast themselves foremost as bearers of constitutional principle, not wholly unlike the justices of the Supreme Court. Wilson's new chord was more romantic and visionary. The president was to try to give a voice, a coherent aim and attitude, to the diverse and inchoate motives that had swept him to power. He was now a kind of democratic oracle, tasked with expressing not just the ground rules of constitutional community but its emotional—even sensual—quality and the people's active power to redefine their political life through action.

Inaugural language has always addressed the theme of dignity: what gives a citizen a place to stand and esteem in his or her own eyes and those of others, and how does the political order help make this dignity real? This question is nested within a more general one: what gives an individual life its value? It also contains a more specific question: what is the role of the state, the institutional expression of political power, in relation to the value and dignity of life?

THE TEPID CONSENSUS

For nearly twenty years, since the election of George H. W. Bush in 1988, the main themes of American political language have not been political at all. Instead, they have concentrated on private virtue, the personal qualities that uphold good families, workplaces, and civic organizations. Although there is precedent for this kind of talk, it is new in important ways. Its central ideas—character, responsibility, and service—have never before figured so prominently or in such apolitical ways as they do now.

The major landmarks in this consensus, the two inaugural addresses each of Bill Clinton and George W. Bush, took place in decades of political animosity. Partisans on both sides learned to disdain the other party's president as a moral or intellectual degenerate and to suspect his adamant supporters of being not fully American—or, maybe, the wrong kind of American. But imagine you were to read both presidents' addresses as a visitor from another century, unfamiliar with local partisan cues, such as Republicans' propensity to mention charter schools in a positive light while Democrats keep silent because of their debt to teachers' unions. You would notice a difference in the frequency of religious language: God figures in the critical moments of Clinton's speeches and throughout Bush's. Of course, Bush's second inaugural includes a great deal of war talk. Otherwise, you would probably get the impression of a profound moral consensus, where the same terms and ideas anchor both parties' rhetoric. You might also suspect that you had come across a political culture whose members had no idea what their political life was for—none, anyway, that they could take seriously themselves.

Recent presidential language takes its shape around a few landmarks. *Responsibility* is a touchstone word for both Clinton and Bush. In his first inaugural, Clinton defined "what America does best: offer more opportunity to all and demand more responsibility from all." It was time, he said, "to break the bad habit of expecting something for nothing, from our government or from each other," and time to "all take more responsibility, not only for ourselves and our families but for our communities and our country." Four years later, he announced that "we need a new sense of responsibility for a new century" and, again, that "every one of us, in our own way, must assume personal responsibility, not only for ourselves and our families, but for our neighbors and our nation." George W. Bush dedicated his 2000 nomination address to the theme of responsibility, urging a "responsibility era." In his first inaugural, he called America "at its best . . . a place where personal responsibility is valued and expected." He celebrated responsibility as "a call to conscience" that, although "it requires sacrifice," brings us into "the fullness of life not only in options but in commitments."

Service, too, is a central term in both presidents' language. In his first inaugural, Clinton challenged "a new generation of young Americans to a season of service," called "serving" the key to the "simple but powerful truth" that "we need each other," and declared, "From this joyful mountaintop of celebration, we hear a call to service in the valley." In 2001, explaining that "what you do is as important as anything government does," Bush urged citizens "to serve your nation, beginning with your neighbor," and to build "communities of service and a nation of character." *Character* is another defining word in this lexicon. In an alliterative catalogue of personal virtues, Bush's 2001 speech called for "a new commitment to live out our nation's promise through civility, courage, compassion and character." Four years later, he explained, "In America's ideal of freedom, the public interest depends on private character—on integrity, and tolerance toward others, and the rule of conscience in our own lives. Self-government relies, in the end, on the governing of the self. That edifice of character is built in families, supported by communities with standards, and sustained in our national life by the truths of Sinai, the Sermon on the Mount, the words of the Koran, and the varied faiths of our people." Clinton did not rely in the same way on the word *character,* but he did declare in 1997, "The greatest progress we have made, and the greatest progress we have yet to make, is in the human heart. In the end, all the world's wealth and a thousand armies are no match for the strength and decency of the human spirit."

This constellation of virtues is at once personal, residing in individuals, and interpersonal, essentially concerning their ties with others. Interdependence is the key moral insight for both presidents and unites their language across partisan differences. While Clinton announced the "simple but powerful truth" that "we need each other" and "we must care for one another," Bush explained that "the exercise of rights is ennobled by service" because "liberty for all does not mean independence from one another." In keeping with this emphasis, this political language also leans heavily on *community* and *communities,* not merely as descriptive words, but as moral terms for groups of people who recognize their responsibility of service to one another. *Character,* similarly, is employed not to describe good, bad, or merely quirky personality but as a moral word for the qualities of responsibility and service that make such communities possible.

These personal and social virtues are good and important. But such undeniable values are not the basis of an idea of political community. Rather, they are a substitute for it, a confection of irresistible facts about human beings in general that is very little help in thinking about human beings in a political community—at least, in this political community.

One of the first things to appreciate about this political vocabulary is how new it is. To be sure, George Washington held that a country's political institutions depend ultimately on the virtue of its people, but for roughly the first two centuries of American independence, political language concentrated on specifically political ideas. *Character* was a description of personality or outlook, not a moral term, and *virtue,* its obvious cognate, tended to mean such political virtues as love of liberty and respect for rule of law. *Responsibility* and *service* overwhelmingly referred to the duties of public office, usually the presidency itself. The language of sacrifice and dedication, famously associated with John F. Kennedy's inaugural call to "ask what you can do for your country," was reserved for wartime and the geopolitical struggle of the cold war, which was how both Kennedy and Dwight Eisenhower used it. (Kennedy's famous sentence was a bridge in a series of exhortations to advance the cause of American freedom around the world.) Before the cold war, such language was mostly absent even from wartime inaugurals: presidents did not dwell on the grim prospect of sacrifice in the speeches intended to define national community. Even Lincoln's Gettysburg Address is a call not to sacrifice—the melancholy and humane president was out of appetite for that, if he had ever had any—but to political hope in sacrifice's aftermath. *Community* was a neutral noun rather than a moral concept; it designated communities of interest, political jurisdictions, and the international community of civilized nations.

Private virtue began to occupy the center of political language only with Richard Nixon. Nixon's inaugurals form a kind of bridge between the old, political register of virtue and the new, private register. Nixon first used *responsibility* in its private sense, arguing in 1969 that national greatness rested above all on "those small, splendid efforts that make headlines in the neighborhood newspaper instead of the national journal." Pressing the theme further in 1973, he urged the country to turn away from "attempting to gather all power and responsibility in Washington. Instead, he insisted, "A person can be expected to act responsibly only if he has responsibility. . . . Let us locate responsibility in more places. Let us measure what we will do for others by what they will do for themselves. . . . Let us remember that America was built not by government, but by people—not by welfare, but by work—not by shirking responsibility, but by seeking responsibility."

The way Nixon introduced the theme is a second key to understanding our present political language. Private virtue, particularly responsibility, was the counterpoint to Washington and "government." Responsibility filled the void that opened up when the ambitions of government receded. It was a major theme of both of Nixon's inaugurals, especially the second, that Americans had asked too much of government and not enough of one another and themselves. Characteristically, he managed to sound small-spirited as he self-consciously echoed Kennedy: "let each of us ask—not just what will government do for me, but what can I do for myself?" Nonetheless, he pioneered a formula that pervades today's political speech. Clinton's language of service and responsibility was a way of working out the idea that government, while not the source of all problems, "is not the solution." "We, the American people," he argued, "we are the solution." Clinton's insistence on the limits of government was louder than Bush's, perhaps because he was pressing against the stereotype of the big-government liberal, while Bush does not labor under that shadow. The exile of government from civic identity, which Nixon set in motion, is nearly complete in Bush's speeches.

This highlights the third key to understanding our political language. It is not just that private virtue is now honored as a necessary strut of a working public life. Instead, the most important part of political language, connecting government and public life to people's sense of life's meaning and purpose, now relies almost entirely on a vision of private and social virtues. In this vision, circles of concern work outward, through affection and interdependence, from the family through church, friendship, and other concrete forms of moral community. Participation in these relationships is the civic and moral dimension of the personal life that the language of private virtue expresses. The only political quality about this language is that the speaker occupies the country's most powerful and visible political office. This language speaks to people as complex animals, moral and social beings, but not as citizens, unless *citizen* means simply a person who is aware of the interdependence that social life brings and takes it seriously.

It may be a symptom of exhausted political language when intense partisan hostility sits alongside large agreement about the moral vision of politics. This is even more so when political language sets out the inferiority of political acts and values to personal ones. This language is certainly truthful in one important respect. Americans today mostly feel that the best and highest goods in life come through family, friendship, spiritual development, and other parts of personal experience. We do not tend to believe that a thing is ennobled because it is collective, touched by state power or a partisan movement, or otherwise political. We like our values concrete, embodied in our own experience and in people that we can see and touch and name.

This political language is remarkable for its remoteness from distinctly political questions, those about the purposes and limits of the unique power of the state. How did we come so far from those? The answer involves the whole story of American political language, from the earliest efforts to describe the connection of political community to individual dignity through a long, hard struggle to redefine that connection for the complex economy and hugely expanded government of the twentieth century. In important ways, the leading figures of American politics abandoned that struggle in the 1970s and, especially, the 1980s. We are living in the remnants of a collapsed rhetorical tradition. Our intensely personal language of political community, composed in the absence of political vision, is what we have left.

FREEDOM AND DIGNITY IN NINETEENTH-CENTURY AMERICA

In his first inaugural, Thomas Jefferson described Americans as "possessing a chosen country, with room enough for our descendants to the thousandth and thousandth generation." By *chosen,* he meant not that the country was divinely ordained but that Americans had chosen their country by coming to North America and creating a nation out of revolution and constitutional politics. They had conquered, occupied, and shaped a continent of plenty, where westward expansion would enable them to inhabit free, self-governing communities into the indefinite future. There would be no need for the hierarchy and dependence of feudal orders, where men, crowded together in old countries, won their wealth and freedom from the subjection of others. Nor would North Americans suffer the chaos and predation of cities, those crucibles of dependence and exploitation. The chosen country was ample, and every American could have a life worth living there.

In such a country, the role of government was clear and modest. Jefferson continued, "A wise and frugal government . . . shall restrain men from injuring one another, shall leave them otherwise free to regulate their own pursuits of industry and improvement, and shall not take from the mouth of labor the bread it has earned. This is the sum of good government, and this is necessary to close the circle of our felicities." Jefferson envisioned a government of what we would call negative liberties, securing citizens from violence and theft and otherwise leaving them free to organize their own lives. His embrace of negative liberty arose from a vision of the positive powers of individuals to engage in "industry and improvement" to "regulate their own pursuits" without impeding one another's freedom, as well as to make a good living by labor. This version of negative liberty began not in abstract principles but in a picture of the social lives of Americans in a continent of plenty. It contained principles for a nation of the upright and strong, able to take advantage of economic opportunity and use reason, judgment, and energy to give their lives the shapes they wanted. The dignity of such Americans lay in their powers of free action and self-mastery. Threats to their dignity came mainly from government itself: censorship of opinion, excessive taxation, improper arrest and prosecution, or failure to administer what Jefferson called "equal and exact justice."

In this vision, the American political community, unlike the feudal orders of old countries, honored each (white, male, property-holding) citizen as master of his own life, standing foursquare with all others. This was an important part of what Jefferson and his contemporaries meant when they called the United States "republican." A second meaning of that term—and another source of citizen dignity—was the idea that each American had an equal part in the sovereignty of the United States, the body of political power. The idea that power flowed from the whole political community to the government, which held it in "trust," as Jefferson put it, was central to American political language in the nineteenth century. American rhetoricians contrasted this republican idea of sovereignty with the monarchical vision of political power as descending from the king. So Franklin Pierce held that any American citizen could "stand unabashed even in the presence of princes, with a proud consciousness that he is himself one of a nation of sovereigns." Defending the principle of universal male suffrage even for uneducated former slaves, Rutherford Hayes put the contrast even more starkly: "If in other lands it is high treason to compass the death of the king, it shall be counted no less a crime here to strangle our sovereign power and stifle its voice." In this image, the least able and most scorned citizen had the same sovereign dignity as European royalty. In many domains, a racist and recently slaveholding society would impose hierarchy among its people, but in the American ideal of sovereignty, each citizen contributed to the shape of the nation.

These ideas had profound affinities with the social vision that became the unofficial ideology of the Northern states before the Civil War and, in the aftermath, formed the centerpiece of American identity. This was the idea of free labor: that American freedom rested on the power to choose and pursue a career, acquire property, and trade one's time and talent for whatever pay they could command. It was an ideal of individual self-mastery linked to a vision of social mobility, in which nearly everyone—following Jefferson's picture of life in a plentiful and chosen country—would end up as a prosperous property holder. Ralph Waldo Emerson sketched the life course of free labor in his essay "Self-Reliance," where he praised the "sturdy lad from New Hampshire or Vermont, who in turn tries all the professions, who teams it, farms it, peddles, keeps a school, preaches, edits a newspaper, goes to Congress, buys a township, and so forth, in successive years." It is impossible to miss either the ideal of self-mastery in this sketch, one of the most concrete passages in Emerson's paean to "self-trust," or the expectation of plenty: a township is waiting for a purchaser. This ideal carried a demanding, sometimes merciless counterpart: those who fail must deserve it. The largehearted Abraham Lincoln, in the course of defending free labor as a principle of equal dignity appropriate to democratic citizens, paused to assert, "If any continue through life in the condition of the hired laborer [rather than become a proprietor], it is not the fault of the system, but because of either a dependent nature which prefers it, or improvidence, folly, or singular misfortune." In this version, American dignity implied a certain vulnerability, even culpability: if you could not pull off success, the failure was all yours.

There was always a big element of myth in the worldview of free labor, but there was reality, too, in the plentiful opportunity of a continent cleared for settlement in a substantially agricultural economy. The late nineteenth century brought the closing of the frontier. An industrial economy moved production from farms and workshops, which laborers could hope to acquire for themselves, to factories, which they could not. The national economy overwhelmed local markets and produced engorged semimonopolist trusts, which effectively regulated their industries in their own favor. In the face of these realities, espousing free labor came to seem more complacent than dignifying. The most famous expression of this decrepit period is, of course, the Supreme Court's notorious opinion in *Lochner v. New York,* holding that a labor law establishing maximum weekly hours for bakers violated workers' freedom to contract for whatever terms they liked. The real consequence of that principle, if pursued to a consistent conclusion, would have been that workers and other less powerful groups could not resort to politics to change the balance of economic power. Outside the courts, that was exactly the note Grover Cleveland sounded in the Gilded Age at the end of the nineteenth century, denouncing such political efforts as "paternalism." That attitude, he claimed, was "the bane of republican institutions": "It perverts the patriotic sentiments of our countrymen and tempts them to pitiful calculation of . . . sordid gains. It undermines the self-reliance of our people and substitutes in its place dependence upon governmental favoritism. It . . . stupefies every ennobling trait of American citizenship." Cleveland argued that "while the people should patriotically and cheerfully support their Government, its functions do not include the support of the people." When laws for minimum wage and maximum hours could be styled the antithesis of American dignity and when a sometimes brutal industrial economy could be equated with the open frontier of Jefferson's vision, free labor was close to becoming an exhausted political language.

Whatever the experience of earlier generations had actually been, workers, small farmers, and some small businessmen began to feel that they were not masters of their own destinies but playthings of complex systems that they could only partly understand, let alone change. At least among elites, changing ideas also helped to challenge the individualism of free labor. A generation of economists and students of politics returned from the German universities with images of a nation as an organic whole, in which the national spirit or character must be deeply entwined with both political and economic institutions. They tended to deplore the political economy of free labor as illusory atomism, a false image of society as an assembly of "sovereigns" rather than the complex superorganism it really was.

THE PROGRESSIVE SEARCH FOR DIGNITY

Both strands of discontent with the language of free labor reached the center of national politics with the presidencies of Teddy Roosevelt and Woodrow Wilson. The first presidents deeply influenced by the Progressive movement, they believed that government must be large and vigorous enough to control private economic power in the interest of the vulnerable. In a critical respect, their vision of the nation was nearly opposite the image of individual self-mastery that had animated free labor. In its place, they portrayed Americans as profoundly vulnerable to economic and social forces beyond their control, which only government could discipline. The failure that Lincoln attributed to "dependent character" or "singular misfortune" was now the ordinary possibility that haunted everyone. What Cleveland had denounced as "paternalism" the enemy of American dignity, Wilson redefined as the moral justification of government. In 1913, Wilson set out the ways Americans had failed to take account of a changing world. With such ideas as Cleveland's squarely in his sights, Wilson lamented that the country had not "studied and perfected the means by which government may be put at the service of humanity, in safeguarding the health of the Nation, the health of its men and its women and its children, as well as their rights in the struggle for existence." Those "rights" were the negative liberties of free labor. Wilson added to them an almost parental duty for the state to succor to the needy and fragile bodies of its people. He continued, "There can be no equality of opportunity, the first essential of justice in the body politic, if men and women and children be not shielded in their lives, their very vitality, from the consequences of great industrial and social processes which they cannot alter, control, or singly cope with."

This was new language in two ways. It was the first explicit appearance of women and children in an inaugural address. That change expanded the circle of citizens whom the president addressed, to include not just adult men but the whole social body. Wilson's address was also the first portrayal of Americans in the terms the Progressives had pioneered: as limited in their powers of self-mastery and small before vast "industrial and social processes" that would overpower them if the state did not intervene. Wilson took an image of the citizen as a man mastering his own fate and replaced it with an image of human beings of all sexes and ages who were often mastered by the impersonal fates of a complex economy. The same imagery persisted through much of the twentieth century. In 1937, Franklin Roosevelt announced the following purpose for government: "to solve for the individual the ever-rising problems of a complex civilization," problems that "without the aid of government had left us baffled and bewildered," the victims of "blind economic forces and blindly selfish men." Almost thirty years later, Lyndon Johnson cautioned that the American ideal of "a place where each man could be proud to be himself . . . , rejoicing in his work, important in the life of his neighbors and his nation," had "become more difficult in a world where change and growth seem to tower beyond the control and even the judgment of men." The world was too much with us and perhaps too much for us.

The change brought a problem. How did the new description of the vulnerable individual watched over by a powerful state connect with any feeling of personal dignity? Having set aside the mythic imagery of free labor, what could Progressives offer in its place? Presidents attempted several answers in the twentieth century. One approach was to present the nation as a single personality that had fallen into confusion or failed to realize its full potential but was now reaching a new wholeness that would bring moral as well as material greatness. Citizens were supposed to be elevated just by being parts of this improving whole. Wilson portrayed this national personality as holding "a vision . . . vouchsafed us of our life as a whole." He portrayed the self-confident individualism of free labor as a period of callowness and callousness, pointing out "something crude and heartless in our haste to succeed and be great." The new aim would be to overcome these deficiencies, "to cleanse, to reconsider, to restore, to correct the evil without impairing the good, to purify and humanize every process of our common life without weakening or sentimentalizing it." This was the moral purpose that Wilson called "no mere task of politics but a task which shall search us through and through," not a question of power or practical capacity alone, but a challenge at the level of identity. In his second inaugural, in 1917, Wilson pressed this image further, calling authenticity the standard for the country's self-transformation through politics: "The shadows that now lie dark upon our path will soon be dispelled, and we shall walk with the light all about us if we be but true to ourselves—to ourselves as we have wished to be known in the counsels of the world and in the thought of all those who love liberty and justice and the right exalted." In this picture, a nation has not just a character but a true character, which it can fall away from and reattain, and which remains true even when the nation fails to express it. Belonging to a nation that is both moral and true to itself ennobles citizens in a direct way. The quality of America's common life, imagined as a shared moral personality, figures here as a source of meaning and purpose in the lives of individuals.

Another way of talking about the dignity of citizens was the language of mobilization, in which social reform became what William James called "the moral equivalent of war." In this imagery, collective action brought clear purposes and dramatic effect, more charismatic than the scattered acts of individuals. Wilson's language of national vision and insight had portrayed the nation as a single mind and spirit, able to mature and become more authentic. The language of mobilization drew the country as a single body composed of millions of parts, each contributing to the power and discipline of the whole. Interestingly, such images did not appear during or after the Civil War. Lincoln's spirit was profoundly nonmartial, and in major speeches, he chose to portray war as tragedy, not heroism, and ascribed final agency in the North's victory to God's inscrutable will as much as to the efforts of Union soldiers. Only after the country's second experience of warfare involving mass mobilization, in World War I, did presidents begin to envision Americans in peacetime as an army on the march. It was Warren Harding, speaking well after the armistice but seeming to savor his vision of another war, who first spoke of combat's power to "unify our collective and individual strength and consecrate all America, . . . , body and soul, to national defense . . . , all in the sublime sacrifice for country."

Franklin Roosevelt picked up this strand of language in his 1933 inaugural, well before real war returned to American consciousness. In the worst period of the Great Depression, Roosevelt announced,

> If we are to go forward, we must move as a trained and loyal army, willing to sacrifice for the good of a common discipline, because without such discipline no progress is made, no leadership becomes effective. We are, I know, ready and willing to submit our lives and property to such discipline, because it makes possible a leadership which aims at a larger good. This I propose to offer, pledging that the larger purposes will bind upon us all as a sacred obligation with a duty hitherto evoked only in time of armed strife. With this pledge taken, I assume unhesitatingly the leadership of this great army of our people dedicated to a disciplined attack upon our common problems.

The image of war was the key to the psychological appeal that mobilization offered. Roosevelt promised his listeners "the warm courage of the national unity," "clear consciousness of seeking old and precious moral values," and "clean satisfaction that comes from the stern performance of duty by old and young alike." This lucid, vigorous, effective action, undertaken by the people as a whole, was what Roosevelt called "the future of essential democracy." It required a leader to provide voice and coherence. Thus Roosevelt argued that the American people proved their democratic vitality when they "asked for discipline and direction under leadership" and "made me the present instrument of their wishes." Roosevelt evoked a country ready to "submit our lives and property" to the "discipline" of his leadership.

This collectivist image was not Roosevelt's only vision. His more lasting contribution was the effort to find new, twentieth-century expression for the dignity of nineteenth-century individualism. Addressing the Commonwealth Club in San Francisco, Roosevelt identified two timeless American rights: free conscience and judgment, on the one hand, and protection of property, on the other. He described the first as unchanged since the time of Jefferson, whom Roosevelt invoked as his model. The second, however, had changed in the industrial era. The point of property rights, Roosevelt said, was to enjoy personal security, which included assurance against starvation, sickness, and old age, as well as a place to stand in the world without abject dependence on others (which made a master of one man and a slave of the other). In the twentieth century, that security was not as simple as it had (allegedly) been on the frontier. Roosevelt referred to "the highly centralized economic system" as "the despot of the twentieth century, on whom great masses of individuals relied for their safety and their livelihood, and whose irresponsibility and greed (if it were not controlled) would reduce them to starvation and penury." Just as arbitrary political authority, feudal prerogative, and enslavement had once denied men security in their property, now an economic system built out of property rights paradoxically did the same. The only solution was to limit the power of wealthy interests and provide new kinds of economic security and opportunity to ordinary people. That, however, was not an anti-individualist position: it was only a way of doing for self-reliance in the industrial era what simpler property rights had done for it in the agrarian age. Americans needed "a more permanently safe order of things . . . not to hamper individualism, but to protect it."

DEEPENING CIVILIAN DIGNITY

Lyndon Johnson picked up and refined two notes that earlier Progressive presidents had sounded, but he found ways to connect them with personal experience in more concrete and plausible fashion. First, in describing the purposes of "the Great Society," he moved Roosevelt's image of broad mobilization back to the level of individual mastery. He declared in 1965, "I do not believe that the Great Society is the ordered, changeless, and sterile battalion of the ants. It is the excitement of becoming—always becoming, trying, probing, falling, resting, and trying again—but always trying and always gaining." Johnson was echoing Roosevelt, who had described the founding spirit of the United States as the power to begin the world again in one's own life, to "create upon this continent a new life—a life that should be new in freedom." But Johnson, more than Roosevelt, portrayed this same urge as the signal quality of his contemporaries, the citizens he addressed. In an address dedicated to setting out the idea of the Great Society, he portrayed a humanist paradise, "where leisure is a welcome chance to rebuild and reflect, not a feared cause of boredom and restlessness," and "where the city of man serves not only the needs of the body and the demands of commerce, but the desire for beauty and the hunger for community." He evoked a country without poverty or racial injustice, but also one "where the meaning of our lives matches the marvelous products of our labor." The call to substitute meaningful activity for "soulless wealth" was familiar from Roosevelt and even Wilson, and the image of "becoming" was Roosevelt's as well, but the register had moved, subtly but unmistakably, to individual activity. In this respect, Johnson's language came closer than earlier versions to integrating the original American impulse of individual freedom and dignity with the Progressive vision of a strong state in a complex society.

Johnson's other major advance on the Progressive inheritance was his treatment of race. This was his occasion to pick up Wilson's language of national "vision" and Franklin Roosevelt's "spirit." Johnson placed these ways of identifying morally with the nation in the charged, personal, and everyday experience of racial division. In a special address to Congress on the 1965 Voting Rights Act, he asked, "How many white lives have been scarred by fear, because we wasted energy and our substance to maintain the barriers of hatred and terror?" In asking this question, Johnson aligned himself with the "I have a dream" speech of Martin Luther King Jr., in which the civil rights leader praised whites who "have come to realize that their destiny is tied up with our destiny and their freedom is inextricably bound to our freedom." Like Wilson and Roosevelt, Johnson proposed to connect individuals with a moral vision of national community. He evoked this experience of connection more concretely, by referring to personal diminishment and degradation in a society of fearful and resentful hierarchy and to personal enlargement and grace in a society of openness and mutual respect. Whereas Wilson began the modern language of citizens' moral identification with the nation on a nearly mystical tone, and Roosevelt carried it into the ominous terrain of military mobilization, Johnson kept it concrete and savingly individual.

ROLLBACK AND RENEWAL

All these forms of political language were attempts to make sense of national community—and particularly to define the role of government—in a complex economy with a large state. Each of these presidents tried to avoid the specter that haunted Wilson's first inaugural and the whole Progressive view of society: the image of women and men as flotsam on the seas of economic change, passive objects of the state's solicitude, lacking the mastery that had always been the touchstone of American dignity. Sometimes presidents tried to adapt the old tradition of dignity to new circumstances, recasting mastery as Roosevelt's mobilization or Johnson's "becoming." At other times, they offered new registers of dignity, such as Wilson's identification with the moral growth of the nation and Johnson's image of integration as not just a demographic change but a moral and emotional reunion of parts that history had split apart.

It was inevitably tempting to reject this excursion in political language and instead reassert old, familiar ideas: that men and women were naturally the masters of their own lives, that government was usually a threat to that mastery, and that there was no need for a new way to put together personal dignity with citizenship. Such skepticism persisted through the high-water period of the New Deal, of course, but Richard Nixon returned it to presidential language. Ronald Reagan then brought force and clarity to the themes, reasserting the nineteenth-century idea of civic dignity and rejecting outright the whole vision of government and society that Teddy Roosevelt and Wilson had introduced.

In his first inaugural, Reagan rejected wholesale the twentieth-century idea that a modern vision of freedom required a place for strong government. He declared, "From time to time, we have been tempted to believe that society has become too complex to be managed by self-rule, that government by an elite group is superior to government for, by, and of the people." This "temptation" was the doctrine of presidents from Wilson to Johnson, which Nixon had also mostly accepted: that the size, complexity, and power of impersonal systems outstripped individual will and, often, understanding. This was nonsense, Reagan answered: common sense would suffice as well as ever to grasp and master the social world. It might be true that people felt displaced or overwhelmed by powers greater than they, but Reagan could explain that experience: "It is no coincidence that our present troubles parallel and are proportionate to the intervention and intrusion in our lives that result from unnecessary and excessive growth of government." What held people back, cast them aside, and failed to show due respect for their values and hopes was government itself, which Reagan would tame and master. It was a perfect reversal of the presidential role that Wilson and Franklin Roosevelt had pioneered: Reagan remained the master interpreter of American experience, but he would turn his energy against expanded government, not toward it. By blaming government for the loss of individual mastery that Progressives had put at the center of modern politics, Reagan acknowledged that loss while placing the blame for it on the one culprit that seemed possible to overcome. Reclaiming lost mastery only required getting government out of the way. His language returned to denunciations of "paternalism" from the end of the nineteenth century, delivered with the rhetorical skill of a twentieth-century entertainer turned to politics.

This picture cleared space for Reagan to reassert old images of individual freedom and dignity without struggling to reconcile them with modern politics. "It is time for us to realize," he said, "that we are too great a nation to limit ourselves to small dreams." Instead, "We have every right to dream heroic dreams." Whereas Roosevelt had offered himself as general in a national mobilization, Reagan proposed to be the vessel of a newly expansive imagination: "Your dreams, your hopes, your goals are going to be the dreams, the hopes, and the goals of this administration, so help me God." Reagan gave voice to a vital faith that the world exists to make our wishes real. Moreover, he called that magical condition not a quality of the state, nor an achievement of politics, but a natural feature of being American, which an aggressive government could inhibit but not destroy. Reagan's first inaugural address was a rhetorical Battle of Iwo Jima. He reclaimed American innocence by force.

By 1985, the reclamation was complete. Reagan argued that the century had been marked by capitulation to government, which went hand in hand with failing self-confidence and will. The end of that decline came in 1980, when "we knew it was time to renew our faith, to strive with all our strength toward the ultimate in individual freedom consistent with an orderly society." That meant—contrary to eighty years of political language before him—that "there are no limits to growth and human progress when men and women are free to follow their dreams." By rolling back government, Reagan would spur "a new American emancipation—a great national drive to tear down economic barriers and liberate the spirit of enterprise in the most distressed areas." Tearing down was also what citizenship demanded—the tearing down of self-doubt. It required, Reagan concluded in 1981, "our willingness to believe in ourselves and to believe in our capacity to perform great deeds." "Why shouldn't we believe that?" he asked, saying, "We are Americans." Self-trust was our duty and our privilege.

In the nearly twenty years since Reagan finished his second term, our politics has lived in the landscape he created. It has been nearly impossible to speak of a special role for government, let alone to link it to personal dignity and freedom. Bill Clinton attempted some of Roosevelt's political optimism in his first inaugural, calling on the country to embrace change and adapt to the new challenges of globalization—an implicitly political task. After his party lost control of Congress in 1994, he returned, chastened, to the images of personal and social virtue that he later shared with George W. Bush. This language is a kind of protopolitics, a recognition that Reagan's endlessly hopeful individuals exist in communities and families—which Reagan himself hinted at with praise of "compassion" in both inaugurals. The vision of interdependence that it conjures up, however, has no space for the more vexed dependence that ties personal fates to institutions and the sweeping trends of economic life—the original rationale of twentieth-century government. As a matter of politics, our political language is a socialized, rhetorically humane version of nineteenth-century individualism, and the president, as interpreter in chief, reminds us of the virtues we are charged to maintain.

A CHALLENGE FOR LANGUAGE

There is a human appetite for connection, membership, and righteousness (which is not the same as self-righteousness). This produces a persistent desire for a vision of national community and the common good. Self-concern, self-regard, and even a certain amount of self-involvement are all resting places for human feelings. Selfishness and isolation are not. That is why political language remains essentially engaged in trying to find a language of common good that feels alive, contemporary, genuine, and American.

What might such language sound like today? First, it would have to take seriously what Reagan saw when he triumphantly dispatched decades of doubt: there is no American appetite for diminution and bad conscience in political life. We listen to be affirmed and celebrated. We are not interested in being called to sacrifice for sterner limits and firm reproach. In this respect, we are the spiritual descendants of Walt Whitman, who announced that he celebrated himself and, in that act, celebrated every American and the country as a whole. Reagan's inaugurals were tableaux of American dreaming and striving for a heroic ordinariness that had more of Whitman in it than any previous president's.

Second, a renewed language of common good would have to accept some of the consensus on personal virtue that united Bill Clinton and George W. Bush. Americans do experience freedom, purpose, and satisfaction most immediately in family and individual life. These are, by and large, our archetypes for understanding what it means to be connected with others, to have commitments and identity beyond ourselves. We have not so much "mystic chords of memory" as felt, inhabited bonds with others whom we have seen healthy and sick, elated and sad, and at all hours of day and night. It is not just that these are what we live for, although that is true: they are also how we know what it means to live for something, rather than just to exist. Clinton and George W. Bush went into the realms of family and community because they understood that these realms held undeniable shared values, based in the concrete reality of interdependence. Their difficulty—more frustrating, probably, to Clinton than to Bush—was that they had nowhere to go from there.

Third, it would have to be a language of common good for a country that is much more diverse and, in some ways, equal, than any previous America. The New Deal, the greatest American political experiment in social solidarity, worked its wonders for a national community with struts in white supremacy. Roosevelt held his indispensable congressional majority only through concessions to Southern Democrats who refused to have their system of racial caste dismantled. The part of the Great Society that we remember—the War on Poverty—had genuine flaws, but it was broken partly on racial resentment, precisely because Johnson would not limit its reach by the racial lines that Roosevelt accepted. Decades of growing tolerance and openness have made the country a much better one but have also made us more nearly a nation of strangers. I would take that combination in a heartbeat over a country of racial oppression, sexual inequality, and cultural conformity. But taking it means taking its costs. The equality of tolerance is not that far from indifference and is very far from the equality of opportunity that Johnson envisioned. There is no reason to conclude that diversity and solidarity cannot coexist, but we have not yet found a convincing register for their coexistence in American politics.

Finally, a language of common good would have to contend with the elaborate development of Lyndon Johnson's spirit of "becoming" in private life. The search for a fuller and more adventuresome life is underway everywhere but in government: it is the personal utopianism of yoga and Pilates studios, pharmaceutical labs and psychotherapy clinics, Rick Warren's church and the editorial offices of *Saveur*—the hundreds of thousands of places where billions of dollars and hours go into the unending search for meaning and satisfaction. Americans have always been amateur specialists in self-transformation, but the practice has never been more elaborate, mainstream (to the point of near universality), or sorted into lifestyle-compatible market segments. If there was a hint of unique adventure and transformative possibility in the politics of past generations, it is harder to find now, in contrast with the multifarious growth of possibility elsewhere in life.

At least some of a political language that worked might extend Johnson's image of citizens whose free personal activity is enabled by shared institutions. Our personal utopianism often clashes with the same constraints that made individuals vulnerable in the Progressive theory of modern society. On one hand, we experience ourselves as vessels of infinite possibility, and we have more tools and techniques to make that possibility real than any of our ancestors had. We feel correspondingly entitled to make good on at least a generous portion of what we might become, and we are disappointed and wronged if we find we cannot. On the other hand, we are not much less buffeted by economic and institutional fate than earlier Americans. Household income fluctuates—and falls dramatically—more often than it did in the decades of Carter and Reagan. Every year, more Americans lack health insurance and are thus more likely to go undiagnosed or untreated when their bodies turn against them. Globalization, the end of private-sector unions, and new corporate models all make unemployment an ordinary interruption for the fortunate and a long-term threat for the unlucky. It is fashionable to praise the flexibility and self-revision that these changes necessitate, and there is some basis for the praise; but "reinventing" yourself is much more fun when you choose the time, place, and manner than when circumstances pick you out for reinvention. The Progressive criticism of laissez-faire began in the clash between the ideal of self-mastery and the growing reality of dependence on impersonal institutions and events whose dictates could feel as arbitrary as the Greek Fates—institutions and events that, like those iconic powers, made a mockery of human will. The world has changed since 1905: we are much richer, and real deprivation is less likely. Nonetheless, the psychic whiplash that hits when our vast sense of possibility meets unyielding constraint is as acute as ever. A competent, innovative government might pick up this part—the politics of the American dream—where Johnson set it down when the Great Society yielded to bureaucratic overreach, racial anger, and, above all, a war the country was coming to hate, which the president did not know how to end.

There would have to be more, however: a way for citizens to identify with the life of the nation and feel their dignity enhanced by it. For a sample of recent political language that has pressed in this direction, consider the following fragment of Barack Obama's keynote address at the 2004 Democratic National Convention. The freshman senator from Illinois, soon to be a presidential candidate, called on "a belief that we are connected as one people."

> If there's a child on the south side of Chicago who can't read, that matters to me, even if it's not my child. If there's a senior citizen somewhere who can't pay for her prescription and has to choose between medicine and the rent, that makes my life poorer, even if it's not my grandmother. If there's an Arab American family being

> rounded up without benefit of an attorney or due process, that threatens my civil liberties. It's that fundamental belief—I am my brother's keeper, I am my sister's keeper—that makes this country work. It's what allows us to pursue our individual dreams, yet still come together as a single American family.

This language did not describe the practical interdependence that has been so important to the last century of liberal politics, which insists, for instance, that you are less free in a country where there is more crime, more disease, or worse schools than otherwise. That practical idea of interdependence rests on the fact that we live in a complex ecology of cause and effect, where someone else's problem can always become our own. Obama went beyond this argument, to call up a purely moral interdependence. He did not say that our lives go better, on the whole, if other people's lives also go better. He said our lives actually are better if others' lives are better, worse if others' are worse. His point was not that the senior citizen who could not afford medicine would raise a criminal grandson or pass on a drug-resistant flu strain to one of Obama's daughters or that the same government that held Arab American suspects indefinitely might eventually do the same to half-black Christians with African names. It was that anyone's abuse and deprivation was also, in some way, his. The impulse in this language was moral connection to the national community: if America is unjust, every American is diminished; if America rights itself, every American is greater for that. This is what has recently been so hard to say, let alone believe.

One vein of American political language has special promise for citizens' identification with the nation. This is the language of constitutional prophecy. In the mainstream of American politics, particularly in presidential rhetoric, fidelity to the country's founding principles has always been important. The language of fidelity is common to conservatives and reformers. Woodrow Wilson, proposing a great change in the American idea of government and society, described his task as "a work of restoration." Franklin Roosevelt, too, called for a "restoration" of "the temple of our civilization" to "the ancient truths" and promised to "reconsecrate our country to long-cherished ideals in a suddenly changed civilization." Of course, what those ideals were was vigorously disputed. Thus, when Lyndon Johnson assured his listeners in 1965, "Our destiny in the midst of change will rest on the unchanged character of our people, and on their faith," he was making a profoundly partisan argument—but one in the grammar of American political history, with its powerful belief in an unbroken line of principle. So Reagan, rejecting much of the political vision that defined Johnson's life, promised that Americans would remember his second term as "when the American Revolution was reborn, when freedom gained new life, when America reached for her best"—an image of progressive, reformist fidelity in service of a conservative project. A common language, as much as anything, links these presidents at two poles of twentieth-century ideology, each in his own mind and words a restorationist reformer.

The difference, then, is not between static originalists and change-embracing reformers, as it is sometimes styled in rarefied arguments over interpreting the constitutional text. In American politics, taken more broadly, all are originalists and all reformers, drawn to this partial paradox by deep habits of language and imagination. The difference lies in ideas of what history teaches. For some, the essence of American freedom was an accomplished fact from the beginning. The problems along the way were lapses or failures in application. Getting over those was about purification, setting right in detail what was always right at core. Restoration really was restoration. This attitude toward American experience was central to the language of the New Right in the middle of the twentieth century. Barry Goldwater, accepting the Republican presidential nomination, assured listeners in July 1964, "We Americans understand freedom. We have earned it: we have lived for it, and we have died for it. This nation and its people are freedom's models in a searching world. We can be freedom's missionaries in a doubting world." He did not say that, along with these historical achievements, Americans had learned about the meaning of freedom. That we already knew, from the time that "the Good Lord raised this mighty Republic to be a home for the brave and to flourish as the land of the free." Freedom could be defended, preserved, and expanded—all important in a time when "the tide has been running against freedom" and "our people have followed false prophets." It could not, however, reveal itself in new qualities, new forms, a new spirit through history's experiments. American freedom needed defenders and missionaries, not doubting yet hopeful experimenters. These were the themes that Reagan would bring to his first inaugural address, less than two decades later.

For a different attitude toward history, consider again Lyndon Johnson's address on the 1964 Civil Rights Act. In that speech, the failures of American history figured as inseparable from the understanding that Americans in 1964 should have of their national identity. Johnson identified the present moment as "a turning-point in man's unending search for freedom." That continuing search defined the United States as "the first nation in the history of the world to be founded with a purpose," but the standard of freedom was also the measure of national failures. More than a century after the Emancipation Proclamation, Johnson argued that "the Negro . . . is not fully free tonight" and that "emancipation is a proclamation and not a fact." That situation presented the country with a question to "bare the secret heart of America," the question of what freedom meant for membership in a nation whose members often feared and hated one another. As a question of self-definition, it meant the country could fail "as a people and as a nation," gaining "the whole world" and losing its "own soul." This was the language, too, of Martin Luther King Jr., who had called the broadest phrases of the Declaration of Independence and the Constitution "a promissory note" for a later generation to make good when it would "rise up and live out the true meaning of its creed." The principles were a challenge to the living, a challenge set at the center of what it meant to be American.

Both attitudes understand any great moment in American politics as a challenge of continuity, with elements of preservation and of restoration. Johnson's version, however, adds another note: the idea that only by repudiating something we have been from the beginning can Americans become more nearly what we were always meant to be—meant by the moral ambition the country staked itself to at the beginning and has revisited in crises since. Setting ourselves free from a cramped vision of the country is, in this idea, the first step in entering a larger one. It is never possible simply to identify American life with a fixed idea of freedom. What is possible—and right—is to see the country as animated partly by an impulse to freedom, whose meaning is always the way it is embodied in the facts and practices of a national life. Finally, the meaning of American freedom is the measure and kind of dignity and mastery it provides to Americans, as well as the ways we carry those together. Abjection, constraint, and the violent forms of mastery that depend on these, such as white supremacy, paradoxically comprise part of the meaning of these values, because we discovered the meaning of the values by rejecting and overcoming their opposites, the violations that defined them.

Words cannot command experience, but they do help to shape it. Language like Johnson's might enrich personal identification with the nation. It takes the country's failings as real and basic, but instead of calling for guilt or diminution, it treats failings as a starting point for appreciating what it would mean for the country to be greater. This is true to national history and also to the experience of any reflective person, who must know that life—for an individual as for a country—is a braid of aspiration, disappointment, and change that combines loss and progress, that success is not a perfect resting point but a steady tack toward betterment. It may be that in this age in which so much is personal, we will be best able to believe about the development and prospects of the country what we know is true of our own lives.

This rhetorical tradition also has some potential to make American diversity a point of strength in national community. One of the basic themes of American history, from both the standpoint of Lyndon Johnson and that of Ronald Reagan, is the extension of equal citizenship from the small group that first claimed it to (some version of) everyone. The more complex tradition of Johnson and King offers a difficult insight: that the meaning of citizenship—and thus the meaning of American freedom—changes as its limits move outward. A country that extends civic dignity to those who once formed a slave caste has changed the kind of dignity that being American implies. Gone is the pride of racial supremacy, of belonging to a master caste and lording it over others with the small humiliations that the powerful exact in any caste system. One part of what takes its place is belonging to a country that drew a new version of fairness and reciprocity from a history that had joined the freedom of some to the brutal subjection of others. This is a familiar—even commonplace—idea of what it means, morally, to be American, a version of the legacy any American can claim as a point of personal dignity. It is also a triumph of moral and political imagination, which requires citizens to set themselves loose from an old idea of national identity and find their way into another. That kind of self-transforming consummation is the special gift of this way of thinking and speaking about the country.

This rhetorical tradition has weak points as well as strengths. It falls too easily into bad conscience or self-righteous hectoring. It lacks the appeal of robust self-confidence that Reagan's tradition exudes: it marks a version of national greatness that passes through doubt, introspection, and failure, and it locates these not just in the other side of the partisan divide but in everyone. Indeed, it makes them—or at least their acknowledgment in a country where they are real—a precondition of greatness. As the starting point for an American public language, it remains the best we have.

NOTE

This essay appears in a revised form in Jedediah Purdy, *A Tolerable Anarchy: Rebels, Reactionaries, and the Making of American Freedom* (New York: Alfred A. Knopf, 2009).

Democracy and Prophecy

M. Cathleen Kaveny

A distinction between what can be called "prophecy" and "casuistical reasoning" runs deep in Western history. Exemplars of prophecy include not only the Hebrew prophets but religious and political reformers ever since, those who see what they regard as a central unseen moral truth about their culture and articulate it with insistence. Exemplars of casuistical or practical reason include most philosophers (from Aristotle on), most lawyers, most politicians, and most of us most of the time.

As M. Cathleen Kaveny observes in this essay, our own era has lots of speech of both kinds, on the right and on the left; in addition, much confusion, in religion and politics alike, arises from our common failure to understand the differences between these two genres of expression and the criteria appropriate to judging them. Sometimes, prophecy is indeed called for, or prophecy of a certain kind; sometimes, the occasion does not justify prophecy, or even if it does, a particular exercise of the prophetic voice is not justified by the criteria that should shape the genre. Kaveny explores these issues both as a theoretical matter and by comparing two prophetic works of our own era, Martin Luther King's "I have a dream" speech and Father Frank Pavone's "Open Letter to Michael Schiavo."

In *Political Liberalism* (1993), John Rawls argued that when citizens are engaged in public discourse about fundamental political questions, they must conform to the ideal of public reason. In particular, they must refrain from offering arguments that depend ultimately on exclusively religious premises or insights or other controversial commitments not shared by the vast majority of citizens.[1] Rawls's book sparked a rich interdisciplinary discussion about the role of religion in American public life. While appreciating his concern for civil discourse in a pluralistic society, many religious believers and those sympathetic to their claims worried that Rawls's conception was too restrictive of religiously based arguments. In response to these concerns, Rawls modified his position to allow for more flexibility for religious believers and others to offer arguments in explicitly religious terms.[2]

Still, not everyone was satisfied. For example, philosopher of religion Jeffrey Stout has suggested that even the new and improved Rawls operates with an unacceptably narrow notion of what counts as being a reasonable person in the public square. More specifically, Stout highlights both the rigor and flexibility of what he calls "immanent criticism," which is essentially the process of giving reasons for one's own views and requesting reasons for the views of other participants in critical, dialogical fashion. Stout contends that immanent criticism is "both one of the most widely used forms of reasoning" in political discourse and "one of the most effective ways of showing respect for fellow citizens who hold differing points of view." Religious people, Stout notes, can give reasons for their views and request reasons from other participants in the discussion in ways that do not differ essentially from secular participants. We are a community of reason requesters and reason givers, believers and nonbelievers alike.[3]

While Stout's criticism of Rawls is entirely accurate, it is not, in my view, sufficiently radical. A distinct and additional flaw in the Rawlsian framework is that it fails to grapple with a common form of American religious discourse that is not straightforward discursive argument, although it does possess its own inner logic and structure. More specifically, the Rawlsian concept of "public reason" does not give us a way to deal with the place of prophetic discourse in the public square. Rawls's framework tacitly assumes that everyone discussing matters of public concern in the public square will be employing discursive practical reason; religious believers will differ from others only in that their conclusions will depend to some degree on distinctively religious premises. Stout's critique, as powerful as it is, does not challenge this assumption, although his account of the practice of immanent criticism provides a richer and more capacious account of what type of reason giving ought to count as reasonable in the public square.

Discursive practical reasoning is certainly a key part of the tradition of public rhetoric in the United States and in Western culture more generally. In *Culture and Anarchy,* Matthew Arnold (1822–88) called it the language of "sweetness and light," finding the roots of its dispassionate progression of argument and analysis in ancient Greek philosophy's pursuit of truth. But Arnold also points to another type of rhetoric equally important in the

American political tradition. It is not cool reflection on carefully defined premises and delimited conclusions; it is, rather, the heated and unwavering commitment to absolute moral truth. Arnold describes this passionate rhetoric of moral witness as the "fire and strength" of the Hebraic tradition; it is found most vividly in the great prophetic books of the Hebrew Bible, which is also the Christian Old Testament.[4]

To deal adequately with the role of religious discourse in the public square, it is not enough to come to terms with "sweetness and light"; we must also come to terms with "fire and strength." We need to reflect on the appropriate use of prophetic discourse in the discussion of controversial moral and social issues. Why? In my judgment, some of the key reasons why Rawls is worried about the introduction of religious claims in the public square—the potential for such claims to cause social divisiveness can result in the marginalization of the individuals who disagree with the people asserting those claims—are particularly applicable to religious rhetoric of "fire and strength." Reasons calmly stated, no matter what their premises, do not usually provoke conversation partners to retaliation, verbal or otherwise. Prophetic indictments, however, do tend to attract harsh invective in return, at least from those members of the audience who do not consider the prophetic indictment fair. Furthermore, by their very nature, prophetic indictments rhetorically marginalize those who do not comply with their demands for reform.

In my view, some forms of prophetic rhetoric are necessary, on some occasions, to the moral health of the American polity. Think, for example, of Martin Luther King Jr. and the nineteenth-century abolitionists; they traded in prophetic rhetoric. Their uncompromising moral demands reshaped American society on the race question. At the same time, however, this kind of rhetoric is also dangerous to the bonds of civility that allow diverse groups to live peaceably together as one people. All prophetic rhetoric can be divisive—even the rhetoric of Martin Luther King and the abolitionists. Furthermore, not every would-be prophet is Martin Luther King; not every cause is abolitionism.

Those of us interested in the role of religion in the public square need to grapple with both the usefulness of prophetic rhetoric and its dangerousness. Doing so requires us first to understand how prophetic indictments of "fire and strength" operate rhetorically. On the basis of this understanding, we need to develop criteria for the appropriate use of prophetic discourse, criteria that would endorse the use of its "fire and strength" in appropriate cases, while discouraging that use in cases where it is inappropriate or disproportionately destructive. Furthermore, we need to do so in a way that is not politically biased toward either "liberal" or "conservative" prophets. Finally, the criteria for the appropriate use of prophetic language ought not to be imported from outside that realm of discourse but, instead, ought to be organically developed from reflections on the central cases of its use.

In this essay, I attempt a few small steps toward these goals. In the first section, I briefly address the role of prophetic discourse in American political history. In the second section, I identify some key characteristics of prophetic discourse, which help explain why such discourse is both necessary to maintain the moral health of a community and potentially dangerous to the peaceful coexistence of the members of that community. In the third and fourth sections, I begin to develop some criteria for the appropriate use of prophetic discourse by reflecting on two recent examples of the genre in American public life: Martin Luther King's "I have a dream" speech (1963)[5] and Father Frank Pavone's "Open Letter to Michael Schiavo" (2006).[6]

PROPHETIC DISCOURSE IN THE AMERICAN TRADITION

From the very beginning, American political speech has been inherently religious. As recognized by scholars of American religious history, such as Perry Miller,[7] Sydney Ahlstrom,[8] and Jon Butler,[9] political sermons reflecting on the state of the covenant between God and the people were common in colonial New England, as settlers articulated their vision of themselves as a "new Israel," living out a new and eternal covenant with God. In *The American Jeremiad*,[10] social historian Sacvan Bercovitch traces the uniquely American development of a form of prophetic speech regularly used by Puritan preachers in order to call their flock to live up to their obligations under the covenant. Named in honor of the prophet Jeremiah, whose passion it both imitates and channels, the jeremiad is defined by Bercovitch as "a lament over the ways of the world": "It decried the sins of 'the people'—a community, a nation, a civilization, mankind in general—and warned of God's wrath to follow."[11] The Puritans put their own stamp on this genre, mixing anxiety with a conviction of America's divinely given mission and promise to propel their flock forward on their theological and political mission. Impressed by its power, Bercovitch is nonetheless fundamentally wary of this form of discourse—he emphasizes the nationalism and divisiveness that this form of rhetoric can produce.[12]

Not everyone is quite so negative about the role of prophetic discourse in political community. In his brilliant and highly original study *The Prophetic Tradition and Radical Rhetoric in America,* James Darsey offers a different perspective.[13] Fully recognizing its potential for divisiveness, he nonetheless laments the dearth of prophetic rhetoric in contemporary American public argument. After exploring the use of prophetic language in the work of American political activists ranging from pamphleteers for the American Revolution to abolitionist Wendell Phillips and communist Eugene Debs, Darsey maintains that this form of discourse is no longer widely available or accessible in American political life. Taking the gay rights movement as his case study, he contends that contemporary political activists now attempt to produce moral and social change by mustering their commercial power, not their moral power. This change in political discourse both reflects and reveals a real loss—our loss.[14]

According to Darsey, the availability of prophetic rhetoric within a particular political community depends on a bedrock sense of common values, on which prophetic speakers can ground their cause in a common dedication to moral righteousness.[15] Our nation is increasingly pluralistic and materialistic; it is held together largely by self-interest rather than firm and unwavering moral commitment. In this context, gay activists in the 1980s made a strategic decision to minimize their appeals to fundamental rights and concentrate their attention on the conjunction between their own purchasing power and the monetary greed of the economic sphere. This strategy, while successful in one sense, could also be seen as a cause for some regret. Appeals to monetary self-interest might win benefits and remove burdens, but they cannot convert the heart. They cannot gain fundamental moral acceptance. "There is no communion," observes Darsey, "in money."[16]

But Darsey spoke too soon about the demise of effective prophetic rhetoric in the American public square. In the 1960s, prophetic language was used by so-called religious progressives; in our era, it is used primarily by religious conservatives. The resurgence of explicitly religious discourse, especially prophetic discourse, after the 2000 presidential election is too prominent to be ignored. For example, the rhetoric of the "culture of life" versus the "culture of death," brought to the fore by Pope John Paul II in his 1995 encyclical *Evangelium Vitae,*[17] has been adopted by a wide range of cultural conservatives of all denominations to encapsulate their moral and political demands. That language is prophetic language; it is an uncompromising moral demand to do good and avoid evil, in accordance with God's law. There is no reason to think that prophetic speech is not an enduring aspect of American public life. Those who want to come to terms with the place of religion in the American public square cannot avoid coming to terms with prophetic discourse. I now turn my attention to this task.

THE USE AND ABUSE OF PROPHETIC INDICTMENTS

What is prophetic speech? The short answer is that it is speech in the tradition or style of the Hebrew prophets, but they of course constitute more than one tradition and display a range of styles. So where do we look in order to begin developing a fuller answer? My object here is to look to contemporary scholarship about the Hebrew prophets themselves.

What is a prophet? Here we immediately run into complexities. The precise definition of a biblical prophet, the actual authors of the prophetic books, and the relationship of prophetic insight to other aspects of Hebrew scripture and society are topics that have generated a prodigious amount of scholarship. How Christianity, which began as one of a number of late Second Temple Jewish sects, reshaped the understanding of the prophetic role to correspond to its beliefs about the nature and role Jesus of Nazareth is another multifaceted and highly contested question.

The most common word for prophet in the Hebrew Bible is *nabi.* For our purposes, its root, the term *nab-,* which means "to call," is highly significant.[18] A prophet is someone who is called and commissioned by God to deliver a message to God's people. The message generally reflected God's perspective on the relationship between God and the Hebrew people and, more specifically, on the ways in which his chosen people were fulfilling—or failing to fulfill—their obligations to him at a particular time and place in their history.

Quite frequently, the prophetic assessment of the people's performance was harshly negative—prophets criticized the manifold ways in which the people of Israel and Judah strayed from their covenantal obligations to Yahweh. Abraham Joshua Heschel states, "The prophet was an individual who said No to his society, condemning its habits and assumptions, its complacency, waywardness, and syncretism."[19] This aspect of the speech of the prophets carried its way over into later religious and political thought formed in the tradition of the prophets. Let us call this type of rhetoric *prophetic indictment,* both to be precise about what it entails and to signal the fact that prophetic speech is not exhausted by indictments. This fact will be important to my argument later in this essay.

One does not have to be called by God by name to employ prophetic discourse; many of those who use prophetic discourse see themselves as following in the footsteps of the prophets. Indeed, the line between true prophets and their successors is not as clear as some like to think. Biblical exegesis, for example, has shown that the books of Isaiah and Jeremiah contain not exclusively the writings of the men whose names they bear but substantial portions written by disciples writing in their name and style. Later religious thinkers appropriated the language of the prophets to reflect on the relationship of their own communities to God and divine law. To borrow an image from theologians George Lindbeck and Hans Frei, these thinkers absorbed the world into the biblical text;[20] they inscribed the trials, tribulations, catastrophes, and controversies of their own time into the biblical drama of the frequently difficult relationship between God and God's beloved people, the ancient Jews. Preachers in post-biblical times saw themselves as preaching God's word to their own communities, as refracted through God's word to the ancient Israelites and Judeans.

Is there a strict correlation between religiosity and the invocation of prophetic indictments? No. There is, of course, a correlation, but it is not strict. In one sense, Jews and Christians have a natural affinity for the use of prophetic rhetoric, since its exemplars are embedded in their sacred scriptures. At the same time, both of these religious traditions have branches, denominations, or schools that do not encourage the appropriation of prophetic discourse as a means of addressing contemporary problems. These groups prefer the rhetoric of "sweetness and light," as reflected in the precise distinctions that characterize moral reasoning in both the Jewish rabbinic tradition and the Catholic casuistical tradition. For example, for many years, rather than decrying the "culture of death" in global and undifferentiated fashion, Catholic moralists spent a great deal of time arguing whether certain medical procedures resulting in the death of a fetus (e.g., a craniotomy performed to save the life of the mother) counted as morally prohibited "abortion" or not.

Furthermore, as Darsey's work demonstrates, thinkers who are not ultimately motivated by belief in God and a manifestation of God's will for their society can nonetheless fruitfully employ prophetic indictments. Darsey, in my view, also correctly identifies the basic requirement for their nonsectarian use: the belief in a set of foundational moral and social commitments, whose purpose is to constrain, infuse, and inspire all subsequent decisions on the part of the society in question. While not requiring religious belief, the invocation of prophetic rhetoric requires an unwavering commitment to a set of foundational moral values, which becomes analogous to religious commitment in its depth and force.[21]

What are the characteristics of prophetic indictments as a rhetorical form? The Protestant ethicist James Gustafson noted three characteristics. First, "they usually, though not always, address what the prophet perceives to be the root of religious, moral, or social waywardness, not specific instances in which certain policies are judged to be inadequate or wrong."[22] Second, prophetic indictments use "language, metaphors, and symbols that are directed to the 'heart' as well as to the 'head,'" and the prophet "usually does not make an argument; rather he demonstrates, he shows, he tells."[23] Third, prophetic indictments are usually utopian in nature. Gustafson does not use the term *utopian* technically; he merely employs it to indicate that "prophets sometimes proclaim and depict an ideal state of affairs which is radically in contrast with the actual state of affairs in which we live together in society."[24] Prophetic indictments frequently decry a social evil without providing a clear plan for its amelioration.

Prompted by James Darsey's analysis I would add a fourth characteristic: those who use prophetic discourse tend to presuppose, tacitly or explicitly, that they are speaking to a moment of communal crisis—a moment of decision with enormous consequences for the community. Quite often, this moment of crisis is presented in the starkest possible terms: either turn from your wicked ways or be destroyed. There is no time to waste.[25]

What is the relationship of prophetic indictment to ordinary moral discourse? The first point to make is that it is not ordinary moral discourse—it is radical discourse. Prophetic indictments are radical in the original sense of the term. The overarching goal is to call the community back to its roots in its fundamental moral commitments—to renewed dedication to the bedrock principles on which the society is based.

Prophetic discourse is, in an important sense, about the foundations of moral discourse—not its upper floors. If the foundations are not steady and strong, any moral reasoning grounded on them is likely to be unstable and dangerous. The definitive example from the Hebrew Bible is the sin of idolatry, excoriated again and again by the prophets. If an Israelite does not understand why idolatry is a sin—and a serious sin—he or she is not likely to make any progress in more subtle matters of moral reasoning. Those who do not realize why idolatry is a grievous offense against Yahweh clearly do not perceive who Yahweh is—the one true God, who led the Israelites out of captivity and provided for them through their wanderings in the desert. They do not understand the exclusive nature of the covenant between Yahweh and his people concluded on Mount Sinai/Horeb. They do not understand either the folly or the betrayal involved in chasing after false gods. Having shown themselves blind to the fundamental nature of that covenant, they are in no position to adjudicate more difficult questions of loyalty and obedience that are to be decided on its basis.

The covenant between God and Israel is sometimes analogized with a marriage covenant. By pursuing other gods, Israel is behaving like a flagrantly and serially unfaithful spouse. Nowhere is this framed more powerfully or poignantly than in the book of Hosea, who was instructed by God to take a temple prostitute for a wife, in order that he might more vividly experience and convey God's sense of outrage and betrayal at Israel's dalliances.[26]

> Protest against your mother, protest!
> for she is not my wife,
> and I am not her husband.
> Let her remove her harlotry from before her,
> her adultery from between her breasts,
> Or I will strip her naked,
> leaving her as on the day of her birth;
> I will make her like the desert,
> reduce her to an arid land,
> and slay her with thirst.

In addition to calling people back to the fundamental commitments of their moral and political world, prophetic indictments also serve a second basic purpose. They are frequently used as a form of moral shock treatment. In their very harshness, they force people to recognize the truth about thoroughly corrupt patterns or practices of behavior, a truth to which they have become blind or callous. This function of prophetic indictments is illustrated by the second overarching theme in the Hebrew prophets: the scandalous exploitation of the poor by the privileged upper class. In many cases, this exploitation was not due as much to maliciousness as to moral senselessness; consequently, the prophets assailed minds and hearts numb to the tribulations of other people. Nothing is more powerful than the words of the prophets themselves. Consider Isaiah 3:13–17:

> The Lord rises to accuse,
> standing to try his people.
> The Lord enters into judgment
> with his people's elders and princes:
> It is you who have devoured the vineyard;
> the loot wrested from the poor is in your houses.
> What do you mean by crushing my people,
> and grinding down the poor when they look to you?
> Says the Lord, the God of hosts.
> The Lord said:
> Because the daughters of Zion are haughty,
> and walk with necks outstretched
> Ogling and mincing as they go,
> their anklets tinkling with every step,
> The Lord shall cover the scalps of Zion's
> daughters with scabs,
> and the Lord shall bare their heads.

For the ancient Israelites, the prophets were both religious and political figures; indeed, the idea of separating religion and politics in modern liberal fashion would have been unfathomable to them. Their political community was constituted by a divine gift that was simultaneously a divine call. Rescuing the sons and daughters of Jacob from their Egyptian captivity, Yahweh agreed to be their national god, protecting and guiding them in exchange for complete and exclusive loyalty. They believed that Moses, unique among the prophets in that he saw Yahweh face-to-face, received a revelation that provided them with a detailed blueprint for their society. The covenant between God and Israel was their fundamental political constitution; keeping the covenant meant keeping the commandments.

How do prophetic indictments properly function with respect to our ordinary moral and political discourse? In my view, the best way to encapsulate the dual role of prophetic indictments with respect to ordinary political discourse is with an image: such indictments are a form of moral chemotherapy. More specifically, they function with respect to ordinary moral discourse rather as chemotherapy functions with respect to the health of a human body.[27] Just as chemotherapy is not an ordinary form of health care, prophetic indictments are not an ordinary form of moral discourse. They are an extraordinary form, aimed at a lethal threat to the health of moral discourse within a particular community: either utter disdain for a fundamental moral premise of the community's moral reasoning (e.g., idolatry) or a pattern of utter blindness to a consequence of its fundamental moral commitments (e.g., gross exploitation of the poor).

When a human body is ravaged by cancer, chemotherapy can be the only hope of restoring life and health. At the same time, chemotherapy can have destructive consequences. Unless the physician is extremely judicious in its use, it can do more harm than good—in some circumstances, it can even kill the patient. So it is with the moral chemotherapy of prophetic indictments. They can be absolutely necessary to preserve the fundamental moral fabric of the community. At the same time, they can rip a community apart, setting mother against son, sister against brother. Any reflection on the function of prophetic indictments must come to terms not only with their appropriate use but also with their great potential for abuse. This destructive potential is intimately connected with the inner logic of prophetic indictments; it arises from the way in which prophetic interventions affect the ongoing conversation. Let me sketch, therefore, four key characteristics of this inner logic.

First, by their very form and content, prophetic indictments radically constrain the possibilities for acceptable response on the part of the listeners. Remember that the true prophet is claiming to be a messenger of God; the prophet also claims that the message he or she is delivering is divinely mandated. From the prophet's perspective, therefore, the only acceptable response is obedience and repentance on the part of the audience. How else can one respond to an unequivocal message from the Supreme Being? Hearers who do not obey and repent are functionally in the position of making an ad hominem attack on the prophet. In effect, they are calling the prophet a liar or, at the very least, an unreliable messenger. Their very recalcitrance proclaims their belief that the prophet is not, indeed, a messenger from God or that the prophet distorted or truncated the message in some significant way.

Second and relatedly, it is important to note that by their nature, prophetic indictments forestall the possibility of dialogue or compromise. This is the case with respect to the substance of the message. The prophet believes that he or she is uttering God's own message; it cannot, therefore, be quibbled with or debated. Consider, for example, the following passage from Jeremiah:

> Therefore, I will give their wives to strangers,
> their fields to spoilers.
> Small and great alike, all are greedy for gain,
> prophet and priest, all practice fraud.
> They would repair, as though it were nought,
> the injury to the daughter of my people:
> "Peace, peace!" they say,
> though there is no peace.
> They are odious; they have done abominable things,
> yet they are not at all ashamed,
> they know not how to blush.
> Hence they shall be among those who fall;
> in their time of punishment they shall go down,
> says the Lord.[28]

There is no conversational space in this indictment for an interlocutor to ask, "Well, wait a minute, now. What exactly counts as 'greedy'?" Moreover, the questions "Do you have anything specifically in mind with the term 'abominable things'?" and "Is their commission a specific intent offense?" are not likely to be met with a measured and thoughtful response from the prophet. Those who ask such questions merely prove that "they know not how to blush."

Third and consequently, prophetic indictments leave scarce room for careful, casuistical distinctions common both in the law and in the analysis of day-to-day moral problems. Consider, for example, the prohibition against idolatry, which I identified earlier as the fundamental moral prohibition of the ancient Israelites. Does it count as "idolatry" to eat meat sacrificed to idols if the eater does not actually believe in other gods? This is a casuistical question, probing the precise boundaries of the definition of "idolatry." It was a live question for St. Paul.[29] It is not one, however, with which the writers of the biblical books of Isaiah or Jeremiah or Hosea would have had much patience. To ask the question would be to demonstrate that one had not fully grasped the full horror of the sin of idolatry; anyone who did recognize that horror would want to stay as afar away from it as possible, not only in internal beliefs, but also in external acts.

Fourth and finally, the use of prophetic indictment generally marks the end of civil discussion. Those who, for whatever reason, do not acknowledge the speaker's identity as a true prophet are likely to react with indignation to the prophet's stinging words. Consider the foregoing passage from Jeremiah as an example. The experience of being called "greedy" or "odious" by a person one does not consider a true prophet is likely to produce indignation and insults in return, at least from the vast majority of people not blessed with saintly patience. The prophet, filled with righteous anger, calls for obedience and repentance. One or two members of the audience might comply. But the rest are incredulous and skeptical; they feel they have been calumniated and respond accordingly.

Prophetic indictments are thus rhetorically coercive; indeed, they are generally meant to be so. Their goal is to narrow the hearers' options to two: either obey and repent or be damned, literally or figuratively. Under the best of circumstances, prophetic indictments will rend the moral fabric of the community, provoking resentment, recalcitrance, and, sometimes, retaliation in response. Like chemotherapy, if they are not used as a last resort, carefully, and with proper precautions, they will do more harm than good. But there is a crucial difference between actual chemotherapy and moral chemotherapy. Physicians charged with the care of persons' bodies are not generally tempted to overuse chemotherapy; it has no intrinsic fascination as a form of medical treatment. There is, however, a certain attraction to the use of prophetic indictment on the part of those who are tempted to view themselves as spiritual physicians, charged with the care of the soul of America. There are three basic sources of temptation.

First, the status of the Hebrew prophets and the history of prophetic rhetoric in the American political tradition play no small part in the attraction to this form of discourse. Against the temptations of self-aggrandizement, self-proclaimed prophets need to be cognizant of the spiritual danger of assimilating one's own mission to that of a biblical prophet or an acknowledged successor. Such an assimilation frequently precludes healthy self-criticism; it encourages the would-be prophet to interpret criticism and qualification as misunderstanding and moral turpitude.

Second, self-proclaimed prophets ought to be cognizant of the attraction of the easy way out. Homiletic classes in divinity schools regularly hear the joke about the preacher who writes in the margins of his sermon, "Point weak—bang on pulpit." Prophetic indictments can be the rhetorical equivalent of pounding on the pulpit. If one's argument is weak, if one's capacity for dialogue and exchange is uncertain, it can be tempting to invoke prophetic indictments prematurely rather than engaging in the difficult work of strengthening one's discursive argument.

Finally, there is the dangerous allure of unconsciously procuring a righteous cover for base motives. One does not need to be an expert in international politics or human psychology to recognize that those who are angry at another person or group, no matter what the underlying reasons for that anger, frequently find it convenient to cloak their anger in righteousness. By engaging in prophetic indictments of their enemy, they both give expression to their outrage and proclaim their own moral rectitude. This can be a heady combination.

Prophetic indictments are not the discourse of practical reason. Nonetheless, they have an important and intelligible function in the context of a community's moral conversation and debate. They can call a community back to faithfulness to its most basic values, when those values have been distorted or occluded by the passage of time or the complacency of succeeding generations. They can break through self-indulgence and indifference to the suffering of others. At the same time, however, prophetic indictments can also be dangerous, threatening social harmony on a basic level. They can also be misused, and their inexorable demands can be marshaled for the wrong reasons, such as shoring up a weak argument or artificially enhancing the status of the speaker.

CRITERIA FOR THE RIGHT USE OF PROPHETIC INDICTMENTS

I now turn my attention to the task of articulating some basic criteria for the right use of prophetic indictments in the public square, criteria that would encourage the benefits of this form of rhetoric while discouraging the liabilities. In my view, successful criteria for the use of prophetic rhetoric need to be developed from an internal perspective—a perspective sensitive to the inner logic and purpose of prophetic speech—rather than imposed from outside, in an arbitrary fashion. Consequently, I propose to use the books named after the great Hebrew prophets themselves for the development of criteria guiding the appropriate use of prophetic indictments. These books reveal that the indictment is not the only form of prophetic speech; in fact, prophetic books contextualize indictments with other forms of speech in ways that maximize the beneficial effects of the indictment while minimizing deleterious consequences. For prophetic indictment to function to heal, rather than to harm, a community, would-be prophets need not only to reflect on the conditions under which its use is appropriate but also to contextualize their indictment in ways that mitigate its harm to the broader community.[30]

To lend specificity to my quest for normative criteria for the use of prophetic indictments, I shall explore, in comparative fashion, two proclamations about issues of political morality and law, made by religious figures in the public square. The first is Martin Luther King's "I have a dream" speech, delivered at the Lincoln Memorial on August 28, 1963, to more than 250,000 people at the March on Washington for Jobs and Freedom.[31] Martin Luther King was a Baptist minister, the president of the Southern Christian Leadership Conference, and a linchpin of the civil rights movement, which drew on black churches to mobilize support and inculcate the character traits necessary for the discipline of nonviolent civil resistance. The second proclamation I will consider is Father Frank Pavone's "Open Letter to Michael Schiavo," written to the widower of Terri Schindler Schiavo in March 2006, a year after her death, and published on the World Wide Web. In a highly publicized case, Mr. Schiavo authorized the withdrawal of artificial nutrition and hydration from his forty-two-year-old wife, who had been in a persistent vegetative state for almost fifteen years. This decision was forcefully opposed by Ms. Schiavo's parents, in part on the basis of their Catholic faith. In the fall of 2004, Father Pavone intervened in the moral and legal controversy, on the side of the parents. A contemporary culture warrior, he founded a new Roman Catholic religious order called Priests for Life, dedicated to combating abortion, euthanasia, and other manifestations of the "culture of death" as described in Pope John Paul II's encyclical *Evangelium Vitae.*

In the section that follows, I will argue that Reverend King's speech constitutes a model for the proper use of prophetic indictments whereas Father Pavone's open letter falls far short of the mark. A reader might well question whether this comparison is fair. King's speech, after all, is an undisputable high point of American political and religious rhetoric; who among us could expect to survive a comparative scrutiny that used it as a touchstone? My response is twofold. First, it is, I think, important to consider precisely why King's speech is effective, not merely as a general example of political rhetoric, but also more specifically as a particular example of prophetic rhetoric in the public square. Comparative analysis facilitates this task. Second, one ought not to minimize either the political significance of the Terri Schiavo case in American political life or the role of Father Pavone in stirring the sentiments of religious people across the nation against the withdrawal of Terri's feeding tube. Thanks in part to the intervention of religious conservatives, a Republican Congress passed "Terri's Law,"[32] which took the extraordinary step of giving de novo jurisdiction over one particular case—her case—to the federal courts, despite the fact that family law and medical treatment decisions are quintessentially matters for state courts. "Terri's Law" was an extraordinary manifestation of political power, much of it motivated by religious conviction. Father Pavone helped to galvanize that conviction.

A TALE OF TWO PROPHETS

I begin my account of King and Pavone by identifying something they share: namely, they ground their prophetic speech in a claimed violation of law or covenant. This is not surprising, for ever since the work of the great German biblical scholar Claus Westermann, who emphasized the parallels between prophetic speech and the ancient forms of lawsuit,[33] it has been clear that the law, particularly as a fundamental agreement or covenant binding on the parties in question, often provides the basis for a prophetic indictment, in biblical times as well as in (or perhaps therefore in) our own. Not surprisingly, therefore, when we examine both King's speech and Pavone's open letter, we find the rudiments of a claim of breach of contract.

First, the opening paragraphs of both documents ground their critique in a fundamental covenant or compact to which their audience can be presumed to have assented. More specifically, Martin Luther King invokes the Declaration of Independence and the Constitution as constituting a "check," a "promissory note" extending rights to African Americans.[34] Father Pavone invokes the marriage covenant that bound Michael Schiavo to care for and protect his wife Terri.[35]

Second, each prophet proceeds to develop the factual basis for the indictment, drawing on vivid imagery to do so. King surveys the plight of black citizens in America, charging that "one hundred years later, the Negro is still languished in the corners of American society and finds himself an exile in his own land."[36] Pavone describes Terri Schiavo's death: "I watched her face for hours on end, right up to moments before her last breath. Her death was not peaceful, nor was it beautiful. If you saw her too, and noticed what her eyes were doing, you know that to describe her last agony as peaceful is a lie."[37]

Third, each proceeds to draw the legal conclusion on the basis of the law and the facts. King proclaims, "It is obvious today that America has defaulted on this promissory note insofar as her citizens of color are concerned. Instead of honoring this sacred obligation, America has given the Negro people a bad check; a check which has come back marked 'insufficient funds.'"[38] King is charging the American polity with a type of fraud. Pavone, in contrast, excoriates Schiavo for murdering his own wife: "We watched, but you had the power to save her. Her life was in your hands, but you threw it away, with the willing cooperation of attorneys and judges who were as heartless as you were. Some have demanded that I apologize to you for calling you a murderer. Not only will I not apologize, I will repeat it again."[39]

If one compares these two prophetic indictments, it is clear that both aim to provide a type of moral chemotherapy. Both King and Pavone are using these communications to attack what they perceive as a type of moral cancer invading the body politic—a racist regime in the case of King and the "culture of death" in the case of Pavone. It is also clear that neither prophet leaves much room for legitimate disagreement with their diagnosis. As I argued earlier in this essay, these features are inherent in the very rhetorical structure of prophetic indictments. Further comparisons, however, reveal illuminating differences in the two sources, which may help us develop criteria to determine both when the moral chemotherapy of prophetic indictments is justified and how to minimize its inevitable dangers to the body politic. More specifically, I think comparison on three points generates three criteria for the appropriate use of prophetic indictments.

First, look more closely at the basis of the prophetic indictment in the two cases. Martin Luther King was focused on the injustice of a whole pattern of laws that was deeply subversive of the full citizenship of African Americans—the Jim Crow regime, which had thwarted the full implementation of the antislavery amendments to the Constitution. Like the biblical prophets, he used a solid foundation—our basic constitutional values—to call attention to the rotting superstructure.[40]

In contrast, the basis for Frank Pavone's indictment is far more restricted. More specifically, the problem he saw was not with the legal regime but with the application of relevant law in a particular instance. There is no doubt that Terri Schiavo was recognized as a legal person by all those involved in the dispute. Euthanasia was and remains illegal in Florida. Moreover, the state's legal framework regarding guardianship and withdrawal of medical treatment—including artificial nutrition and hydration (ANH)—was sound.[41] Father Pavone and his supporters might argue that the result in the Terri Schiavo case exemplifies callousness toward people of compromised physical and mental state. Yet an examination of the case file, which runs over a thousand pages long, demonstrates that this is not so.[42] At bottom, the legal dispute between the two sides turned on divergent views regarding whether Terri Schiavo would have wanted ANH to be discontinued were she able to make the decision for herself, as well as divergent views about who should make that decision since she could not. Father Pavone believes that Mr. Schiavo—and the courts—answered this particular question incorrectly, by not giving enough weight to his view of what Catholic teaching requires in this instance.[43]

It seems to me that the first criterion generated by this comparison is this: do not deploy the moral chemotherapy of prophetic rhetoric without a sufficiently grave cause. There is a significant difference between a systematically unjust legal regime and a basically sound regime that reaches an unjust result in a particular instance.[44] It is one thing to protest a widespread pattern or practice of treating some people as second-class citizens; it is another to focus on one case of problematic decision making. Furthermore, disagreement about the application of law to facts is inevitable in hard cases, even among those who are committed to the same moral and legal principles. To use prophetic indictment to call into question the goodwill and integrity of someone who reaches a different conclusion about what the law requires in a particular hard case may be momentarily gratifying to the self-proclaimed prophet, but it is not likely to be successful or effective, even on its own terms. More specifically, there is no disagreement about the law or its foundational nature as the basis for the decision; there is no conversion of heart to a greater commitment to the integrity of the law that can be gained by the deployment of prophetic rhetoric in such a case.

This criterion, in my view, can be applied to both politically liberal prophets and politically conservative ones. The key is to consider whether, from the perspective of a would-be prophet, the object of prophetic indictment is an isolated problem or a pervasive pattern or practice. For example, it would have been inappropriate for a latter-day civil rights activist to use prophetic invective if O. J. Simpson had been convicted, rather than acquitted, of murdering his former wife and her male friend in 1995. Even if such a verdict would have been unjust, it would have been an individual instance of injustice in the context of a functioning legal system. In such an instance, prophetic indictment would have been destructive overkill. Conversely, it would have been appropriate for Father Pavone to protest prophetically a law that declared all persons in persistent vegetative states to be legally dead, or nonpersons, just as it is rhetorically appropriate, given his convictions, for him to use prophetic language to protest *Roe v. Wade*'s exclusion of unborn life from the category of persons. Given his convictions about the importance of recognizing the equal dignity of all human beings, no matter what their state of disability or dependence, laws restricting personhood in this matter would mark a fundamental deficiency in the American legal system.

Second and relatedly, the ultimate motives and goals of the use of prophetic indictment differ significantly in the two cases. Reverend King's motive is obviously hope-filled and oriented toward the future; he holds before his audience the possibility of justice and peace for the nation as a whole. Nowhere is this more clear than in the last line of his speech:

> And when we allow freedom to ring, when we let it ring from every village and hamlet, from every state and city, we will be able to speed up that day when all of God's children—black men and white men, Jews and Gentiles, Catholics and Protestants—will be able to join hands and to sing in the words of the old Negro spiritual, "Free at last, free at last; thank God Almighty, we are free at last!"[45]

In contrast, Father Pavone's motive in issuing his prophetic indictment against Michael Schiavo on the anniversary of Terri Schiavo's death is not entirely clear. There is no orientation toward the future in his open letter; he is entirely focused on the events of the past, and his tone is predominantly vindictive: "Some have demanded that I apologize to you for calling you a murderer. Not only will I not apologize, I will repeat it again. Your decision to have Terri dehydrated to death was a decision to kill her.

It doesn't matter if Judge Greer said it was legal. No judge, no court, no power on earth can legitimize what you did."[46]

It seems to me that this difference between Reverend King and Father Pavone suggests a second criteria for the appropriate use of prophetic indictment: do not deprive your intended audience of all hope of a better and more harmonious future. Otherwise, they have no incentive to listen to you, much less to change. Moreover, the purely vindictive use of prophetic rhetoric to revisit a past incident is unjustified in terms of the ancillary and inevitable harms of that form of discourse; it also may correlate with the misuse of this form of discourse as a righteous cover for all-too-human motives of anger and self-aggrandizement.

Third and finally, there is a striking difference in the stance that each prophet takes toward the intended audience of his prophetic indictment. Reverend King sees himself as part of the community to whom he is issuing the indictment; he suffers not only with the African Americans whose just claims he advocates but also with the American people as a whole, who have been harmed by the sin of racism. Like the prophet Jeremiah, whom he studied extensively in seminary,[47] he suffers with his people on account of their iniquities; he takes no joy in delivering a message of indictment. He begs Americans to end our shameful history of segregation and racism in order that we might flourish together; the vision of a united, free, and redeemed America with which he culminates his address includes black and white, Jew and Gentile, Northerner and Southerner. His call for repentance and reformation on the part of racists simultaneously holds out to them the possibility of forgiveness and the renewal of community. The beginning of the second half of the speech, where the litany of King's dreams actually commence, decisively establishes this redemptive horizon.

> So I say to you, my friends, that even though we must face the difficulties of today and tomorrow, I still have a dream. It is a dream deeply rooted in the American dream that one day this nation will rise up and live out the true meaning of its creed—we hold these truths to be self-evident, that all men are created equal.
>
> I have a dream that one day on the red hills of Georgia, sons of former slaves and sons of former slave-owners will be able to sit down together at the table of brotherhood.
>
> I have a dream that one day, even the state of Mississippi, a state sweltering with the heat of injustice, sweltering with the heat of oppression, will be transformed into an oasis of freedom and justice.[48]

Father Pavone, in contrast, gives no evidence that he sees himself as having any real bond or commonality with Michael Schiavo. More specifically, in addressing Mr. Schiavo, he sets up a dichotomy between a sinful "you" and a righteous "us": "Your actions offend us. Not only have you killed Terri and deeply wounded her family, but you have disgraced our nation, betrayed the Gospel of Jesus Christ, and undermined the principles that hold us together as a civilized society."[49] At the end of the open letter, he issues a call for repentance, with a mention of forgiveness, but it is brief and perfunctory. In this call, Father Pavone proffers no possibility of living in a reconstituted community with Michael Schiavo; the God whom he invokes is a distant scorekeeper. He does not reconstitute a redeemed world. Father Pavone writes, "You have made your mark on history, but sadly, it is an ugly stain. In the name of millions around the world, I call on you today to embrace a life of repentance, and to ask forgiveness from the Lord, who holds the lives of each of us in His hands."[50]

It would be wrong to say, however, that Father Pavone's approach has no analogue in the prophetic books. In his contempt for Mr. Schiavo, as well as his apparent inability to conceive of sharing a common community with him, Father Pavone's approach to prophetic rhetoric echoes what are commonly called the "oracles against the nations"—prophetic indictments of Israel's enemies that predict and sometimes applaud their destruction rather than their redemption. Whereas the Hebrew prophets frequently demonstrate sympathy for the fate of Israel and Judah at the hands of a just God, they are far more parsimonious in their expressions of fellow feeling for the suffering of the denizens of Assyria, Babylon, Moab, and Edom.

Nonetheless, the oracles against the nations are part of the prophet books, but they are not the whole of them. The majority of prophetic indictments are directed (sometimes reluctantly) by the prophets of Israel and Judah against their own people. Their words of woe are balanced in the prophetic books by words of weal, or consolation and hope. Furthermore, contemporary biblical scholarship has emphasized the way in which the prophetic hope for divine deliverance, for the triumph of God's mercy, contextualizes even the indictments in the oracles against the nations. In the book of Isaiah, for example, we find the statement "I will give you as a light to the nations, that my salvation may reach to the end of the earth." David Petersen argues that this statement "looks to the blessing for all peoples."[51] Petersen also argues that Jeremiah's oracles against the nations are "suffused by a motif of hope," not only for Israel and Judah, but for their enemies.[52] It is a hope rooted not in human endeavors but in God's infinite patience and creative mercy.

From this point of comparison comes my third and final criterion for the use of prophetic indictments. In addressing fellow members of one's political or religious community, it is best not to model the tone of prophetic discourse on the biblical oracles against the nations. In addressing their fellow citizens, the Hebrew prophets did not set themselves over and against them; in an important sense, they stood with their people as much as they stood with the God whose words they spoke. Still less should a prophet speaking to his own community depict himself as on the side of a God who has utterly and completely rejected them. The Hebrew prophets preached divine mercy as well as divine judgment; as Abraham Heschel writes, they force us to ponder "what hidden bond exists between the word of wrath and the word of compassion, between 'consuming fire' and 'everlasting love.'"[53]

NOTES

1. John Rawls, *Political Liberalism* (New York: Columbia University Press, 1993), 212–54.

2. I summarize the modifications in M. Cathleen Kaveny, "Religious Claims and the Dynamics of Argument," *Wake Forest Law Review* 36 (Summer 2001): 423–48, at 425 n. 2.

3. Jeffrey Stout, *Democracy and Tradition* (Princeton: Princeton University Press, 2004), 73.

4. Matthew Arnold, *Culture and Anarchy,* ed. Samuel Lipman (New Haven and London: Yale University Press, 1994), chap. 4.

5. Martin Luther King Jr., *I Have a Dream* (San Francisco: Harper San Francisco, 1993).

6. Frank Pavone, "Open Letter from Fr. Frank Pavone to Michael Schiavo," Terri Schindler Schiavo Foundation, 26 March 2006, http://www.terrisfight.org/news.php?id=86 (accessed 11 June 2007).

7. Perry Miller, *Errand Into the Wilderness* (Cambridge: Harvard University Press, 1956; reprint, New York: Harper and Row, 1964).

8. Sydney E. Ahlstrom, *A Religious History of the American People* (New Haven: Yale University Press, 1972; Image Books Edition, Garden City, NY, 1975).

9. Jon Butler, *Awash in a Sea of Faith: Christianizing the American People* (Cambridge: Harvard University Press, 1990).

10. Sacvan Bercovitch, *The American Jeremiad* (Madison: University of Wisconsin Press, 1978).

11. Ibid., 7.

12. Ibid., 176.

13. James Darsey, *The Prophetic Tradition and Radical Rhetoric in America* (New York: New York University Press, 1997).
14. Ibid., chap. 1.
15. Ibid.
16. Ibid., 9.
17. Pope John Paul II, *Evangelium Vitae* (Boston: St. Paul Books and Media, 1995).
18. See David L. Petersen, *The Prophetic Literature: An Introduction* (Louisville, KY: Westminster John Knox Press, 2002), 6.
19. Abraham J. Heschel, *The Prophets,* First Perennial Classics Edition (New York: HarperCollins, Perennial, 2001), xxix.
20. See George A. Lindbeck, *The Nature of Doctrine: Religion and Theology in a Postliberal Age* (Philadelphia: Westminster Press, 1984), chap. 6; Hans W. Frei, *The Eclipse of Biblical Narrative: A Study in Eighteenth and Nineteenth Century Hermeneutics* (New Haven: Yale University Press, 1974), chap. 2.
21. Some activists on behalf of the environment display such a commitment.
22. James M. Gustafson, *Varieties of Moral Discourse: Prophetic, Narrative, Ethical, and Policy; The Stob Lectures of Calvin College and Seminary* (Grand Rapids, MI: Calvin College and Seminary, 1988), 7–8.
23. Ibid., 11.
24. Ibid., 13.
25. James Darsey emphasizes this aspect of prophetic discourse. See Darsey, *Prophetic Tradition,* chap. 4.
26. Hos. 2:4–5. Unless otherwise noted, all biblical passages are taken from *The Catholic Study Bible.*
27. I have made this argument in more detail in M. Cathleen Kaveny, "Prophecy and Casuistry: Abortion, Torture, and Moral Discourse," *Villanova Law Review* 51 (2006): 499–580.
28. Jer. 8:10–12.
29. See 1 Cor. 8:1–13.
30. I realize my strategy here is incomplete. A complete look at the requirements for the use of prophecy within a flourishing community would need to pay attention not only to the role of prophetic indictments within the context of the prophetic books but also to the broader process of canonization, as well as the liturgical function of the prophetic books in the life of the worshiping community. Obviously, that function would be different in Jewish and Christian communities.
31. For a fascinating account of the composition of the speech, see Drew D. Hansen, *The Dream: Martin Luther King, Jr. and the Speech That Inspired a Nation* (New York: HarperCollins, 2003).
32. *An Act for the Relief of the Parents of Theresa Marie Schiavo,* Pub. L. No. 109-3, 119 Stat. 15 (2005).
33. Claus Westermann, *Basic Forms of Prophetic Speech,* trans. Hugh Clayton White (Philadelphia: Westminster Press, 1967), 129–63.
34. "In a sense we've come to our nation's capital to cash a check. When the architects of our republic wrote the magnificent words of the Constitution and the Declaration of Independence, they were signing a promissory note to which every

American was to fall heir. This note was a promise that all men, yes, black men as well as white men, would be guaranteed the unalienable rights of life, liberty, and the pursuit of happiness" (King, *I Have a Dream,* 4–5).

35. "A year ago this week, I stood by the bedside of the woman you married and promised to love in good times and bad, in sickness and health" (Pavone, "Open Letter").

36. King, *I Have a Dream,* 3–4.

37. Pavone, "Open Letter."

38. King, *I Have a Dream,* 6.

39. Pavone, "Open Letter."

40. "The History of Jim Crow," a very helpful set of resources on the Jim Crow regime, is available online at http://www.jimcrowhistory.org/ (accessed 11 June 2007).

41. In essence, every person of sound mind has the right to reject whatever form of medical treatment or procedure they wish to reject, including ANH. This right is grounded not in a right to commit suicide but in a right to prevent battery—the unconsented touching of one's body, for any reason whatsoever. Furthermore, the state specifies an elaborate system of surrogate decision makers for incompetent persons, such as Ms. Schiavo; the decision makers' task is to decide for the patient according to what they believe the patient would have decided for himself or herself if able to make the decision. The state of Florida has specified a higher burden of proof if a surrogate decision maker wants to withdraw ANH from an incompetent basis; the surrogate must prove that the patient would have desired this result by "clear and convincing evidence," not merely by a preponderance of the evidence. The relevant legal framework can be found at Fla. Stat. Ann. §§ 765.101–.404 (West 2005 and Supp. 2007).

42. Ms. Schiavo's parents attempted more than once to have Mr. Schiavo removed as Terri Schiavo's guardian on the grounds of unfitness; they were unsuccessful in their efforts. For a good history of the early years of the case, see the report submitted by guardian ad litem Jay Wolfson, "A Report to Governor Jeb Bush and the 6th Judicial Circuit in the Matter of Theresa Marie Schiavo," 1 December 2003, http://abstractappeal.com/schiavo/WolfsonReport.pdf (accessed 11 June 2007).

43. The question of whether Catholic teaching requires the continuation of ANH in this instance is disputed by Catholic moralists. Furthermore, even if it were the case that Catholic teaching so requires, it is not self-evident that Ms. Schiavo would have followed that teaching, despite her Catholicism. Even in Pavone's expressed view, the relevant question is what she would have wanted, not what the church teaches.

44. This criterion corresponds to the second mark of prophetic indictments identified in Gustafson, *Varieties of Moral Discourse,* 7.

45. King, *I Have a Dream,* 31–33.

46. Pavone, "Open Letter."

47. King wrote a term paper on Jeremiah while at Crozer Theological Seminary. See Martin Luther King Jr., "The Significant Contributions of Jeremiah to Religious Thought" (1948), in Clayborne Carson, Ralph E. Luker, Penny A. Russell, and

Louis R. Harlan, eds., *The Papers of Martin Luther King, Jr.*, vol. 1, *Called to Serve, January 1929–June 1951* (Berkeley: University of California Press, 1992), 181–95.

48. King, *I Have a Dream,* 21–23.

49. Pavone, "Open Letter."

50. Ibid.

51. Petersen, *Prophetic Literature,* 87.

52. Ibid., 128. Petersen notes that Babylon is an exception—which shall "sink, to rise no more" (Jer. 51:64, New Revised Standard Version).

53. Heschel, *Prophets,* 27.

Ennobling Politics

Robin West

As Robin West tells us in this essay, a great deal of constitutional scholarship in the past half century has proceeded on a set of related assumptions: that the processes of democracy are unruly, irrational, inherently subject to corruption, and just plain inelegant; and that the processes of law, especially constitutional law, can, in the right hands at least, be orderly, rational, incorruptible, and highly elegant. We scholars and judges, if we are of the proper persuasion, are priests in this civic religion, the center of which is what West calls an "adjudicated constitution," a constitution, that is, which lives through lawsuits and judicial opinions.

In this essay, West challenges these assumptions.

Even in its own terms the traditional view addresses only the active wrongs of the government, not its inaction, and the abandonment of responsibility by the government is as serious an issue today as its violations of established rights. Moreover, the adjudicated constitution cannot effectively regulate the processes of politics; what is needed is not a removal from politics but an engagement in politics—and an engagement that uses the Constitution not just as a set of rules limiting what the government can do but as a set of principles and values that can guide the government when it is acting, or refusing to act, beyond the zone of any possible adjudication. How such a politics might be imagined is West's subject here.

Over the last half century, we American lawyers have been congenitally worried, sometimes alarmed, and occasionally frightened out of our very skins by the specter of democratic politics, both our own and others: the faux democracies that might spawn global fascism, communism, and terrorism to be sure, but also our homegrown and at least somewhat genuinely majoritarian deliberations. That lawyerly concern has not been without good reason. Democratic deliberations in the past century have notoriously reflected as well as entrenched a vicious race hatred that poisoned domestic life for generations of Americans, the beginnings of a cure for which came not through democratic process but through Supreme Court action.[1] In just the first decade of this new century, democratic deliberations have yielded the Patriot Act,[2] a military commissions act,[3] and amendments to various surveillance acts[4] that collectively strip us all of individual rights; have paved the way for calamitous and ill-considered foreign policies;[5] have prompted sanctimonious exercises that gratuitously offend religious minorities or nonbelievers;[6] have cruelly extended the life of a severely disabled and long-unconscious individual for no earthly reason;[7] and have expended precious resources on foolish projects to nowhere that do nothing to promote anyone's conception of the public good.[8] Even democratically pristine political will, we lawyers fear, can be rooted in fanaticism, greed, fury, or calculated self-interest; can inspire clannish loyalties that prove genocidal; can sow familial fellow feelings of community and shared identity that prove to be the stuff of fascism; can give voice to a purported generosity that masks authoritarianism; can take the shape of a concern for well-being that is in fact contempt for the individual's self-sovereignty. The problem with ordinary do-it-by-voting democracy is not, American lawyers of the past half century might be read as collectively proclaiming, that of which John S. Mill and other sympathetic liberal critics of majoritarianism warned: the mediocrity of the minds of the undistinguished mass.[9] The problem, as increasingly assumed as gospel by the constitutional dogma we are carrying from the last century into this one, is that politics itself is a debased, ignoble endeavor that elicits our worst instincts. The political animal within must be stopped.

So, stop it we do, or try to. The framers of our Constitution famously worried as well over the political animal and designed a familiar political structure they thought might tame it.[10] Equal state representation in the Senate would put that institution at odds with rank majoritarianism; separation of the powers of enforcement and legislation would counter ambition with ambition; power shared, dispersed, limited, and divided between state and national governors would create political competitions that would ultimately further the common good. Not content, however, with those quaintly hardwired political safeguards, constitutional lawyers have done Madison and company one better: we stop the political animal dead in his tracks with the full force and rhetoric of constitutional law. That is a very different thing. The Constitution, as employed and deployed by American lawyers and courts from Justice Marshall's time to our own, is not simply a blueprint of good governance for a nation cautious about political ambition. Rather, the Constitution is a source of law, the very point of which is to counter the political impulse with a legal one and at times negate the fruit of politics with the power of a legal pronouncement.

Stopping malignant politics with benign law—curbing the excesses of the dangerous branches with the words, the collaborative thought, the collective wisdom, and the judicial good reason of the least dangerous—has long seemed, to American lawyers, to be the most felicitous way to honor the spirit of Simone Weil's[11] and now Jim White's[12] pressing moral demand: that if we wish to live lovingly and justly, we must find a way to disrespect the destructive instincts and disastrous policies of the world's empires of force, including the one in which we all live and work. Lawyers collectively answer Weil and White that here in America, we counter our "empire of force" with judicially created constitutional law. We do not just counter ambition with ambition—rather, we counter the whole mess with reasoned law. When lawyers voice a worry over the adequacy of our legal response to the empire of force, it is likely to be the worry that—for various reasons—our constitutional response is not sufficiently robust to meet the dangers posed by an overreaching, dangerous, voracious political state. Perhaps the Supreme Court has been politically co-opted and has lost its claim to neutrality. Or perhaps the legal commands of the Constitution themselves are not sufficiently clear. Perhaps conditions have changed such that amendments are in order; maybe the legal apparatus with which we counter the political has grown creaky or dysfunctional. For any of these reasons and plenty of others, the legal, constitutional, reasoned response to the state's overreaching, intrusive, destructive political inclinations might not be adequate. If so, then we will have reached a dangerous imbalance in the relation of force to reason, of politics to law, and of the political to the judicious animal, both in our governing constitution and in our human souls. If any of this is true, then we lawyers need to turn our attention pronto to the dangerously overreaching political state. The best way to do that—maybe the only way, or at any rate, the way American lawyers instinctively explore—is through revitalizing our constitutional culture. The papers prepared for the conference that produced this book sought in large part to do just that.

I do not wish to disagree with White and Weil that we are right to fear what they call the empire of force or that it is imperative that we learn how not to respect it, if we are to live lovingly and justly. I also do not disagree with the near-unanimous consensus of my liberal colleagues in the law schools that bucking the empire of force with the tools of constitutional law is one way to do just that. I do, though, want to complicate that picture. Over the last decade—and particularly in the short two years that have passed in Katrina's wake—our cocitizens have been increasingly voicing a very different worry about the current state of our democratic politics than that implied by the legal community's response to the moral charge voiced by Weil and White. A political leviathan untamed by law—an empire of force—is indeed a frightening spectacle. But a state that is too shrunken—that does too little, that fails to act, that is seemingly impotent, or that willfully neglects its political charge—also impoverishes and imperils lives. The political animal within us might become hyperactive, reckless, and destructive. But it can also be slothful, neglectful, and distracted, and when it is, the consequences can be equally lethal.

The worry increasingly voiced by American citizens, particularly in Katrina's wake, is that our domestic politics and the state that is its product have become too wan, not too voracious, even as our foreign policies have become monstrously outsized. Our shrunken state, incapable of either preparing for or mounting an adequate response to a hurricane, incapable of repairing deteriorating bridges or crumbling schools, incapable of responding to public health crises or to a dangerously warming climate, seems, to many of our cocitizens, to be in breach of the most basic, fundamental duties central to a sensible construal of virtually any social compact. Thus, where lawyers look at our government and see the empire of force of which Weil spoke, in violation of any number of constitutional norms, many of our cocitizens see, at best, an empire of sloth—an empire that is failing or willfully refusing to live up to its most basic obligations.[13] This worry likewise is not without reason. Over the past decade or so, our legislators, who spend such extraordinary sums of money to be elected to their jobs, have "worked," we learn, only a few "weeks" a year, with a "week" defined as Tuesday to Thursday. Handguns proliferate on city streets and in rural towns both, leaving many in fear not of a state untamed by the Constitution but of drug empires unrestrained by law. Balmy December, January, February, and March days are worrisome reminders of a looming and largely unaddressed environmental crisis, not a sweet reprieve from an unchangeably cold winter. The costs of health care and food force bizarre budgetary accommodations and trade-offs in the individual households of the working class: dental visits are sacrificed for rent payments; new clothes are foregone for weekly groceries. For vast numbers of poor, working-class, and middle-class families, the protection against risk that is the leviathan's raison d'être, as argued by liberal theorists of the state from Hobbes to Rawls, is just nowhere in sight. The government—or at least the lawmaking first branch of it—seems to be broken[14]—not much of an empire at all. The social compact has seemingly been breached.

So, against the risk of a shrunken state rather than a hyperactive one—a state that leaves our public lives diminished; that leaves our health, safety, and old age at risk; that leaves levees unbuilt and public schools in disrepair—what do constitutional lawyers, ever alert to the dangers of empire, distinctively assert? Nothing, really. Some of us regret it. We vote for change. But virtually no one of us asserts a professional, disciplined role for constitutionalism—and hence a role for constitutional lawyers—in the work of *tikkun* that is necessary to mend that broken first branch of our government. There is, then, this profound asymmetry in our American constitutional culture. We pit constitutional law, constitutional lawyers, and of course constitutionalism itself against the errant, overreaching, dangerously destructive leviathan. We are virtually as one in this collective effort. Almost no one, though, asserts even a theoretical—much less an enforceable—constitutional breach when the state the Constitution constitutes fails to act. Our constitutional law, we collectively assume, is just not implicated or breached by a state's passivity. The consequence of all of this in terms of our own identity is that we lawyers feel a heightened legal obligation—a constitutional obligation—to repel the bestial, aggressive, political animal when he starts to run amok, and we feel we must do so through the persuasive power of sweet reason manifested in law. Yet we recognize no professional constitutional duty whatsoever to prod that same political animal when it kills through slothfulness. No higher law—or at least no higher law with which we are familiar—is breached by a state that fails to act. That is just politics. It is not law's work.

This sharply delineated contrast between our sense of constitutional obligation to struggle against the malfeasant state and our insistence on our own utter lack of responsibility when faced with the nonfeasant one, right at the heart of our professional legal culture, is worth pondering, if we are worried, as Jim White correctly says we should be, about the current state of our law and democracy. Against the overreaching, intrusive state and the political animal that moves it, constitutional lawyers pit a higher law and all its constituent parts: the Constitution itself, the Bill of

Rights, the Supreme Court, the federal judiciary, the rule of law, the rule of precedent, stare decisis, judicial review, strict scrutiny, substantive due process, procedural due process, individual rights that "trump" policy, penumbral rights to complement the enumerated ones, neutral principles, fundamental interests, liberty interests, balancing tests, formal equality, and so on. It is quite an arsenal. Against the neglectful, inattentive, passive, inactive state and its sometimes lethal indifference, we lend a shrug of our collective shoulders. The state, the Court tells us again and again, is under no constitutional duty to affirmatively act, or if there is such a duty, it is unenforceable.[15] There is just no legal remedy for any purported breach of these most likely nonexistent duties, when the state allows the levees to collapse; fails to move the elderly, infirm, and poor to high ground when the waters rise; or fails to fund the schools, to repair the nursing homes and veterans hospitals, to address a deteriorating environment, to provide a poor child with a dentist who might prevent an infection from an abscessed tooth from entering his brain and killing him, and so on. Citizens have no "positive rights" to any of these provisions, the courts instruct, and likewise, legislators are under no affirmative duty to protect people from crime, guns, and violence; to compensate for tortious wrongs; or to provide a public education. Much less must it guarantee food or shelter for poor people or get people out of the way of a hurricane. The state could simply cease performing all of these functions entirely and breach no constitutional duty upon doing so. If the people choose, through their elected leaders, to let their schools' bathrooms rot and their infrastructure decay, to let levees fall into disrepair, children die, and the earth sicken, then that is their choice; that is politics. It is not the place of law and not the duty of lawyers to waken the sleepy animal. The voters can, and they will, if they so choose. Again, it is just not law's work.

This essay first argues that both the promise of the Constitution, as understood by the legal profession (that constitutional law, as interpreted by judges, is a meaningful check on egregious politics), and its limit (that the Constitution, so understood, is no response at all to state sloth) are deeply and perhaps inextricably interrelated. Both, I will argue in the first part, are rooted in a particular conception of the Constitution and a particular understanding of its role in democracy: a conception that stresses the legalistic nature of the Constitution and its amenability to judicial enforcement and interpretation. Here as elsewhere, I call this conception of constitutionalism the "adjudicated constitution." When lawyers put their faith in the Constitution as a check on the malfeasant state, and when lawyers collectively claim that there is no constitutional breach when the nonfeasant state fails to act, they are typically referring to the Constitution as understood by courts. Lawyers, then, to refine the point, have tremendous faith in the adjudicated constitution as a response to the empire of force but see no role for it when the state harms through inaction. That somewhat complicated faith—faith in the Constitution as enforced by courts—I believe, is overstated. It is not illogical or incoherent or internally contradictory. It is simply overstated. The second and major part of this essay simply highlights some of the moral and pragmatic costs of our reliance on that promise—and our acquiescence in its limit.

In the third part of this essay, I offer a different sort of constitutional response to White's and Weil's charge than the one currently embraced by our constitutional community. The heart of my answer to White and Weil is that constitutional lawyers should at least attempt to use their talents so as to ennoble politics, rather than try so relentlessly to stop it, if we want to disrespect the empire of force in the way that makes it possible for us to live lovingly and justly. Lawyers, I suggest, have much to offer the collective effort of reinvigorating our lawmaking processes in a direction more consonant with social justice, just as we have, collectively, in the past, offered much to the task of invigorating adjudication with a sense of legal justice.

By no means, furthermore, should we turn our backs on the Constitution as we engage this effort. Thus I am not arguing that the Constitution itself is a hindrance to the work of ennobling politics. We might, though, want to not rely quite as heavily as we have in the past on the adjudicated constitution. This is not an effort to which the rhetorical tools, powers, and virtues of adjudication can be put. It is, though, a constitutional effort all the same, to the necessity and urgency of which our undue adherence to adjudication may have made us blind.

THE PROMISE AND LIMITS OF CONSTITUTIONALISM

Why are constitutional lawyers, ever vigilant to the dangers of state malfeasance, so silent with respect to state nonfeasance? Why are lawyers so convinced that the Constitution has nothing to say about state failures to act? Whatever might be the lessons of doctrine, as a matter of political theory, this just seems peculiar. A constitution—any constitution—constitutes a government, after all, in order for it to do things. Indeed, both the original form of our own Constitution and the postbellum reconstruction amendments were born of the conviction that the federal government in particular ought to be doing a good bit more than it had been doing in the period preceding its enactment. Does the Constitution really impose on our lawmakers no affirmative duties at all to promote the general welfare?

Neither the text nor the history of the American Constitution provides a full explanation of the contemporary consensus view in the legal profession that as a matter of doctrinal constitutional law, the Constitution is one of negative rights only and does not speak to state nonfeasance. First, as numerous scholars over the last quarter century have repeatedly pointed out, the Constitution itself contains more than just a few passages suggesting the existence of positive obligations, both of the individual states and of the federal government.[16] The Constitution itself was "ordained and established," according to its very first sentence, in part, to "insure Domestic Tranquility" and to "promote the general Welfare."[17] Those sound like things the federal government is being tasked to do. The states, furthermore, are required, by Section 1 of the Fourteenth Amendment, to provide both due process and equal protection of the laws—that "no state shall deny" these rights, if we take out the double negative, seems to mean that all states shall grant them. It is not clear from the text what we are to be protected from, but the syntax and grammar of the sentence seem to quite unambiguously charge the states with the duty to protect citizens against various risks and to do so equally.[18] Congress is empowered to respond if they fail to do so, by Section 5. States and Congress are both likewise required by the same amendment to accord to persons born in the U.S. territory all the rights, privileges, and immunities of full citizenship.[19] We do not know what those privileges and immunities of citizenship might be, but that is because the Supreme Court largely cut off the inquiry, not because it would be so hard to determine what the framers meant by this.

Our political history likewise is filled with examples of both individual patriots and large political movements employing the language and rhetoric of the Constitution to urge that states are obligated to act in accord with the mandates of social justice. Tom Paine saw in the U.S. Constitution and in the constitutions of the various states an attempt to articulate the basic rights of man, rights that he argued ought to include what we would today call welfare rights;[20] some abolitionists saw in the original articles of the Constitution affirmative rights to liberty, happiness, and equality that precluded its implied endorsement of slavery; many prominent statesmen of the immediate postbellum era saw in the various reconstruction amendments constitutional obligations of the state to provide means of support for newly freed citizens, as well as the protection of the laws against the violence of white mobs.[21] Franklin Roosevelt famously urged a second Bill of Rights that would explicitly include a duty to provide for "welfare rights";[22] late nineteenth-century and early twentieth-century unionists, suffragists, and feminists all saw in the Constitution affirmative rights of labor,[23] of suffrage and equality for women, and of reparations for slavery; and a goodly number of contemporary scholars and activists find in the Constitution's general phrases more than sufficient textual support for the claim that the Constitution requires the national and state governments to attend to the basic welfare needs of poor citizens.[24]

Whence, against the evidence of text and history, came the persistent judicial claim—the certainty—that the Constitution is one of negative rights only? What accounts for its appeal? One possible explanation for the widespread acceptance of this canard, which I believe is relatively unexplored in even the contemporary scholarship that is most critical of it, concerns the nature of the law that constitutional law has become. Constitutional lawyers typically see the Constitution as a source of entirely ordinary, positive, judge-made (or adjudicative) law, and they typically see it as nothing but that. Put differently, according to this understanding, our country's constitutional principles—including the entire panoply of rights, duties, liabilities, aspirations, and powers, as well as their limits—are properly recognized, articulated, embroidered, embellished, trimmed down, overturned, or abandoned through ordinary judicial method. The law that stems from the Constitution is therefore subject to the ordinary judicial constraints of process, stare decisis, and whatever professional culture might exist at the time, which curbs interpretive excess. Constitutional content is discerned by judicial acts of reason. Its force, its rhetoric, and its reasoning are all invoked in restraints on the will of actors, in a way that is common to all judge-made law. Constitutional law, then, unsurprisingly comes to share the attributes of that general class of which it is a member. It may be a Constitution that is being expounded and an extraordinary one at that, but it is being expounded by judges, justices, and lawyers in ordinary courts of law and in quite ordinary legal ways. The claim that this is the proper understanding and function of the Constitution in our scheme of government is what I mean by the term *adjudicated constitutionalism*. The Constitution is law—the Constitution itself of course says so—and what follows from this, American lawyers virtually all believe, is that the judicial branch of government creates, interprets, and enforces the law that the Constitution is.

What difference does this make? What is constitutional law by virtue of its being judge-made? What features might constitutional law share with all judge-made law by virtue of its inclusion in that class? I think there are several, but most important for these purposes, virtually all branches of judge-made law, including judge-made constitutional law, target aberrant, occasional misdeeds rather than systemic social wrongs. Adjudicative law is alert to that which wreaks havoc: the willful discriminator; the homicidal murderer; the negligent, reckless, or intentionally malfeasant actor; the police officer acting in bad faith. It is much slower to respond, if it does at all, to the adverse impact on the weak of a cruel status quo, to the casually lethal corporate boardroom that knowingly kills, to the police officer who follows (whether in bad faith or not) an invasive and discriminatory social script, and so on. Basically, the more aberrant or occasional the wrong, the more easily and readily adjudicative law responds. On the other side of the ledger, the more systemic, ordinary, or pervasive the injustice, the less the law responds.

Think, for a moment, of other fields of adjudicative law. Tort law—the classic—perceives and responds to the assault and battery that disrupts the social order, not to the subordination and the petty or massive oppressions that are the social order. If one is fired from a job for no discernible reason, no legally recognized wrong has occurred—that is part of the white noise of life. If one has been fired for a noticeable wrongful reason, then maybe there is case. Sexual harassment on the job might be a tort or a civil rights wrong if it is so extraordinarily odd as to stick out like a sore thumb. Ordinary, daily, nonsexual harassment—and a good bit of the "ordinary" sexual kind likewise—is just part of the job. And of course, sexual harassment at home is what we call domestic life. If one is hit and injured by a negligent driver, there may be recovery; for the asthmatic child that suffers from air pollutants or stays in all summer to avoid a dangerous outside environment caused by them, there likely is not. Again, the more ordinary and widespread the assaultive behavior, the less likely it is to be viewed or compensated as tortious. We have all sorts of jargonistic phrases for this entire class of distinctions. In tort law, we identify as tortious the malfeasant but not the nonfeasant; in criminal law as developed, although not authored, by judges, we sanction the bad act but not the bad failure to act; in civil rights law as developed by judges, we compensate for discriminatory state action that harms the few but not for state inaction that adversely impacts the many. In private and public judge-made law, we compensate the victims of individual acts of destruction. Victims of widespread corruption, domination, or injustice are rarely noticed and far less often compensated.

These distinctions are fundamental to the nature and goals of judge-made law. Adjudicative law seeks restoration of a status quo; it seeks to rebalance what has gone awry. It seeks to preserve the social order against disruption. That is the nature of the "legal justice" it seeks, to which it is committed. It only fitfully and only rarely successfully seeks to upset the status quo or challenge injustice that is embedded within it. It is a cliché that the killer of one serves a life sentence or worse while the killer of thousands only suffers the verdict of history. With respect to adjudicative law, this is hardly mysterious or even ironic: such law sees, registers, notices, deters, and compensates the exceptional and the errant. It responds to the actor that breaches the king's peace, not to the injustice of the king's peace itself. Less metaphorically, it does not see, deter, or compensate for injustices occasioned by the norm. Adjudicative law—the law that our courts make—exists, largely, to preserve the norm; in a very concrete sense, such law is the norm. It is at least a part—a substantial part—of the normalcy and ordinariness of life that law seeks to reestablish, after the tortious or criminal act that threatened it. The unjust social subordination that is a part of the normal becomes a part of what such law protects. It will never be its target.

So, what happens when we turn constitutional law in toto, so to speak, over to courts to develop? Over time and, of course, with notable exceptions, the Constitution loses transformative meanings, and its preservative meanings become entrenched. This occurs not because of the nature of the Constitution, which clearly has both preservative and transformative potential, and not because of the nature of law, including the law the Constitution declares itself to be in the supremacy clause, a phrase that can have—and surely had at the time it was authored—any number of meanings. Nor is it because of the text itself—much of which seemingly counsels or requires state action rather than restraint—and surely it is not because of the history of its use. Nor, for that matter, is it because of the political orientation of particular judges or justices charged with its interpretation. Rather, constitutional law has the deeply conservative form and content it has, including its reluctance to countenance the existence of positive rights or state duties, because in ordinary times, which is most of the time, it is a body of judge-made common law. It was not always such and need not always be such, but it has become such, and as a result, its content has been molded to fit the deep premises of that form of law. Like all such law, judge-made constitutional common law responds to the occasional, aberrant misdeeds of identified actors by compensating, retributing, and restoring order to their victims. The actors that are its subject, of course, are state actors rather than individual criminals or tortfeasors—that is its distinction. But its jurisprudential stance toward those wrongdoers is no different in this field of law than in any other. Constitutional law addresses the oddly aberrantly malfeasant, invasive state, just as criminal law addresses the oddly aberrantly malfeasant criminal that disrupts the king's peace, while tort law addresses the irresponsible citizen who invades the ordinary rights of cocitizens.

Like adjudicative law quite generally, then, constitutional law specifically is relatively blind, whether willfully or not, to the systemic injustices that permeate a social order. In some respects and during some periods, it is even more blind or considerably less blind than other forms of judge-made law, for reasons that are indeed quite distinctive to it. Unlike the rest of judicially created law, constitutional law cannot be readily changed politically. That fact alone puts considerably more pressure on both its preservative and transformative functions. At times, if the judicial politics are right, the relative permanence of judicially created constitutional common law creates a felt moral imperative for judges to in effect merge their functions with the legislative one and respond to pervasive injustice through constitutional law. At other times, given the political zeitgeist, that same entrenchment seemingly implies the opposite to the justices themselves and many of the rest of us: the self-same permanence of constitutional law, unlike other fields of judge-made law, suggests that judges should more jealously guard its preservative function. But these are differences over large periods of time, and they are differences at the margins; the consistencies with other forms of adjudicated law are far more striking than the occasional departures.

Like adjudicated law quite generally, constitutional law attends to malfeasance but is inattentive to nonfeasance. It notices, deters, and compensates wrongful acts, but not the wrongs brought on by the failure to act;

it is alert to the dangers posed by overactive states but inattentive to the harms occasioned by the passivity or negligence of states and state actors. We enshrine all of this in doctrine, here as elsewhere: in constitutional law, we distinguish between the public sphere, which can be targeted by constitutional law, and the private one, which cannot be; we draw a firm line between de jure acts that might be unconstitutional and de facto acts that largely are not, between state action that might be compensable and state inaction that mostly is not, and so on. All of these distinctions in constitutional law insure that the judicial gaze will stay focused on the exceptional while preserving the social, cultural, private, and legal norm. The state that kills or injures by failing to act, then, gets a pass from our judicial constitutional enforcers, as does the proverbial stranger of tort and criminal law who blithely walks by the baby drowning in the puddle of water. Whatever might be true of the Constitution itself, adjudicated constitutional law is silent with respect to the state that fails to act, just as criminal law and tort law are silent with respect to the citizen who does likewise.

Yet adjudicative law—precisely because it is adjudicative—can and does react to the bad act and the bad actor that disrupts a status quo, and constitutional law is no exception. Judge-made law responds effectively to individual aberrance—to sharply delineated, individuated, occasional acts of malfeasance. Again, look at tort and criminal law: they are constituted by almost nothing but particular applications of this general norm. Intentionally, recklessly, and negligently harmful individuals get the book thrown at them, while newfangled doctrines that seem to cut against this grain in either field—such as strict liability norms of liability in tort or "syndrome" sorts of defenses in criminal law—are virtually by definition marginalized and are always in danger of disappearing altogether. In this regard, all that is distinctive about constitutional law, as contrasted with other genres of judge-made law, is that it is the political malfeasance of state actors, rather than the individual malfeasance of citizens, that elicits the legalist response. Indeed, this says quite a lot: it makes possible the values we typically associate with the rule of law. Thus, in this field of law, it is the malfeasant state, the malfeasant state actor, and, on occasion, the product of malfeasant state action—statutory law—to which the law responds. The errant leviathan, rather than the errant private citizen, triggers the concern and attention of the law. The promise at the heart of constitutional law and at the heart of the legal constitution is that it extends the ordinary judicial-legal impulse to counter aberrant behavior with law to the realm of the aberrant political actor, leader, and executive—to the sovereign itself, to the empire of force.

So, adjudicated constitutional law has at its heart both an ambitious promise and an implied limit. The promise of the adjudicated constitution is that it can indeed check the abusive empire of force no less than the criminal abuse of force by individuals. Aberrant political behavior—all the way up to the aberrant behavior of sovereigns—is no less subject to the command of adjudicative law than is aberrant individual behavior. Even kings and presidents must bend their behavior to these preexisting norms of conduct. We are a society of laws, not men, here; the law is king here; the tattered monarchical doctrine of sovereign immunity has no legitimacy here (at least, so some of us thought). Adjudicated constitutional law, created by judges, is and can be a potent check on the empire of force—not only because it is a body of constitutional law, but, equally important, because it is adjudicated. It's not only that the judicial branch is "separate." Rather, through constitutionalism, we can apply the deepest and most universal instincts of adjudicative law quite generally—to check, limit, deter, and compensate for aberrant and destructive individual impulses that threaten the status quo—to the aberrant, destructive impulses of state actors. This is rightly considered to be a substantial advance for liberalism and is largely what accounts for the centrality of the rule of law to liberal political theory. Adjudicated constitutional law, understood in this way, homogenizes the expectations and obligations of citizen and state actor—to obey the law. Both citizen and sovereign then must act in conformity, must bring their behavior in line with the norm, must adjust their behavior to the strictures and demands of the "common" law—the law that applies to all.

The limit of adjudicated constitutional law—that the Constitution is perceived as one of negative rights only, that there are no positive constitutional rights and no constitutionally mandated legislative duties—is the implied negative term of that self-same affirmative promise. As long as constitutional law is the province of the courts—as long as we are expounding an adjudicative constitution—pervasive societal injustice and the state inaction that facilitates it will not be its subject, and changing it will not be its objective. Preservation of societal consensus (including whatever injustice has become a part of that consensus) against particular bad actors—including state actors—will be. That is a substantial promise—the badly acting state might be an entire administration, an entire branch of government, an entire war or foreign policy, or an entire state of apartheid. But it also directly implies a substantial limit: the adjudicated constitution will be no response at all to the slothful state. This is not because we are expounding a constitution, the Constitution, or law; rather, it is because courts are doing the expounding. The distinction between state action, which might be the target of the judicial gaze, and state inaction, which will not be, is simply the doctrinal explanation for this quite fundamental and jurisprudential—not constitutional—feature of adjudicative law. The limited ability of constitutional law to correct or even notice state nonfeasance comes from the same root as its (perhaps limited) potency as a check on the empire of force. Both the limit and the promise of constitutional law, vis-à-vis the excesses or failures of the empire of force, are rooted in the nature and essence of adjudication.

SOME COSTS OF THE ADJUDICATED CONSTITUTION

Constitutional lawyers have a decidedly romantic relationship with the adjudicated constitution. They see its virtue and its beauty. Law can and should restrain the empire of force, and adjudicated constitutional law is the highest expression of that impulse. They are not so good at seeing its costs, the greatest of which, without question, is its implied term: adjudicated law will police against the aberrant, and therefore constitutional law will police against the aberrant state, but it will neither see nor respond to the inactive, nonresponsive state. The consequence is the wholesale political and moral legitimation of the negligent state that fails to act—the constitutional legitimation, in effect, of even quite fundamental breaches of the social compact.

Of course, there are obvious and much noted social welfare costs to the doctrine of "negative rights only—no positive rights." In part, at least, because of it, we do not have universal health care or child care, decent public schooling, guaranteed employment, a robust safety net, and so on. There are, though, less noticed costs as well. Look at what happens when we combine this verity of our constitutional law (that there are no positive constitutional rights and hence no legislative duties to act) with another cornerstone of our constitutional culture: to wit, to paraphrase Ronald Dworkin's famous articulation, that in the American scheme of government, our political morality is fully expressed in an idealized—and to some extent realized—body of adjudicated constitutional law.[25] The adjudicated constitution, Dworkin argued, well reflecting late twentieth-century constitutional thought, contains a full articulation of our moral rights and obligations as they pertain to governance. It is the bridge, he taught us all, between natural and positive law. It is political morality rendered positive. If that is true—maybe it is and maybe it is not, but it is certainly widely believed—then this certitude shared by so many in the legal community (that legislatures are under no constitutional obligations to provide basic welfare for the poor, to educate children adequately, to see to the health needs of the public, and so on) comes with a tragic coda: as go constitutional duties, so go moral duties as well. Our adjudicated constitution, after all, is not only a font of law; it is also our code of political morality. This leads to an unfortunate syllogism: if there is no constitutional duty to legislate toward the end of public welfare, and if constitutionalism exhausts our political morality, then there are likewise no moral duties.

Thus one of the least noticed but most consequential costs of the adjudicated constitution is just this: the constitutionalization of our political morality, combined first with the legalization of the constitution and then with the limits of adjudicative law, yields, over time, a political branch that views its distinctively moral obligations, no less than its constitutional obligations, solely as obligations of restraint and never as obligations to act. The unreckoned cost of the lawyerly insistence that the passive state is in breach of no constitutional duty is a state whose lethargy is not only legally but also morally and politically fully legitimated. There is a second and related cost as well. The adjudicated constitution in fact misstates—as it trivializes and minimizes—deeper lessons of our constitutional text and history. It is, again, a mainstay of our adjudicated constitutional law that states are under no affirmative duty to act and are only under duties not to act badly. But it simply does not follow that the Constitution itself is so limited. That the Constitution is one of only negative rights seems true, these days, largely within the context of and because of the nature of and limits of judicially created common law. Courts—because they are courts, not because they are conservative courts or regressive courts or reactionary courts—respect the past, aim to harmonize current realities with historical verities, look for patterned consistency, and seek to minimize upheaval. They are as ill-equipped now as they were disinclined a hundred years ago to flesh out the meaning of citizenship or privileges and immunities so as to specify the content of social justice. Likewise, our modern courts are not just ill-equipped but likewise disinclined to impose on states an obligation to educate all citizens up to a standard of adequacy, to feed hungry children, to criminalize violence against women, or to ensure decent health care. It does not follow, though, that the Constitution does not require of Congress or states or municipalities that one or all of them do exactly those tasks. The conclusion to draw from the limits of the adjudicated constitution is not that the Constitution itself contains no mandate that our states live up to the demands of social justice. The better conclusion is simply that the Constitution may have meanings and impose obligations beyond those the courts can impose as law.

Thus the adjudicated constitution not only entails the moral legitimation; it also and quite perversely entails the constitutional legitimation of the passive, inactive, negligent state. If there are moral or constitutional obligations on state actors to live up to the social compact, they are badly obscured by the judicialization of constitutional meaning. The adjudicated constitution not only obscures but perversely nullifies, rather than reinforces, the obligations of the social compact.

Now let me turn to the other side of the ledger. The question is not only whether the adjudicated constitution comes with these costs. The question is whether it is worth the price. The promise of the adjudicated constitution is that precisely because of its adjudicative nature, it can act as an independent, nonpolitical, legal check on the empire of force. It is surely possible—even likely—that we just cannot have the promise for free. So, how well does the judicial constitution perform its core function? What is the value of the promise? If the adjudicated constitution does fantastically well at this, the cost might be worth it: if the danger of the overreaching leviathan is that much greater than the danger of unchecked private power, then perhaps a judicial constitution that can aggressively police against the former while legitimating the latter might not be a bad trade. If the danger of the intrusive state is great enough, in other words, then perhaps we should put up with a legitimated social order, if that is the cost of an effective adjudicated check on malign politics.

A bit of skepticism regarding the efficacy of the promise might be in order. Let me just list some reasons. One reason for skepticism was famously argued by James Bradley Thayer over a hundred years ago: aggressive judicial review, Thayer worried, might inhibit, rather than spur, the development of a constitutional conscience.[26] Take a rough analogy. Surely parents and school boards all realize that the more we rely on law and legalism to ensure compliance with virtue, the less our children will ever rely on the pull of conscience—and the less reason we will have to instill conscience or to create the social conditions that are essential to the development of one. This might be true of our political actors no less than it is clearly true of our adolescents. Thayer's famous objection to an overly aggressive judicial review and an overly legalized constitution was simply that both would have the undesirable consequence of weakening the felt obligation of lawmakers to respect constitutional guarantees, with the net result being less, not more, constitutional fidelity. Thayer has surely not been proven wrong by events of the last century, particularly the last decade. Even with judicial review and a Supreme Court that has not been overly hesitant to use it, our country is still willfully violating the Geneva Conventions; we still live with the shame of the Bybee torture memorandum; Guantanamo is still in business; extraordinary renditions continue; habeas remains, for all practical purposes, suspended; executive signing statements are still on the table; Congress continues to fund an illegal war; the privacy of our cocitizens is still being invaded without warrants; and so on. Both the legalization of constitutional safeguards against a dangerous leviathan and the trust we now place in the judiciary to police it have not unambiguously left us with a properly chastised, constitution-abiding executive branch. It has left us with an executive willing to push the constitutional envelope and with a legislative branch freed of any felt need to abide constitutional restraints or even attend to the niceties—freed from responsibility in part by virtue of the rhetorical certitude that any constitutional infirmity is the courts' business. It has left us with political branches occasionally checked by law but totally unchecked by either constitutional conscience or constitutional politics, as neither the lawmakers nor the governed feel or act on any felt obligation to abide constitutional mandates.

Are there other reasons beyond Thayer's speculative thesis to be skeptical? Perhaps. Since *Brown v. Board of Education*[27] and even more so since *Roe v. Wade,*[28] liberal constitutional lawyers in particular, but all of us more generally, have come to rely on courts far more than Thayer could have foreseen, not only to limit unconstitutional legislative and executive actions taken in pursuit of national security, but also to police unconstitutional legislative actions that are taken in pursuit of social and moral ends as well—such as the criminalization of abortion, contraception, and homosexuality; the illegalization of same-sex marriage; and the separation of the races in schools, parks, and marriages. The adjudicated constitution, as deployed by liberal and libertarian constitutional lawyers, is meant to save us from the pernicious effects of these unconstitutional legislative adventures, no less than from executive malfeasance. Now, since the Court is doing the constitutional reasoning, the lawmakers themselves—reckless bad actors all—need not. That is basically Thayer's point, albeit updated for modern circumstances. Surely, though, not only lawmakers but citizens likewise should worry over whether our moral and social inclinations to outlaw contraception, regulate abortion, criminalize flag burning, allow prayer in schools, and so on are or are not consistent with the commitments to liberty, equality, and a secular state that lawyers and courts find reflected in constitutional phrases. Whether these laws do or do not comport with liberty and equality are important questions of political morality, no less than of constitutionality. Constitutional norms ought to matter to citizens, simply because and to the extent that they are good norms of governance, not only because they are constitutional requirements. Judicial review and the adjudicated constitution that is its product suggest that although these norms matter greatly, they need not matter at all to citizens; they need not be a part of public deliberations.

There is yet a third problem with the adjudicated constitution's promise to check the empire of force, also not noticed by Thayer (as far as I can tell). As Jeremy Waldron has argued for the past decade, the constitutional-legal discourse that preoccupies the Court threatens to swamp not only the constitutional awareness of everyone else but moral deliberation about these issues likewise.[29] Look at just the most obvious example of this general phenomenon. One reason—there may be others—that we do not have a particularly reasoned and mutually respectful public debate about either the morality of a woman's decision to abort a pregnancy or the morality, wisdom, or practicality of legislating against abortion is that the constitutional argument in the Court has in effect monopolized the debate, not only over the constitutionality of such legislation, but also over its morality and practicality, leaving nothing but a residue of irrationality in the court of public opinion. Waldron suggests a worrisome consequence of aggressive judicial review of social and moral legislation: not only does constitutional argument in the Court trump constitutional argument among citizens and legislators, but by so doing, it obviates public debate about the morality, wisdom, or prudence of constitutionally suspect laws as well. There is not much point in arguing over whether or not a proposed course of action is a good idea if someone else is going to decide, on quite different grounds, whether it is to be permitted. You may as well save your breath.

So, rather than argue over either the sensibility of regulating abortion or the morality of having one, we leave it to courts to discuss whether *Casey*[30] is consistent with *Roe,* whether *Roe* is required by *Griswold,*[31] whether *Griswold* follows from *Pierce v. Society of Sisters,*[32] whether amendments to constitutions can have penumbras, what liberty requires, what (if anything) is substantive about due process, and, most recently of course, whether states can constitutionally subordinate women's health to their own need to express a symbolic respect for fetal life (they can).[33] Rather than talk about pornography's harms, we leave it to courts to discuss rules, community standards, balancing tests, fighting words, and state action, to determine whether states can constitutionally ban this stuff, rather than whether or not they ought to. Rather than talk about end-of-life deliberations and who should make them and how, lawyers and judges discuss substantive due process rights—whether states can legislate on these issues, rather than whether or not they ought to. Rather than engage in a public discussion, if one is warranted, about the value or harms of same-sex sex, lawyers and courts talk about the limits of formal equality—again, whether or not states can intrude here, rather than whether or not they ought to—and so on. In this way, issues of political morality become constitutional issues, which in turn become legal issues, which then must be decided by courts. Congressional and public discussion of pressing issues of political morality—how we ought to govern ourselves and why—is thus doubly or even triply diminished by legal constitutionalism: neither the constitutionality of these laws, nor their wisdom, nor the morality of the actions they aim to prohibit is ultimately determined—if even discussed—in public and political venues. Discussion of the morality of the citizens' conduct, the political wisdom of regulating against it, and the constitutionality of any attempt to do so are all diverted away from public and legislative fora by the identification of questions of political morality with constitutionality, of constitutionality with legality, and then of legality with court-centered adjudication. If we boil this down to a moral, both Thayer and Waldron's objection to aggressive judicial review is this: at least in a democracy, the adjudicated constitution does not look like a very promising way of going about the business of checking the empire of force. It leaves citizens with no incentive and no responsibility to do so themselves.

I want to suggest a final and purely rhetorical cost of the adjudicated constitution, which I do not think has been well explicated in either contemporary or older critiques of judicial review. The rhetoric that is so central both to the promise that the adjudicated constitution can check the errant leviathan and to its silence in the face of state inaction badly degrades politics, by which I mean the utterly ordinary, nonconstitutional, legislative, city hall, do-it-by-voting, let's-make-a-deal, compromising machinations of majoritarian democracy. Constitutional law, in our legal culture, rhetorically soars. The pinnacle of law and legal rhetoric both is the constitutional case and question, and our debates on such cases and questions are intoxicated with this sense of moral purpose. Talk about life, death, marriage, family, liberty, and equality is the bread and butter, so to speak, of constitutional law. Constitutional law—in courts, chambers, and law offices—concerns itself centrally with these existential and profoundly political moral questions. But what is left for politics once the law that asserts itself as politics' antithesis has cornered the market on moral profundity or simply moral seriousness? It is not reasoned deliberations over the meaning of life or death, what equality requires of states, what liberty means to individuals, and so forth. That, after all, is the content of our constitutional law—the law that trumps, checks, and limits politics; the law that is by definition not politics; the law that is reason not passion; and so forth. What is left of politics when law monopolizes reason and idealism both is horse trading, histrionics, legislative irrelevance, free riders, rent-seekers, a market for votes, and speeches to empty chambers. What is left is a politics that is utterly devoid of moral ambition.

Apparently, legislators should not concern themselves, in their ordinary "deliberation," with moral questions—at least according to our now conventional constitution-legal logic. Look at what not only our public choice theorists but our most morally generous, Rawls-inspired, deeply political constitutional and liberal theorists say about of what the legislative process, in contrast to the adjudicative, should consist. Lawmakers, we are told, act—they do not reason. And when they act, they act on the basis of either their own or their constituents' preferences. Those preferences are as morally arbitrary as the patterns in the sand made by the sea's tides. The preferences and the actions taken on the basis of them are constituted by whim, passion, emotion, hysteria, public fears, short-term desires, discriminatory biases, petty bigotry, and so on. Legislators act on the basis of what they want, and those wants are basic, primitive, infantile, and beyond scrutiny—they are just facts of being. Actions taken on the basis of them are justified, assuming they are constitutional, because they are in turn a fair approximation of the equally infantile desires of their constitutents. The infantilization of politics is the rhetorical cost of guarding the chicken coop through the adjudicated constitution.

This infantilization of legislative process is the death knell of the nobility of politics. Infants cannot and should not be trusted. Nor can they be expected to think or care beyond their wants and needs. Our dominant constitutional discourse—the philosophical, reflective backdrop of the adjudicated constitution—characterizes the lawmaking political realm as, essentially, infantile. We have been doing this for a long, long time, and now the chickens are coming home to roost.

This is a profound loss, albeit a cultural and rhetorical one. We Americans have in a sense lost our awareness of the generosity, tolerance, neighborliness, and fellow feeling that must be a component of ordinary politics, as well as awareness of the goodness of the ordinary law that can be its product. Decent, pragmatic, honest discussion and sincere compromise on public issues of reproductive policy, public health, sexuality, education, and the use of the public space between persons of very differing views on the meaning of life requires a healthy dollop of fellow feeling—of fraternalism—and it can certainly engender it as well. Ordinary politics need not and indeed should not invoke "constitutional" dimensions and tones to have this nobility. There just are no good reasons and more than a few bad ones to decide who we are as a people, what our intergenerational commitments should be, what our American essence is, or what might be the moral content of the shining City on the Hill when deciding what our laws should be on matters of health, reproduction, education, or welfare. What we have to do is decide what our policies on the latter should be, what our needs are, and how they can be addressed within the context of our conflicting beliefs. Our intergenerational commitments, our American essence, and all the rest of it should be the result of this process. Agreement on it should not be its precondition.

There is of course a need to confront our differences in ordinary discussion within ordinary political life, including our differing moral views. But there is also a need to create a community—in part through negotiation, deliberation, consensus, or compromise—in order to resolve political issues. This sort of very ordinary political exchange and the state it creates—not constitutional deliberation between elites in private chambers on the meanings for all time of liberty, equality, identity, and virtue—is the political sensibility that Aristotle lauded as the highest collective human achievement. Ordinary politics done well and the ordinary law that is its product should earn our respect. Ordinary politics done well, in fact, may be the best check against an empire of force worthy only of disrespect, and if it is, we should worry that adjudicated constitutionalism threatens it. Americans have in a sense forgotten why this political activity is central to a decent and shared human life, and liberal legal constitutionalists have in effect applauded the amnesia. Decades of degradation of the political, by the legal and constitutional, have taken their toll.

THE POLITICAL CONSTITUTION

Let me suggest one way to turn the tide on all of this, if only a bit. The American degradation of the political is a deeply ingrained national cultural tendency, and it cannot be turned on a dime. But liberal lawyers and liberal law professors have had something to do with entrenching it, and law professors in particular wield some power that might be put toward correcting it. I do not think we do that by pronouncing the judicial constitutional project to be incoherent or contradictory. It is not. Nor do we do that by declaiming adjudicated constitutionalism and the fear of the empire of force that motivates it, as a pernicious or legitimating or corruptive lie. It is not. What adjudicated constitutionalism is, for which it can be faulted, is incomplete. It is an incomplete rendition of our constitutional history. Our Constitution has been much more than a legal document. It is an incomplete accounting of our constitutional ideals. The Constitution and our constitutional tradition most assuredly contain ideals that go beyond those enforced or enforceable by courts. It is even an incomplete reading of the bare text. Mostly, though, it is an incomplete accounting of the vices, dangers, risks, promise, and virtues of politics—and it is therefore an incomplete rendition of the social compact between state and citizen that it encapsulates. It misstates, badly, the relation between politics and law. By so insistently imbuing law with virtue, politics with malignancy, it inclines us to constitutionally legitimate state neglect of basic political responsibilities. It also inclines us all to simply neglect the art and nobility of politics.

What might law professors do? I think we could make a number of changes in the way we teach and study constitutional law, all of which collectively might make a difference. First and most important, we could begin to take seriously, in teaching and scholarship both, what some now call the "political constitution," giving it equal billing, so to speak, with the adjudicated constitution that has for so long been the subject of our professional lives. Thus we might study, teach, and take seriously not only the Court's interpretations but also both legislative and public interpretations of constitutional guarantees, particularly those guarantees that seemingly speak directly to the state's obligations to provide for the public welfare. The Social Security Act,[34] the civil rights acts,[35] the Voting Rights Act,[36] the Age Discrimination Act,[37] the Americans with Disabilities Act,[38] the clean air and water acts,[39] the proposed Anti-Discrimination Act,[40] various pieces of labor-protective legislation, and the pioneering living wage laws[41] in the one state and the handful of municipalities that have them are all central embodiments, not just peripheral glosses, of our constitutional protections of public welfare, liberty, and equality, and we ought to treat and teach them as such. They are the manifestations of a politics that takes very seriously not only its obligations under the social compact to tend to the general welfare and promote domestic tranquility but its constitutional obligations to do so as well. If we treated, honored, and taught them as such, we might, as a side product, instill in ourselves, students, and cocitizens an awareness of those constitutional traditions—whether inside or outside the courts—that have counseled a robust role for politics in the securing of social justice and the general happiness, no less than the role of law on which we have tended to bestow so much attention: securing individual rights, through law, against politically malignant goals.

Second, were we to take seriously the possibility that the political constitution—even if not the adjudicated one—requires of lawmakers that they attend to the demands of social justice, then we will need to ask of what that justice might consist. Law professors might take up this question, not just as an interdisciplinary question borrowed from the humanities, but as a central and long-neglected question of any decent education in law. Does social justice require of lawmakers a Benthamic regard that sees all of law's subjects as rigorously equal in assessing the utility of proposed legislation? Or does it require of lawmakers a Rawlsian commitment to the well-being of the worst off? Does it require a Kantian transparency of means and ends? Does it require a state that promotes the general capabilities or the basic functionings of all citizens—the ability to work, to enjoy intimacy and family life, to age with dignity, to have some modicum of good health and a reasonable life span, to expect safety in one's home and on the streets, and so on—that are necessary to the living of a minimally good life, as argued by Armatya Sen, Martha Nussbaum, and now an increasing number of Aristotlean welfarist philosophers? Does it require some measure of all of these, if they can be made consistent, or does it require something else entirely? A serious regard for the political constitution, in short, might require the recapture and articulation and revitalization of this long-neglected thread of our "natural law" tradition. We would have to ask, or reask, as a matter of constitutionalism, of social compact, and of direct moral obligation, not only what a good state or state actor must not do, but also what such a state and state actor must do. This would require a substantial broadening of the ambitions of our current understanding, not only of the breadth and compass of constitutional law, but of jurisprudence as well. Jurisprudence, even capaciously understood, has not asked questions about the political virtues of states—rather than the political dangers they pose—in a very, very long time.

Lastly, broadening our understanding of the Constitution to include its political, as well as adjudicative, interpretations and functions might entail considerably more skepticism than we have managed to muster, not over the coherence of constitutionalism—there has been plenty of that—but over its ultimate value. As I have tried to argue here, lawyers and law professors ought to consider the possibility that even if our adjudicated constitution fails to urge our legislators to promote social justice in their work, the political constitution might well do so. We should also consider the possibility that if the political constitution fails to require what social justice demands of lawmakers, then it follows that we ought to change it or at least view it skeptically. Taking seriously the broadest possible understanding of our constitutional traditions, rather than the narrowest, would require us to examine the possibility that the American Constitution itself is simply morally inadequate, in deep and perhaps irreversible ways. If we reach such a conclusion, we should treat that as the very real constitutional, moral, and political crisis it would surely be. What we ought not to do, should we so conclude, is tailor our moral aspirations for our politics and our governance to fit the fashion of the constitutional day.

Let me end with one institutional suggestion. If law professors were to take seriously the political constitution, the most immediate implication might be in our career counseling. We might consider advising some of our graduating law students that they in turn consider taking a one- or two-year legislative internship after graduating, in lieu of those highly coveted and sought-out judicial clerkships. We have idealistic, smart students brimming with constitutional ideas about what politics should be for and what government should be and do—not only what government must not do. We have a broken legislative branch that could use good legal advice and aspirational political vision informed by just those legal ideals. We need our legislators to exhibit precisely those virtues—reason, idealism, conviction, and principles—that we have come to expect of the participants in the branch we used to think was the least dangerous. These are legalist virtues to be sure, but they are not only legalist virtues—they embrace substantive principled commitments to equality, to liberty, and to the general welfare that are the heart of liberal democracy. Those ideals ought to inform and ennoble our politics and our community, whether or not they inform our law. Lawyers have the capability to see that they do, and we ought to consider this both a moral and a constitutional obligation.

CONCLUSIONS

What good might come from any of this? Is respecting, recognizing, studying, and perhaps teaching the political constitution a credible way to disrespect the empire of force? Does it answer Weil and White's charge? It is surely not sufficient. It might, though, go some small way toward directing both our own and perhaps our students' constitutional passions, energy, interpretive creativity, and thoughtfulness toward the project of prodding the state to fulfill its very positive obligations—moral and constitutional both—to legislate in the public interest, for the public welfare, and toward the end of creating and maintaining a socially just state. Minimally, interpretation of the political constitution, unlike the adjudicative, would not be bound by the conventions of adjudicative law, including the conventional limit of that law to address malfeasance rather than nonfeasance. More broadly, the political constitution, unlike its legal sister, at least might address the slothful state, as the adjudicative constitution does the dangerously forceful empire. If we were to develop it, we might close the gap between our lawyerly sense of the constitution and what constitutes a violation of it, on the one hand, and, on the other, our cocitizens' sense of the social compact and when it is and is not breached.

Attendance to the political constitution, as well as the adjudicative, might also indirectly bolster even the adjudicative constitution's affirmative promise as lawyers now understand it—that the Constitution, interpreted by judges, can act as a check on the empire of force. Recall Waldron's and Thayer's objections to the practice of judicial review. Both, I think, are largely obviated by complementing—not replacing—the regard we show for the adjudicative constitution with regard we might show the political. First, recall Thayer's objection to judicial review: that robust review "disincentivizes," as we would now say—or discourages, as he might have said—the development of a constitutional superego. The natural implication of his argument, however, is not necessarily that we limit judicial review—although that was the implication for which he argued—but, rather, that whether or not we do so, we intensify civic education. If law professors studied, argued over, heeded, and taught the political as well as the adjudicative constitution—and did so throughout public education, not just in law schools—we might instill in our future governors a sense of constitutional obligation, thus lessening what might be a crippling overreliance on judicial vigilance. A little constitutional superego might go a long way, particularly in the executive branch of government.

Second, recall Waldron's modern argument against judicial review: that judicial review interferes with straightforward moral and political argument over the wisdom of various sorts of state actions. Even if true, this does not necessarily lead to a critique of judicial review—although that is the inference Waldron drew. It might also be read to imply a bit more respect for the political constitution—a greater regard for the role of both legislators and citizens in crafting moral arguments regarding the wisdom and legality of various legislative schemes of good government. Thus a focus on the political constitution might instill in future legislators a sense of moral as well as constitutional responsibility to act in such a way as to further some defensible conception of the public good—rather than only a sense of responsibility not to act in malignant ways. If we attended to the political as well as the adjudicated constitution, we might trigger a more broad-based conversation not only about the constitutional necessity but also about the political wisdom—or lack thereof—of social legislation intended to further that good, from antiabortion statutes to marriage laws, schemes for school funding, and policies of affirmative action. We do not have to supplant judicial review to do this. We would only have to complement it.

Lastly, if we were to attend to the political constitution and not just the adjudicated one, we might ennoble politics as well as humanize—and thereby dignify—constitutionalism. Even here in America, politics itself, debased though it now is, might emerge, from the local to the national level, as a potent response (rather than law and only law) to the dangers of the various empires of force with which we contend. This is not as fanciful as it might first sound. Clearly, if we could imbue political discourse with even a fraction of the apparent regard for moral purpose and high-minded ideals with which the justices of the U.S. Supreme Court routinely purport to treat issues of liberty and equality in their decision making—and with a fraction of the apparent moral seriousness with which that body approaches its own deliberative processes—that alone might deepen the moral seriousness with which we embark on, approach, or criticize legislative lawmaking effort. More ambitiously, if we could instill in legislators a sense of obligation to promote the general welfare, insure domestic tranquility, and protect the rights, privileges, and immunities of citizenship, that might go a good ways further. A state that actually promotes the general welfare and insures domestic tranquility is a nobler state than one that does not. One that at least attempts to do so is nobler than one that feels no obligation to even give it a try.

What would happen to constitutionalism, constitutional law, and constitutional consciousness were we to alchemize it with ordinary, do-it-by-voting politics, from school boards and city halls to Congress? It seems to me that the constitutional discourse that might play a role in our openly political fora might be more earthy and less ethereal, more lowbrow and midbrow rather than so relentlessly high-minded, more normal and ordinary rather than so relentlessly exceptional. It might rhetorically give counsel to the resolution of particular disputes or issues rather than aim for the universal pronouncement. It seems to me that all of this might be rather a good thing. Perhaps, if we could just loosen it up a bit and spread it more generously, a politicized "constitutional law"—the "law of the governors," as Tom Paine metaphorically understood the phrase—could facilitate, rather than limit, political dialogue, political compromise, and political imagination, through conscience and felt obligation rather than court order.

Would this be a good thing, overall, for constitutionalism itself? Constitutional law and rhetoric both might become less authoritarian, with its normative authority at least somewhat, sometimes, horizontally spread and used through the community rather than imposed on it. Constitutionalism, generally, I would think, could remain inspirational and aspirational both but nevertheless also be—and be understood to be—changeable, malleable, and utterly human, not so wedded to ringing declarations of timeless truths, not so dependent on sweeping declarations of what it does and does not mean to be an American, or to be free, or to be equal, or to have liberty, and so forth. A more, rather than less, majoritarian, democratic, localizing, normalizing, and ordinary constitutional consciousness might actually lend our constitutional dialogue some of that dignity that ought to come from being of and from the people. If so, then for that reason, if no other, we might want to consider this rather different path for our constitutional law to take. Of late, adjudicated constitutionalism's increasingly isolated high-mindedness, its overwrought identitarianism, and its distorted sense of American exceptionalism, have conspired to make our Constitution look just a tad trashy.

NOTES

1. Brown v. Board of Education, 347 U.S. 483 (1954).

2. Uniting and Strengthening America by Providing Appropriate Tools Required to Intercept and Obstruct Terrorism Act of 2001 (Pub. L. No. 107-56), known as the USA PATRIOT Act or simply the Patriot Act; USA Patriot and Reauthorization Act of 2005, Pub. L. No. 109-177, 120 Stat. 192 (9 March 2006).

3. United States Military Commissions Act of 2006, Pub. L. No. 109-366, 120 Stat. 2600 (17 October 2006).

4. Foreign Intelligence Surveillance Act, 50 U.S.C. § 1801 et seq.

5. The Authorization for Use of Military Force against Iraq Resolution of 2002, Pub. L. No. 107-243, 116 Stat. 1497-1502 (11 October 2002).

6. In 2002, following a ninth circuit case finding the Pledge of Allegiance's inclusion of the phrase "under God" to be an unconstitutional endorsement of religion, approximately 150 members of the House of Representatives stood on the Senate steps to recite the pledge, shouting the phrase "under God" for emphasis. The Senate voted a resolution unanimously supporting the pledge. See http://archives.cnn.com/2002/LAW/06/26/pledge.allegiance/index/.

7. See Charles Babington and Mike Allen, "Congress Passes Schiavo Measure; Bush Signs Bill Giving U.S. Courts Jurisdiction in Case of Fla. Woman," *Washington Post,* 21 March 2005, A01.

8. See Michael Grunwald, "Pork by Any Other Name," *Washington Post,* 30 April 2006.

9. John Stuart Mill, *On Liberty* (New Haven: Yale University Press, 2003).

10. See James Madison, *The Federalist Papers,* No. 47, chapter 10, 323–31, 30 Janu-

ary 1788 (on Separation of Powers); No. 51 (on bicameralism); Nos. 22 and 17 (on federalism).

11. Weil writes, "No one can love and be just who does not understand the empire of force and know how not to respect it" ("L'iliade, ou le poeme de la force," first published in *Cahiers du Sud,* December 1940–January 1941). The translation is J. B. White's. The quote appears in the epigraph of White's somewhat surprising book *Living Speech: Resisting the Empire of Force* (Princeton: Princeton University Press, 2006).

12. White, supra n. 11.

13. Many thanks to Lisa Heinzerling for suggesting the phrase *empire of sloth.*

14. See Orenstein and Mann, *The Broken Branch: How Congress Is Failing America and How to Get It Back on Track* (New York: Oxford University Press, 2005).

15. See, e.g., DeShaney v. Winnebago County Social Services, 489 U.S. 189 (1989).

16. See, e.g., Susan Bandes, "The Negative Constitution: A Critique," 88 *Mich. L. Rev.* 2271–2331 (1990); Charles L. Black Jr., *A New Birth of Freedom: Human Rights, Named and Unnamed* (New York: Grosset/Putnam, 1997).

17. U.S. Const. preamble.

18. I have argued elsewhere that the most natural interpretation of the equal protection clause requires the states to take affirmative acts to protect all citizens against certain risks, including, most centrally, the risk of private violence. See Robin West, *Progressive Constitutionalism: Reconstructing the Fourteenth Amendment* (Durham, NC: Duke University Press, 1994), 9–45. See generally Jacobus Ten-Broek, *The Antislavery Origins of the Fourteenth Amendment* (Berkeley: University of California Press, 1951), reissued as *Equal Under Law* (Berkeley: University of California Press, 1965).

19. U.S. Const. amend. XIV, § 1.

20. Thomas Paine, *Agrarian Justice,* in *The Life and Works of Thomas Paine,* ed. William Van der Weyde, Patriot's Edition (New Rochelle, NY: Thomas Paine National Historical Association, 1925); Paine, *The Rights of Man* (Dover: Dover Publishing, 1999). See generally Robin West, "Tom Paine's Constitution," 89 *Va. L. Rev.* (October 2003), 1413–61.

21. See Akhil Amar, "Forty Acres and a Mule: A Republican Theory of Minimal Entitlements," 13 *Harv. J. L. & Pub. Pol'y* 37–43 (1990).

22. See generally Cass Sunstein, *The Second Bill of Rights* (New York: Basic Books, 2004).

23. See William Forbath, *Law and the Shaping of the American Labor Movement* (Cambridge: Harvard University Press, 1991); Forbath, "Constitutional Welfare Rights: A History, Critique, and Reconstruction," 69 *Fordham L. Rev.* 1821–87 (2001); Black, supra n. 16; Mark Tushnet and Gary Peller, "State Action and a New Birth of Freedom," 92 *Geo. L.J.* 779–817 (2004); Peter Edelman, "Where Is FDR When We Need Him?" 93 *Geo. L.J.* 1681–92 (2005); Edelman, "Where Race Meets Class: The 21st Century Civil Rights Agenda," 12 *Geo. J. on Poverty L. & Pol'y* 1–11 (2005); Edelman, "Welfare and the Politics of Race: Same Tune, New Lyrics," 11 *Geo. J. on Poverty L. & Pol'y* 389–403 (2004).

24. See, e.g., Larry Sager, *Justice in Plainclothes* (New Haven: Yale University Press, 2004).

25. Ronald Dworkin, *Taking Rights Seriously* (Cambridge: Harvard University Press, 1977).

26. James B. Thayer, "The Origin and Scope of the American Doctrine of Constitutional Law," 7 *Harv. L. Rev.* 129–56 (1893).

27. Brown v. Board of Education, supra n. 1.

28. 410 U.S. 113 (1973).

29. Jeremy Waldron, *The Dignity of Legislation* (New York: Cambridge University Press, 1999); Waldron, *Law and Disagreement* (New York: Oxford University Press, 1999).

30. Planned Parenthood v. Casey, 505 U.S. 893 (1992).

31. Griswold v. Connecticut, 381 U.S. 479 (1965).

32. 268 U.S. 510 (1925).

33. Gonzales v. Carhart, 550 U.S. 127 S. Ct. 1610 (2007).

34. 42 U.S.C. § 301 et seq.

35. 42 U.S.C. § 2000e et seq.

36. 42 U.S.C. § 1971 et seq.

37. 42 U.S.C. § 6101 et seq.

38. 42 U.S.C. § 12101 et seq.

39. 42 U.S.C. § 7401 et seq.; 33 U.S.C. § 1254 et seq.

40. Employment Non-Discrimination Act, H.R. 2015, 110th Cong. 1st Sess. (2008).

41. See John Wagner, "Maryland First to Have Living Wage Law," *Washington Post,* 8 May 2007.

An *Oresteia* for Argentina: Between Fraternity and the Rule of Law

Martin Böhmer

Why has it been so extraordinarily difficult for Argentina to establish a reliable rule of law, from the beginning of its formal existence almost until the present? How, in turn, can the more promising changes that have recently taken place be explained and understood? These are the questions that concern Martin Böhmer in this essay.

He approaches them by way of several different kinds of material: straightforward political history; folk stories and folk songs; the analysis of the ritual that is acted out, even today, when an automobile driver is stopped by the police for speeding; careful readings of stories by Borges, including the famous "Pierre Menard, Author of the Quixote*"; and an application of Aeschylus' great* Oresteia *to the cultural circumstances of Argentina today. His object is to understand both the cultural forces that have inhibited the development of the rule of law and the nature, force, and meaning of important changes that have taken place since the reestablishment of democracy. This essay may also serve as an instance of a kind of cultural analysis that might have great value in the examination of other political and national systems.*

> . . . the horrible way in which our worst reality
> strives to copy our best fiction.
> Carlos Gamerro[1]

Radical Evil

Argentina's own rendezvous with the empire of force can be described, in the peculiar, already canonical language of post-Holocaust Western thought, as an event of radical evil.[2] For almost a decade, the Argentine state used its monopoly of force to secretly kidnap, torture, and eventually kill tens of thousands of Argentines. We Argentines even coined our own word for them: *desaparecidos.* Videla, the military dictator, defined it in his own cynical words at a press conference: "It is a mystery, a disappeared, a nonentity, it is not here" (Es una incógnita, es un desaparecido, no tiene entidad, no está).

The peculiarity of this event in our history is related to its illegality. In effect, the strategies of our dictatorship were illegal, even within the framework of norms imposed by the regime. There were no Nuremberg Laws in Argentina, no written orders, no procedures to impose death penalties. The crimes were performed clandestinely, in the dark, mostly at night, far from courts and judges; and they were denied in public by the same people who gave and carried the orders. In this sense, Argentina's incarnation of radical evil was inscribed in an old tradition of disobedience and anomie, the ever-present lack of the rule of law.

In what follows, I will try to trace the origins of disobedience in Argentina through its politics, law, and literature. I will argue that the political project that created our nation-state was built on the exclusion of a large part of Argentina's population, thus imposing an authority that was (or was perceived as) illegitimate. I will also show that those who were left out of politics resisted violently but also in an illegitimate fashion. This tragedy of illegitimate force against illegitimate force is also played out in our literature, and I will use some of Borges's stories and his critics' appraisals to claim that our language also plays an important role in creating this tragic political environment. This essay will trace the emergence of an incipient rule of law with a different way of adjudicating, drawn from Borges's stories and recent political and legal developments.

TWO STORIES

A comparison of two stories of similar circumstances illustrates some of the cultural forces working against the rule of law in Argentina today. Here is the first story: When a driver runs a red light in Argentina and is stopped by the police, a dialogue begins. This exchange develops with the predictability and certainty of a script that everybody knows. The dialogue goes like this:

Police: Good afternoon. Documents, please.
Driver: Good afternoon. Here they are . . .

Until here, this is an indispensable exchange. Although legal norms indicate that this dialogue should not exist, good manners ensure it does.

According to the law, what should follow is silent police action: to write the ticket imposing a fine and give a copy to the offender. Excuses or justifications must wait for the hearing in front of a judge. Nevertheless, surprisingly, the exchange continues, in general with the policeman making a statement that takes the situation away from the institutions that define his role, away from the law.

This extension of the dialogue, this excess material, leads inevitably to the offer and acceptance of a bribe. The dialogue continues:

Police: You ran a red light.
Driver: Yes, what happens is that . . .

Here an excuse is presented, such as "I was arriving late to look for the children," "It was yellow," or "Nobody was trying to cross," which could make room for a more or less extensive exchange about its soundness. The excuse, however, is not effective at stopping the dialogue or helping the driver to avoid the sanction.

Police: I will have to fine you.

This description of the legal obligation of the policeman is simultaneously a threat of a sanction and an invitation to continue the dialogue. The announcement of the sanction does not necessarily imply its enforcement. Thus, the phrase becomes an invitation that allows the following question to arise:

Driver: How can we fix it?

This is an ambiguous question. It could be the ratification of an agreement that began the moment in which the dialogue extended beyond what is legally necessary and that will lead inevitably to the bribe. It could also imply a resigned acceptance by the victim of the illegal coercion. Or it could be, as the use of the plural ("we") seems to suggest, the acceptance of belonging to a community of two people who fight (to "fix") against the power of a norm that forces them to do things they do not intend to: it forces the policeman to impose a sanction and the offender to pay a fine.

In the latter sense, the bribe, which, in this case, is the waiver of the sanction in return for a few pesos, is a mutual favor between equals, a fraternal exchange or, as it is said in Argentina, a *gauchada.* Therefore, the bribe constitutes a mutual form of salvation: the policeman saves the driver from paying a fine, and the driver saves the policeman by increasing his salary. The Argentine *gauchada* is a demonstration of generosity and is associated with hospitality values and a way of showing kindness to someone who is suffering an adversity. It is a means of taking mercy on someone, showing empathy. It is also a way of recognizing that one could always be in the same disadvantageous situation as the other. This Argentine virtue explains much of what we cherish about the customs of our country: the informality of visiting a friend without previous arrangements, the flexibility of not imposing time constraints on conversations in cozy bars or around a barbecue, the always available excuse for the fraternal encounter to avoid the obligations and rules that regulate our professional lives.

Here is the second story: An important Argentine government official told me the following anecdote. He was driving in the complicated freeway system in Los Angeles. He was in a hurry because he had to return the rented car before his flight to Argentina. He realized that he was going in the wrong direction. Anxious, he made a U-turn to correct his mistake and was stopped by highway patrol. After a short, strict greeting, the Argentine began to excuse himself by saying that he was in a hurry, intending to start the usual script dialogue with the hope of being recognized as an equal. The police officer commanded, "Silence!" and that was it.[3]

ARGENTINE ANOMIE

The bribe is not an isolated incident in Argentina. Disobedience is a generalized trend. Disregard of transit rules (which causes a world record in number of accidents, injuries, and deaths), bribes to obtain exceptions not only from the state but also from private companies, breach of contracts (even those with international impact, as foreign holders of Argentine bonds well know), and the succession of coup d'états that led to massive human rights violations in the twentieth century are some examples of this tendency. Carlos Nino, in his book on legal disobedience in Argentina,[4] showed that coordination problems, predominantly the free rider effect, could be identified in many instances of this phenomenon. For example, to avoid the annoyance of waiting for one's turn, one way to improve one's situation with respect to those who are waiting is to skip the queue. The coordination problem arises when this exceptional attitude is generalized and everybody decides to jump the queue: the norm to queue disappears, and everybody is worse off, including the free rider.

The solution Nino offered was simply to enforce the law, even if it implies using such methods as whistle-blowing and entrapment. In a brief publication, I attempted to criticize his solution. Among the different arguments that I used, I appealed to what, at that point, I considered a mere adornment in the argumentation, a quote from an Italian author, the famous criminal lawyer Franceso Carrara. The quote seemed pertinent in the context of the topics discussed in my article. In fact, I admitted that, in some cases, it seems inevitable that to respect the law, whistle-blowers must exist, and police have to use entrapments. These strategies are particularly relevant in such crimes as bribery or the illegal sale of drugs to consenting adults, which criminal attorneys call "victimless crimes," because the damage is distributed among a greater number of victims. But, it seemed to me, the proliferation of informers and entrapments could lead to a society that one would doubt whether it is worth living in, which was precisely what Carrara affirmed. Nino responded:

> In contrast to what Böhmer and Carrara think, I do not think that the fight against a Sicilian morality of complicity and in favor of a civic morality is a bad thing. The image of suspicion and mistrust that reminds us of such situations as Nazi Germany and the Stalinist Soviet Union is overwhelming if we do not take into account that everything depends on whether it is legitimate and just to punish the deed we could be accused of and whether due process is respected. If these conditions are satisfied, I would not have any problem in being denounced by a person I know, insofar as I am willing to keep my conduct within the margins of the law.[5]

Nino's answer clarifies the discussion. In fact, the controversy should concentrate on the question of the legitimacy of authority. Those who oppose entrapments and whistle-blowing assume an illegitimate authority, while those who defend them assume its legitimacy. Thus, my defense of the Sicilian morality does not imply a justification of the mafia but, rather, tries to explain it by virtue of a certain way of understanding the history of the relation Sicilians have with authority. One may dare venture to say that since Sicily was always a place subject to invasion and since invasion entails an authoritarian imposition of law, Sicilians refuse to accept any authority as legitimate. Therefore, they disobey and reject informers as mere accomplices of a tyrannical regime. In such circumstances, where there is a contaminated relationship with authority, proposing effective enforcement produces not less but more disobedience.

The preceding story of the driver and the policeman illustrates this point. Imagine that at the moment in which the bribery is taking place, somebody passes by and, after seeing what happened, denounces it in a nearby police station. I do not think I am wrong in predicting that this action would be viewed very negatively, not only by the participants in the bribe, but also by other pedestrians and even by the police officer who takes the complaint. Language serves to help me here. Such terms as *informer* or, in Argentine slang, *buchón, botón, bocón, soplón, batidor, apuntador,* and *ortiba* have a highly negative connotation. They refer to the idea of a traitor, someone who betrays fraternal loyalties, refrains from making a *gauchada,* and favors an authority that is, in the nature of things, illegitimate. This attitude is described in the well-known statement "No te metás" (Mind your own business) and in a more graphical one, "Yo, argentino" (I, Argentine), which means "I have nothing to do with this; I have no role in this drama." In a society in which testifying is a socially vilified act, law enforcement becomes a very difficult task.

Thus, disobedience in Argentina is connected with certain social habits that are translated into a language that undermines the possibility of associating authority with obedience. In this context, I only obey my own will or the fraternal agreement between my own will and that of an immediate neighbor (who is, as we shall see, someone in whom I recognize myself), regardless of any connection that my will or the agreement may have to rules imposed by external authorities. The following sections attempt to tell the story of this language.

BORGES'S *MARTIN FIERRO*

I start with Borges:

> The Argentine, unlike the Americans of the North and almost all Europeans, does not identify with the State. This is attributable to the circumstance that the governments in this country tend to be awful, or to the general fact that the State is an inconceivable abstraction. One thing is certain: the Argentine is an individual, not a citizen. Aphorisms such as Hegel's "The State is the reality of the moral idea" strike him as sinister jokes. Films made in Hollywood often hold up for admiration the case of a man (usually a journalist) who seeks out the friendship of a criminal in order to hand him over to the police; the Argentine, for whom friendship is a passion and the police a mafia, feels that this "hero" is an incomprehensible swine.[6]

Here again, we see the idea that political and social practices sidestep the law and heteronomous authority and that there are only individuals joined by the passion of fraternal friendship. Nevertheless, modern literature offers the following analysis:

> He feels with Don Quixote that "everybody hath sins of his own to answer for" and that "it is not seemly, that honest men should be the executioners of their fellow-creatures, on account of matters with which they have no concern" (*Quixote* I, XXII). More than once, confronted with the vain symmetries of the Spanish style, I have suspected that we are irredeemably different from Spain; these two lines from the *Quixote* have sufficed to convince me of my error; they seem to be the secret, tranquil symbol of our affinity. This is profoundly confirmed by a single night in Argentine literature: the desperate night when a sergeant in the rural police shouted that he was not going to consent to the crime of killing a brave man, and started fighting against his own soldiers alongside the fugitive Martín Fierro.[7]

For those alien to Argentine literature, it is necessary to explain the narrative context in which Borges writes. Martin Fierro is the name of the main character in the poem *El Gaucho Martin Fierro,* which José Hernandez published in 1872. "At the beginning of the poem," one scholar explains, "Martin Fierro identifies himself as a *payador,* a kind of gaucho troubador known for his ability to improvise verses and tell stories in songs," and "states that his is a story of suffering and hardship, that in some sense liberal society has deprived him of everything but his story."[8] He "further notes that his suffering results not from what he has done but from what he is, a gaucho," and "that his is the story of all gauchos."[9]

Hernández's poem starts by remembering a lost paradise of bucolic peace, a golden age. But this tranquility is brutally interrupted, and the account begins:

> A gaucho'd live in his home country
> as safe as anything,
> but now—it's a crime!
> things have got to be so twisted
> that a poor man wears out his life
> running from the authorities.

Why does the gaucho have to run from the authorities? What has he done? Fierro explains:

> Because if you set foot in your house
> and if the mayor finds out about it,
> he'll hunt you like a beast
> even if it makes your wife miscarry. . . .
> There's no time that won't come to an end
> nor a rope that won't break sometime.
>
> And you can give yourself up for dead
> right away, if the mayor catches you,
> because he'll come down on you
> there and then, with a flogging—
> and then if the gaucho puts up a fight
> they call him a hard case.[10]

What is Fierro's crime? Only two stanzas answer this fundamental question, and these tremendously ambiguous lines make sense of the whole poem: "if you set foot in your house / and if the mayor finds out about it." That is pretty much it. "If you set foot in your house" is, among other things that one could guess, a way of saying that you are the owner of your ranch; it means that you own your things. The crime, thus, consists of being autonomous, and when the mayor—that is, the authority—finds out that you are autonomous and own property, then the crime that the gaucho committed is completed, and he will be unavoidably punished for it.

The details are extensive, but the punishment of Fierro includes a draft into the army for the refusal to vote for a certain candidate, military corruption, arbitrariness, torture, desertion, and the loss of everything that the gaucho owned. As a result of these injustices, the gaucho turns evil and murders without justification and with scorn, chauvinism, and racism. The authority is after the gaucho, and Cruz's men surround him, until Cruz turns to Fierro's side and saves him, and they both escape to Indian territory. Thus, in Argentine tradition, Martin Fierro symbolizes the excluded, the unfairly persecuted; and his encounter with Cruz is a symbol of the *gauchada,* of fraternal solidarity, of the courage to rise against the authority and fight with the most vulnerable.

Nevertheless, Borges describes that encounter with words that sound out of tune: "that desperate night in which a sergeant of the rural police shouted that he will not consent to the crime of killing a brave man, and started to fight against his soldiers, with the deserter Martin Fierro." Cruz is a "sergeant of the rural police," somebody with the state mandate to bear arms and with obligations and norms that define his position. Despite this, he fights against his own soldiers, whom he should be protecting from violence and threats from criminals. Cruz instead kills them, injures them, and puts them on the run. This betrayal of his colleagues was not seen as such because, as portrayed in the poem, Fierro is the representation of Cruz himself, of those who have the courage to resist an illegitimate authority. Therefore, to Argentine ears, it is strange to hear about the "deserter" Martin Fierro because it sounds like an accusation, a denunciation—like betrayal.

This new understanding of Fierro attracts a great deal of attention. The Fierro about whom every Argentine reads is a national hero; *Martin Fierro* is the national book; and in Borges's brief final sentence about the encounter, Cruz is the incarnation of the Argentine *gauchada.* Instead, he becomes a traitor to his fellow policemen for defending a criminal and for facing and killing the representatives of the law who had the obligation to enforce it by stopping a deserter, a murderer. This accusatory interpretation of *Martin Fierro* is not only a literary interpretation; it is associated with certain ways of understanding the construction of political authority in Argentina, in which the event in *Martin Fierro* is indeed one of disobedience.

Sarmiento's *Facundo*

Those who built the national state in Argentina in the mid-nineteenth century created, along with the political institutions, literature that tried to generate the necessary narratives to ensure that the institutions worked effectively. One book in this literature, probably the best Argentine literary work of the nineteenth century, is *Facundo,* written by the polymath Domingo F. Sarmiento,[11] an outstanding figure in the process of Argentine state building and one of Argentina's first constitutional presidents. *Facundo* was written in 1845, about thirty years before *Martin Fierro,* and although it was presented as the biography of a bloody caudillo, it is simultaneously a geographic essay, an anthropological study, and, above all, a political diagnosis.

Hernandez wrote *Martin Fierro* when he returned to Argentina from exile after a battle he had fought and lost against the armies of Sarmiento's political party, then in power. The poem was written in a hotel in Plaza de Mayo, in front of the Casa Rosada, the office of President Sarmiento, and against him. The triumphant Sarmiento, thirty years after he had written *Facundo,* is the president of a state whose diagnosis he had helped to imagine and is now a reality. Both writers are opposed literarily and politically. Borges has said that if *Facundo* is the accusation, *Martin Fierro* is the defense. But what was the accusation in *Facundo*? What is *Martin Fierro* defending? The accusation is part of the diagnosis of the intellectuals who constitutionally organized Argentina in the nineteenth century. For them—Alberdi, Sarmiento, and Echeverria, among others—anarchy and poverty were Argentina's problems.

According to their narratives, since the beginning of the nineteenth century, Argentina had been suffering permanent confrontations, starting with the war of independence, proceeding through civil war and anarchy, and ending with Rosas's brutal dictatorship. Argentina had won the struggle to become autonomous from Spain but had dramatically lost the challenge to organize its citizens' peaceful coexistence. Argentina could not create a consensually agreed-on system of authority of rights and respect that would legitimize some kind of social order to defend the rights of its inhabitants. Thus, the first feature of this diagnosis is anarchy, the existence of multiple authorities and rules without an institutional scheme to coordinate collective action. The second feature is poverty, the other enemy it was necessary to defeat. Indeed, crossing the Argentine territory must have been an exasperating experience for that generation. A desert traversed by nonnavigated rivers was all that there was to see, a fertile plain waiting to produce the goods the world needed.

The first problem brought its own solution. The proliferation of authorities had diminished during the repression exercised by Rosas, and the centralization of power in Buenos Aires had proven that it was possible to contain the incompatible ambitions of the caudillos. Therefore, it was thought that anarchy should be opposed by an institutional system designed to concentrate power in a few hands. Alberdi's *Bases*[12] and the Constitution of 1853 are the institutional trademarks of this proposal. Some of the characteristics of such a system include a very strong president (taken from the Chilean constitution); judicial review in a federal supreme court that controls the interpretation of the Constitution; federal codes that limit the capacity of the provinces to create substantive legislation; and a two-chamber congress with very indirect representation, with a small group of senators holding veto power in the House of Representatives, with age and wealth requirements that excluded the majorities, and so on.

Poverty, however, was blamed on living in a desert,[13] barely populated[14] by a race as useless for progress[15] as for democracy.[16] In fact, according to the literary descriptions of *Facundo* and due to a long tradition forged by the needs and opportunities of the desert, *gauchos* developed only the few skills that their environment required: horseback riding, cow slaughter, river crossing, and not much more. These activities did not demand the skills or emotions that both Alberdi and Sarmiento understood as necessary to carry out a capitalist model of development:[17] devotion to work, shame (which comes from the close coexistence in cities), and envy (which inspires competition for a greater quantity and quality of goods). In the generous geography of the "desert," the *gaucho* is not vulnerable to temptation by habits so foreign to his immediate interests.[18]

There were many possible solutions to solve the "problem" of a scarce and nonconvenient race, such as its elimination, the teaching of new habits to future generations, and the incorporation of other races. It is debatable whether the elimination of the *gaucho* at the Indian frontier and in the war against Paraguay was a deliberate policy, but while these confrontations were taking place, Argentina was generating the most ambitious project of compulsory public education ever seen in Latin America[19] and had started the search for an unforeseen number of immigrants who would flood its territory by the hundreds of thousands.[20]

To summarize, if Argentina's problems were anarchy and poverty, the resulting proposal was centralized power concentrated in the hands of a few, education, and, above all, immigration.[21] This political project had nothing to do with democratic pretensions, fear of minorities or majorities, federalist obsessions, or formalities to control discretionary judges.

The project was meant to achieve nothing more than to populate the desert and, thus, to lead to the creation of a national state that would allow governance; afterward, order and progress would become the leitmotif of the generation of 1880.

So the Argentine institutional structure that was finally built in the decade of 1860 constitutes the national state. But the process was not peaceful. Argentina always had, for better or for worse, those who offered resistance. *Martin Fierro* is the denunciation by the defeated in the process of the creation of our national state. Now we can understand Borges's statement about the relation of *Facundo* to *Martin Fierro. Facundo* accuses the gaucho of preventing Argentine progress, of disobedience, of not allowing the creation of an institutional structure that defends the individual rights that will support capitalism and serve to persuade northern Europeans to immigrate. *Martin Fierro* defends the gaucho, claiming that this particular way of building progress is discriminatory, exclusive, and undemocratic. By characterizing Martin Fierro as a deserter, Borges joins the rows of the prosecutors. As additional evidence of this position, Borges famously affirms that "if we had canonized [*Facundo*] as our exemplar book, other would have been our history, and better."[22] Here is the origin of the Argentine tragedy, the violent controversy between those who captured institutional power to the exclusion of others, on the one hand, and those who resist their exclusion by disobeying the law, on the other.

CRUZ

It is interesting to note that the idea that disobedience is legitimate when the authority is considered illegitimate repeats itself. The gaucho disobeys because the authority that claims obedience is illegitimate and complains that it is not understood:[23] "And later they say that it is bad / the gaucho fights against them." This complaint is equivalent to other tragic laments, such as that of Electra, as gathered by Weil:[24] "In these conditions I cannot be not reasonable, my friends, nor good. Those to whom evil is done cannot avoid becoming evil." The inevitability of evil in those whom were mistreated gives rise, in gaucho literature, to an archetype that is known as "the bad gaucho." In the case of the meeting between Cruz and Fierro, the personal history of the first is practically equivalent to what we know about

Fierro: an affront by the authority (in this case, the adultery of his wife with his chief, a commander of the army) gives rise to Cruz's committing murder and then fleeing. After some time and several murders to account for, a friend's favor allows Cruz to come in front of a judge who forces him to become a policeman before the meeting with Fierro.

Thus, the disobedience of both is excused as a resistance to illegitimate, corrupted authority, but this does not lead to the construction of another kind of authority, a legitimate one (as is the case of Robin Hood and in many westerns where the vindictive cowboy finally puts on the star and becomes an authority acclaimed by the community to restore the rule of law). The disobedience of both, like the disobedience of Orestes (and like the one Electra would dream of), is also illegitimate. In the case of Cruz and Fierro, they kill randomly with discriminatory and racist excuses—or even without excuses, without any reason at all. In the case of Orestes, the disobedience to the illegitimate and regicidal authority of Aegisthus and of Clytemnestra, murderers of Agamemnon, is at the same time itself homicidal, regicidal, and matricidal. In this way, the circle of violence continues: illegitimate authority against illegitimate disobedience.

Borges is delighted at the narrative possibilities of the infinite circle of violence once the tragedy has been identified and both antagonists are right and wrong simultaneously. He adds one more ingredient, a tragic component for excellence: destiny. In this way, in "Biografía de Tadeo Isidoro Cruz," Borges surmises the story from Cruz's point of view.

> The outlaw stepped out from his hiding place to fight them. Cruz glimpsed the terrifying apparition—the long mane of hair and the grey beard seemed to consume his face. A well-known reason prevents me from telling the story of that fight; let me simply recall that the deserter gravely wounded or killed several of Cruz's men. As Cruz was fighting in the darkness (as his body was fighting in the darkness), he began to understand. He realized that no destiny is better than the next and that every man must accept the destiny he bears inside himself. He realized that his sergeant's epaulets and uniform were hampering him. He realized his deep-rooted destiny as a wolf, not as a gregarious dog; he realized that the other man was he himself. Day began to dawn on the lawless plain; Cruz threw his cap to the ground, cried that he was not going to be a party to killing a brave man, and he began to fight against the soldiers, alongside the deserter Martin Fierro.[25]

In the face of the excuse of a criminal reaction against the law, based on the illegitimacy of the authority, Borges adds the inevitability—the animality (the proud and fearsome wolf against the lamentable gregarious dog)—of the evil of someone who does not have any other option but to follow his destiny. Therefore, the tragedy does not have an outcome. The illegitimate authority generates the destiny of those who criminally resist. In this way, an endless repetition of violent deeds against violent deeds is generated, and this constitutes the barbaric order (*orden de la barbarie*)—an oxymoron that, in the best tradition of Borges, generates an enumeration of events that becomes infinite.[26] Therefore, the meeting between Cruz and Fierro is no longer just a fraternal encounter between a couple uniting to resist unfair authority, the symbol of the *gauchada* that repeats itself in the scene between the policeman and the transgressor. It is also the inevitable destiny of two people who recognize themselves as equals (they are each other) in their common struggle against their enemy.

THE LUJANERA

Just as Borges explains the position of the gaucho in "Biografía de Tadeo Isidoro Cruz," he also gives voice to the stereotype of urban violence. The character of the *malevo,* the *compadrito,* is to the tango and the city of Buenos Aires what the gaucho is to the folklore and the countryside. In "Hombre de la Esquina Rosada," Francisco Real shows up in a brothel looking for Rosendo Juarez—a *malevo* like himself, but a famous one—with the aim of defying him in a fight. After walking across the dance floor and being humiliated by everybody without reacting, he faces Juarez.

> I've let these poor sons of bitches lift their hands to me because what I am looking for is a man. . . . I'd like to make his acquaintance, so he could show me—me being nobody, you understand—what it means to be a man of courage, a man you can look up to.[27]

To everybody's surprise, Juarez says something, which is not heard, and declines to fight. Juarez's woman, the Lujanera, brings him a knife, which Juarez throws out the window. Real responds with disgust.

> "'The only reason I don't carve you up for beefsteak is that you make me sick," said the stranger. At that la Lujanera threw her arms around

> this Yardmaster's [Real's] neck and she looked at him with those eyes of hers, and she said with anger in her voice: "Forget that dog—he had us thinking he was a man."[28]

Then Real and the Lujanera leave together.

An admirer of Juarez, who tells everything soon after having left the dance, narrates the whole story in first person. Real returns to die from the wound of a dagger on the brothel's floor.

> And just then a stranger appeared and desperately called out the Yardmaster to fight, and he stabbed him, gave him that wound there, and she [the Lujanera] swore she didn't know who the man was, but it wasn't Rosendo. Who was going to believe that?[29]

The arrival of the police causes many to flee. The narrator returns to his ranch and senses the presence of the Lujanera. The story finishes this way:

> And then, Borges, for the second time I pulled out that short, sharp-edged knife I always carried here, under my vest, under my left arm, and I gave it another long slow inspection—and it was just like new, all innocent, and there was not the slightest trace of blood on it.[30]

From the cult of friendship that confronts power, we move into what Borges elsewhere describes as "the sect of knife and courage."[31] Now violence occurs without even the need of an excuse. In the cult of courage, barbarism is the pure order of the infinite succession of deaths and revenges. Violence is infinite and, like destiny, inevitable. Nobody can stop it, and if somebody attempts to, like Juarez, somebody else will take his place, like the narrator. The Lujanera is probably the metaphor of that violent destiny that goes from hand to hand and defines the meaning of being a man, of being somebody. In Borges's words from another story, "war was, like a woman, a test for men."[32]

AGAINST THE LAW

In "El Escritor Argentino y la Tradición," Borges writes:

> What is our Argentine tradition? I believe we can answer this question easily and that there is no problem here. I believe our tradition is

> all of Western culture, and I also believe we have a right to this tradition, greater than that which the inhabitants of one or another Western nation might have.[33]

As previously discussed, Borges states that if *Facundo* had been Argentina's national book, representing the imposition of civilization over barbarism, our destiny would have been different and better.[34] This quote shows a Borges aligned with the elitist imposition of progress, a banally authoritarian Borges. However, Borges's literature saves him from that banality and produces the inevitability of the barbaric order, his infinite repetition, the permanent violation of what the written law dictates. In this sense, Josefina Ludmer says that "one of the foundations of Borges's writings is the transgressive treatment of, or the confrontation with, all normativity, literary and legal."[35]

According to Ludmer, Borges writes his story named, precisely, "The End" as an ending for the legendary *Martin Fierro.* In his story, he violates not only the literary canon of *gauchesca* literature but also the legality that *Martin Fierro* had accepted in the second part of the poem, also precisely called "The Return of Martin Fierro." In "The Return," we find a tamed José Hernández, who tries to return to politics by moving away from violent disobedience and changing his character's destiny. In this sense, Martin Fierro comes back from his life with the Indians to confront—singing—the Negro brother of Moreno, whom he had murdered in the beginning of the poem. After avoiding a quarrel and thus preventing both his enemy from seeking vengeance and the tragedy from repeating, he reunites with his children and advises them to work and to respect the law, not kill and steal. Ludmer explains:

> Borges takes "La Vuelta de Martin Fierro," an Argentine classic, and writes a different ending for it and a different outcome. In "The End," one can see the way he treats the law (against the law) in the two meanings of the term: as literary canon and as legal canon at the same time. "The End" is "a correction" or a reinterpretation of "The Return of Martin Fierro" that functions as law as a canonical text or as a classic. But also, in "The Return," Martin Fierro represents "the law" established by his advice to his sons: man does not kill man, theft is a crime.
>
> . . . "The Return" is a peaceful text about the integration of the gauchos into the national project: the war by knife turns into a purely

> verbal war by way of Fierro's improvised gaucho folk song *y el negro;* in 1879, at the moment of the legal unification and the state constitution, the disputes were resolved with dialogue. And therefore *el negro* could not avenge his brother who had been assassinated by Martin Fierro in 1872 . . . *el negro.*[36]

In "The End," Martin Fierro leaves his children and goes back to look for the Negro's brother, to offer him the possibility of revenge. After a brief dialogue, the Negro kills him in a fight under open sky. Ludmer writes:

> Here Borges intervenes to violate the sacred text. In "The End," Martin Fierro separates himself from his own advice, denies himself, violates the law he transmitted to his sons, assumes ancient justice, and draws the knife. But the black man launches a final attack and avenges his older brother. In 1953, the black man achieves justice: an oral, familiar justice. There Borges adds another twist to "The Return," or invents a real end, which is nothing more than another beginning, because the black man, who kills old Martin Fierro to avenge his older brother, himself becomes Martin Fierro of *La Ida* [The Going] he had killed a man, disgraced himself, and had no destiny on earth. Borges violates and closes the classic and brings it back to the beginning, to *The Ida* of the black man, from a black man to Martin Fierro.[37]

The tragedy does not allow for renouncements. Nobody, neither Martin Fierro nor the Negro, escapes the logic of the inevitable sequence of revenge. In this sequence of events, both end up losing in the end, and, as Cruz and Martin Fierro, both are the same. At the end of "The End," Borges writes:

> He wiped off the bloody knife in the grass[38] and slowly walked back toward the houses, never looking back. His work of vengeance done, he was nobody now. *Or rather, he was the other one: there was neither destination nor destiny on earth for him, and he had killed a man.*[39]

It is the world of literature, once again the mechanism of the oxymoron, that produces the infinite: revenge is imposed onto Fierro as an obligation, as his destiny. It takes away his identity, his decision-making capacity, and (once again) his destiny: "there was neither destination nor destiny on earth for him." But something else is added—"and he had killed a man"—which again creates once more the possibility of revenge (in this case, the revenge of Fierro's sons, who, violating their father's law, will go back looking for the Negro as their father had done, and from there ad infinitum).

Borges does not stop there. He develops his literature through the appropriation of the Western canon, with the whole extension of classic property rights, which comprehends even the capacity of destroying it: "Argentines, and South Americans in general . . . can handle European themes, handle them without superstitions, with an irreverence that can have, and already has, fortunate consequences."[40] The logic of normative destruction also proceeds against the literary canon of Spanish language: the *Don Quixote* of Cervantes.[41] In "Pierre Menard, Author of the Quixote," the narrator tells the story of Menard, a Frenchman who, by the beginning of the twentieth century, tries to write the *Quixote:* "Pierre Menard did not want to compose *another* Quixote, which surely is easy enough—he wanted to compose *the* Quixote."[42] Menard could only write chapters 9 and 38 and a fragment of chapter 22. Ludmer writes of Borges:

> Let us see what he does to the literary canon of the Spanish language: Cervantes's *Quixote.* The classics are the point of departure for Borges's literature because the classic text always functions as a law to be violated in his writing. This is already evident in his first fiction story, "Pierre Menard, Author of the *Quixote,*" where he changes the author or invents an author of the classic text. In the very title, there is a crime against Miguel de Cervantes himself, against his intellectual property rights. And the story reveals another crime against the *Quixote:* a plagiarism of two chapters by a French writer in the beginning of the twentieth century. In other words, "Pierre Menard, Author of the Quixote," a false attribution and a plagiary, is a double attack on the classic text from the legal point of view: against the author's rights and against the inviolable character of the text. In his thinking and writing, Borges departs from the classic of our language in order to violate its title and text. And this is his debut in fiction in 1939.
>
> . . . Two problems then in Borges' writing: on the one hand, the treatment of the literary canon, of the classic text to be attacked, transgressed, plagiarized; its author, sense, and ending to be changed. On the other hand, the treatment of the legal canon or the written law to be attacked in order to exercise revenge: the law always loses, as

in the case of Narciso Laprida, "man of canons and laws," in the "Conjectural Poem."[43]

Now we turn to law. The kind of law that loses in Borges's stories and poems is that which seeks to impose itself as a text, the letter of the law; and the ones who always lose are those who write it, the literate. As mentioned by Ludmer, in Borges's "Conjectural Poem," Francisco Narciso Laprida laments:

> . . . I who studied canon law and civil
> Francisco Narciso de Laprida
> whose voice declared the independence
> of these harsh provinces, am overthrown
> covered with blood and sweat
> without fear or hope, lost,
> fleeing south through the farthest outskirts
>
> . . . .
> I longed to be something else, a man of
> sentiments, books, judgement
> and now will lie in a swamp under the open sky
> And yet, a secret joy inexplicably
> exalts me. I've met my destiny,
> my final South American destiny.[44]

Formalist thinking, which regards law as purely textual, and ideological positivism, which orders the enforcement and the fulfillment of the law without interpretation, do not allow for dialogue. Formalism and positivism tend to impose the pure will of the one who thinks he has the authority. Facing this imposition, there is only subjugation or resistance, not dialogue. Laprida's happiness has found a place in the narrative of South American destiny: violent death. Laprida is now part of the infinite sequence of deaths and revenges. He is the others (the victorious barbarians, the gauchos), and he is nobody.

As in the first two parts of the *Oresteia,* in *Oedipus* and in *Antigone,* the law, as Ludmer puts it, always loses. The tragedy is built on the inevitability of the violation of the law, of any law. If this is the way of building sociability in Argentina, if the *gauchada* is complicity in violating the law, then the possibility of building the rule of law or any kind of legitimate authority becomes impossible. This is so because, in principle, the actor's identities are shaped by their violation of the law, including in their language and literature. Finally, it is easy to note that this is another instance of the emergence of the us-and-them divide, the one that we now know leads to the empire of force. As Weil claims, "the variety of constraints pressing upon man gives rise to the illusion of several distinct species that cannot communicate."[45]

ANOTHER MENARD

Let us briefly return to "Pierre Menard." It is true that "Pierre Menard" tells the story of plagiarism, but it is much more than that. If it were only the narration of a swindle or a fraud, it would not be literature, or it would not be Borges literature. The idea of somebody pretending to write the *Quixote* creates one of Borges's most amazing stories. (Borges reports: "Nor, surely, need one be obliged to note that his goal was never a mechanical transcription of the original; he had no intention of copying it. His admirable ambition was to produce a number of pages which coincided—word for word and line for line—with those of Miguel de Cervantes.")[46] In particular, I would like to refer to Borges's comparison between the identical texts of Cervantes and Menard in the following, which begins by enunciating again the oxymoron and the infinite.

> The Cervantes text and the Menard text are verbally identical, but the second is almost infinitely richer. (More *ambiguous,* his detractors will say—but ambiguity is richness.)
>
> It is a revelation to compare the *Don Quixote* of Pierre Menard with that of Miguel de Cervantes. Cervantes, for example, wrote the following (Part I, Chapter IX):
>
> > . . . truth, whose mother is history, rival of time, depository of deeds, witness of the past, exemplar and adviser to the present, and the future's counselor
>
> This catalog of attributes, written in the seventeenth century, and written by the "ingenious layman" Miguel de Cervantes, is mere rhetorical praise of history. Menard, on the other hand, writes:
>
> > . . . truth, whose mother is history, rival of time, depository of deeds, witness of the past, exemplar and adviser to the present, and the future's counselor

> History, the *mother* of truth!—the idea is staggering. Menard, a contemporary of William James, defines history not as a *delving into* reality but as the very *fount* of reality. Historical truth, for Menard, is not "what happened"; it is what we *believe* happened. The final phrases—*exemplar and adviser to the present, and the future's counselor*—are brazenly pragmatic.
>
> The contrast in styles is equally striking. The archaic style of Menard—who is, in addition, not a native speaker of the language in which he writes—is somewhat affected. Not so the style of his precursor, who employs the Spanish of his time with complete naturalness.[47]

The text itself does not matter. What defines it, what creates it, what gives value to it, is the interpretation, the imposition of a context. If we assume that Cervantes wrote it, it is one book; if Menard wrote it, it is another. There is no text; there are readings, infinite readings. The text is not the script; it is the activity of interpreting it. And if there is no text, there is no plagiarism. As Borges says in the quote at the beginning of the preceding section, "our tradition is all of Western culture, and . . . we have a right to this tradition." We are the owners, not plagiarists; we own it and have a right to read it and transform it.

The formalist idea that the law is a text that is not subject to interpretation, that laws are merely orders that are imposed by force, is hidden behind the accusation that Borges is a transgressor. But in Menard, Borges denies this accusation and supports that law (and literature, too) is only an invitation to a dialogue, a suggestion of the way in which certain texts can be read, a proposal of contexts in which one can understand the meaning of certain symbols. Breaking the assumption that literature is a series of canonical texts, Borges proposes an incredible series of interesting ways of reading the texts. As literature is a way of reading, not of writing, so law is an interpretive, complex social practice, not mere texts.

THE *ORESTEIA*

How does one avoid a seemingly inevitable tragedy? How can an infinite sequence of deaths end? What follows is an attempt to answer these questions from Aeschylus's tragic *Oresteia.* In the *Oresteia,* the tragedy, in the dispute between Apollo and the Furies for Orestes' fate, is once more built on the application of formal laws, which contradict the brotherly honor and the prohibition of matricide. Apollo defends Orestes and justifies the murder of Aegisthus and Clytemnestra because they had killed Agamemnon, Orestes' father. However, the Furies seek to punish Orestes because he committed matricide. Each is both right and wrong. The contradiction between rules suggests that everything is forbidden and that everything is allowed, that there really is no rule; in the end, there is only the anarchy of permanent violence.

Orestes, advised by Apollo, looks for protection in the temple of Athena, and the Furies, at the request of the spirit Clytemnestra, follow him. The Furies are restricted from entering the temple, and the temple serves as a protection for Orestes. Athena interrogates the Furies (here the chorus) about the reasons of the dispute, and the Furies complain that Orestes does not want to confess. The dialogue in the *Eumenides* proceeds as follows:

Chorus Leader
Yes—he thought it right to kill his mother.
Athena
Why? Was he forced to do it? Did he fear
another person's anger?
Chorus Leader
Where's the urge
so strong to force a man to kill his mother?
Athena
There are two sides to this dispute. I've heard
only one half the argument.
Chorus Leader
What about the oath?
He won't deny he did it or accept
the guilt we charge him with.
Athena
Where do you stand?
You wish to be considered righteous,
but not to act with justice.
Chorus Leader
How? Teach me.
You clearly have a mind for subtleties.
Athena
I assert that no one should use oaths
to let injustice triumph.

Chorus Leader

Question him.
Then make a righteous judgment.

Athena

Are you prepared
that I should be the one to do this,
to produce a final verdict?

Chorus Leader

Why not?
We respect your worth, as you do ours.[48]

The Furies enter the dialogue proposed by Athena and agree to play the trial game. It is the beginning of the end. This agreement is followed by a legal process, with witnesses, jurors, and a rule about the final decision: in the case of a tie among the jurors, Athena gets the final vote. Predictably, both party's demands are presented and are equally persuasive: the jury is tied, and Athena makes the final decision. Her decision favors Orestes for a clearly arbitrary reason: Athena, who was not born from a woman, misogynously decides against Orestes' mother.

The Furies are irritated, but Athena's work does not end with the sole announcement of the sentence. She does not just leave the text. The dialogue continues with Athena persuading the Furies to remain in Athens, to enforce justice with their dread powers. The goddess's speech is an oratorical piece of classic persuasion by a stateswoman, consisting of threats, promises of reward, and kind but firm language, spoken in terms that the interlocutor can understand. She displays the skills of a statesperson, of practical wisdom: empathy and distance.[49]

The tragic circle of violence ends when both sides accept a regulated dialogue—when the law is not only the written text but, rather, is shaped by a shared argument, a process that generates rules to be obeyed. These rules become effective authority, the law. Just as the *Quixote* becomes literature when somebody reads it as though in dialogue with the person he or she imagines as the author, rules become the law when people enter into dialogue with the objective of interpreting, enforcing, and obeying them.

What act makes dialogue possible? In Menard's case, it is the acceptance on my part that the text I am reading was written by him, trusting that what the other says is true, the agreement to be equals. In the case of the *Oresteia,* both sides consciously accept that they are tied (in the sense that neither is able to win or escape from the other) in parallel positions:

the Furies cannot kill Orestes; Orestes cannot escape. This position prevents them from escaping: their only option is another tie, the one that leads to the infinite spiral of violence. Athena's suggested solution allows the Furies to accept the tie and reject the belief that they can win. However, if Athena's decision had been final, the problem would remain: either Athena would have become authoritarian and restrained the losing side, or violence would have been used to persecute the opponents. Athena's decision is a confirmation of life, without offering strong reasons. However, Athena does not just stop there. She takes into account the losing side and continues talking. Athena's skills persuade the Furies to transform themselves from pure agents of punishment to Athenian authorities, open to dialogical processes that will allow for laws to be obeyed.

In Borges's *Martin Fierro,* how is dialogue initiated? How can we dismantle the device that Ludmer assembles? In "The End," the dialogue emerges from a sense of hope and perhaps from some incentive. Let us remind ourselves of the scene: Martin Fierro returns to the inexorable appointment with the Negro's brother, who is seeking revenge. He returns to the place of the unfinished fight, which gives Moreno the opportunity to seek revenge on Fierro, who had killed his brother. The following are the brother's first words:

> "I knew I could count on you, sir," he softly said.
>
> "And I knew I could count on you, old nigger," the other man replied, his voice harsh. "A heap of days I've made you wait, but here I am."
>
> There was a silence then the black man spoke again.
>
> "I'm getting used to waiting. I've been waiting now for seven years."
>
> Unhurried, the other man explained:
>
> "It'd been longer than seven years that I'd gone without seeing my children. I found them that day, and I wouldn't have it so's I looked to them like a man on his way to a knife fight."[50]

After Moreno accepts Fierro's apology for the delay, the element that initiates the dialogue is shame. At this point in the story, shame arises from Fierro's reluctance to appear in front of his sons as "a man on his way to a knife fight."

> I understood that, the black man said. I hope they were all in good health.

> The stranger, who had sat down at the bar, gave a hearty laugh at that. He ordered a drink and took a sip or two, but didn't finish it.
>
> I gave them some advice, he said, which is something you can never get too much of and doesn't cost a lot. I told them, among other things, that a man ought not to go spilling another man's blood.
>
> A slow chord preceded the black man's response:
>
> Good advice, too. That way they won't grow up to be like us.[51]

The other man also is shameful of being the type of man who spills the blood of other men, and he expresses hope for different future, one in which the children of his adversary do not share their same destiny. Then, they start fighting, and the Negro kills Fierro. I quote again the memorable ending:

> He wiped off the bloody knife in the grass and walked slowly back toward the houses, never looking back. His work of vengeance done, he was nobody now. Or rather, he was the other one: there was neither destination nor destiny on earth for him, and he had killed a man.[52]

The interpretation previously proposed, as per Ludmer, suggests that here Borges repeats the device of the destiny of nondestiny and the ineluctability of violence. However, the brief dialogue recently quoted can be interpreted in a different manner. The hope of both is based on Fierro's capacity to convince his sons. Was he persuasive enough? Will Fierro's famous advice be as effective as the authoritative exercise of Athena? Perhaps the ending can be given another meaning. On the one hand, the black man "was the other"; he was Fierro. On the other hand, "he was nobody"; he did not have "destiny on earth" because "he had killed a man." The end of "The End" could be, then, a warning, a threat to future generations. If they do not stop the violence, then they will be nobody and will not have, as the Furies, a destiny on earth.

In 1970, at the beginning of the political violence in Argentina and thirty-five years after "Hombre de la Esquina Rosada," Borges wrote "Historia de Rosendo Juarez." In this story, Rosendo Juarez explains his night's behavior to Borges. But before doing so, he tells his own story. Juarez had killed a man in a duel. The reason was banal: the man, drunk, had bothered him and challenged him to fight. The police gave him two options: to put his knife to the service of a political party or to go to jail. Things did not go badly for him. He obtained a woman, the Lujanera, and a good horse. One day, a very good friend of his, a carpenter, asked for advice: his wife had left him for another man, a famous *malevo,* and now the carpenter wanted to fight him. When Juarez advised him against fighting, his friend asked, "But what'll people say? That I'm yellow? That I don't stand up to a man that wrongs me?" Juarez predicted that he will either die or go to jail and asked him, "You mean you are going to base your peace of mind on a stranger you've never met and a woman you don't even love any more?" His friend did not listen to him and died in the duel. A few days later, the story that is narrated in "Hombre de la Esquina Rosada" occurred. Juarez's explanation is the following:

> That was when it happened—what nobody wants to understand. I was looking at myself in a mirror and all of a sudden I was ashamed of myself. I wasn't afraid of him; if I had been, I might've gone outside and fought him. I just stood there. This other guy, this Yardmaster, who by now had his face about this far from mine, raised his voice so everybody could hear him:
>
> "You know what's wrong with you? You're yellow, that's what's wrong with you!"
>
> "That may be," I said. "I can live with being called yellow. You can tell people you called me a son of a whore, too, and say I let you spit on my face. Now then, does that make you feel better?"
>
> La Lujanera slipped her hand up my sleeve and pulled out the knife I always carried there and slipped it into my hand. And to make sure I got the message, she also said, "Rosendo, I think you're needing this." Her eyes were blazing.
>
> I dropped the knife and walked out—taking my time about it. People stepped back to make way for me. They couldn't believe their eyes. What did I care what they thought.
>
> To get out of that life, I moved over to Uruguay and became an ox-cart driver. Since I came back, I've made my place here. San Telmo has always been a peaceful place to live.[53]

As in "The End," but this time more explicitly, shame appears as an emotion that restrains violence. Here and in other Borgesian forms, the infinite succession of shame ends up becoming an oxymoron, but this time, the oxymoron leads to a peaceful solution: to say, "I can live with being called yellow," is to say, "I am so courageous that I am above all violence." In respect to the end of violence, Juarez asks Real, "Now are you calmer?" Like Socrates with respect to Crito, Juarez states, "What did I care what they thought." So, in effect, what the others thought does not invite dialogue. Rather, dialogue is the result of specific community prejudices, which, in this case, imposed a certain manner of being violent; here the authoritarian voice of social authority encouraged dialogue. Juarez, who had lost a friend due to what others thought, was not ready to lose his life or the life of another for the blind demands of others.

The emotion of shame also appears in the myth of Protagoras, when Zeus finally concedes to handing over his political power to mortals. Plato states that when Protagoras refers to politics, he explains it in terms of "shame" and "justice."[54] Shame is connected to the idea of decency, the awareness that there are others with the same claim to dignity as myself, whom my actions could damage and whose actions could damage me. It is awareness of my dependence on others, of being a gregarious dog, and also of the possibility of appearing to others in a way that I do not wish others to appear to me: as a wolf, as Cruz would say.

In "The End," Martin Fierro feels shameful in front of his sons but cannot circumvent his destiny; in "The History of Rosendo Juarez," Juarez feels shameful in front of himself, and his friend's death allows him to circumvent his destiny by changing the meaning of bravery, so that it means not fearing that others will consider him a coward. This change, in fact, continues to make possible Borges's literature. It is the revelation that literature can coexist with peace, that one can write Argentine literature against violence. The artifact, however, continues to be the same: the violation of the canon, this time of the canon of violence through the use of an oxymoron (from having fear to not having fear), which triggers a life of civility.

ALFONSÍN AND THE MOTHERS

How can the history of the violation of rules in Argentina be altered? In the anecdote about the traffic that begins this essay, the *gauchada* led to the banishment of all rules. In effect, in that dialogue, the law has no voice. I have attempted to argue that the silence of both the police officer and the offender condemn the law to be a response to silence, just as the law condemned the Argentines to construct institutionalism in the way they did in the nineteenth century. Disobedience is a response to the authoritarian imposition of the law. The *gauchada* is a distinctly Argentine form of solidarity, a mechanism used by those who have refused to recognize the legitimacy of authority in order to save one another: the "Cruz" (cross) saving the "Fierro" (knife).

This situation led Argentina in the twentieth century to suffer various instances of authoritarian regimes and criminal resistances and the massive violation of human rights in the 1970s, our own encounter with radical evil. Perhaps none of this would have had much consequence without the bravery, stubbornness, and perseverance of human rights organizations, most importantly the Mothers of the Plaza de Mayo and the triumph of President Alfonsín in the 1983 elections. These two events forced the Argentines to accept the existence of human rights violations, which gave rise to the emergence of shame. Various instances of collective complicity accentuate this feeling: for example, such statements as "They should have done something" (blaming those who were disappeared, as Job's friends blamed him) and "We Argentines are right and human" (written on stickers to be seen by the Inter-American Commission on Human Rights when they visited Argentina during the dictatorship). How can we trust ourselves if we are capable of such attitudes of complicity when faced with radical evil?

Perhaps because of this, Argentina has not suffered any more coups d'état since 1983 and has learned many lessons. From the dictatorships, Argentina has learned the importance of democracy, at least in the sense of free elections and freedom of expression and association. From the massive human rights violations, Argentina has learned about the idea of rights and the importance of having countermajoritarian institutions to defend them. Already in democracy, Argentines, especially the leading politicians, have learned about the social cost of inflation; the impact on equality of the inefficient provision of public services; and the effects of corruption, public deficit, the incapacity to maintain order without killing innocents, and structural inequality.

These lessons have translated into innovative institutions. Argentina has signed all international human rights treaties, and as of 1994, the most important are incorporated into its national constitution. Argentina has accepted international jurisdiction not only in the area of human rights but also in issues having to do with commerce and the protection of international investment. It has pursued collective actions to defend human rights and has created a community of associations that legally represent its collective interests, has privatized public services and created regulatory agencies, and has discovered in the judiciary a power that is ready to involve itself in political discussion among other institutional reforms. Compared with that created in the nineteenth century, these reforms constitute a real change in the political system. Reasonably, these changes require some time for institutional adjustment, but more important is the conceptual adjustment. In effect, many of these changes are yet regarded as complications of the normal order of our political tradition. However, some actors are responding in an encouraging manner.

In the international arena, the Inter-American Commission on Human Rights and the Inter-American Court of Human Rights, prompted by organizations of the civil society and public interest lawyers, have mandated changes in public policies that have been appropriated and implemented by the national and provincial governments, in regard to the violation of rights in the prison system and in ruling against those responsible for the human rights violations in the last dictatorship, among other topics. It is interesting that in the implementation of these decisions, some problems of enforcement have become, for some critics, an obstacle that must be overcome with better enforcement systems. However, this is a mistake. Enforcement problems are an opportunity to equalize the parties and force them to sit and talk. The international actors have countermajoritarian legitimacy in applying international treaties of human rights, the victims have an interest in stopping the violation of their rights, and national authorities have democratic legitimacy to decide on the opportunity, costs, and priorities of public decisions. Shame has prompted Argentine citizens to sit and talk. It may well be that Athena is building another temple, in a most surprising place.

NOTES

1. Carlos Gamerro, *El nacimiento de la literatura argentina y otros ensayos* (Buenos Aires: Norma, 2006).

2. See Carlos Nino, *Radical Evil on Trial* (New Haven: Yale University Press, 1996).

3. See the scene of the crossing of the U.S.-Mexican border back into the United States in the film *Babel,* directed by Alejandro González Iñárritu (143 min., Los Angeles: Paramount Pictures, 2006).

4. Carlos Nino, *Un país al margen del la ley* (Buenos Aires: Emecé, 1992).

5. ". . . contra lo que piensan Böhmer y Carrara, no veo tan mal combatir contra una moral siciliana de la complicidad en favor de una moral cívica. La imagen del recelo y la sospecha que nos hacen recordar situaciones como las de la Alemania nazi y la Unión Soviética stalinista, es sobrecogedora si no tomamos en cuenta que todo

depende de si es legítimo y justo penar el hecho por el que podemos ser denunciados, y si se respetan las garantías del debido proceso. Si estas condiciones se satisfacen, yo no tendría ningún recelo en ser denunciado por una persona con la que tengo tratos, en la medida en que estoy dispuesto a mantenerme en los márgenes de la ley" (ibid., 266–67).

6. "El argentino, a diferencia de los americanos del Norte y de casi todos los europeos, no se identifica con el Estado. Ello puede atribuirse a la circunstancia de que, en este país, los gobiernos suelen ser pésimos o al hecho general de que el Estado es una inconcebible abstracción; lo cierto es que el argentino es un individuo, no un ciudadano. Aforismos como el de Hegel 'El Estado es la realidad de la idea moral' le parecen bromas siniestras. Los filmes elaborados en Hollywood repetidamente proponen a la admiración el caso de un hombre (generalmente, un periodista) que busca la amistad de un criminal para entregarlo después a la policía; el argentino, para quien la amistad es una pasión y la policía una *maffia,* siente que ese 'héroe' es un incomprensible canalla" (Jorge Luis Borges, "Nuestro pobre individualismo," in *Otras Inquisiciones,* in *Obras Completas* [Buenos Aires: Emecé, 1974], 658). The English translation in the text is from Jorge Luis Borges, "Our Poor Individualism," in *Selected Non-fictions,* ed. Eliot Weinberger, trans. Esther Allen, Suzanne Jill Levine, and Eliot Weinberger (New York: Penguin, 2000), 309.

7. "Siente con Don Quijote, 'que allá se lo haya cada uno con su pecado' y que 'no es bien que los hombres honrados sean verdugos de los otros hombres, no yéndoles nada en eso.' . . . Más de una vez, ante las vanas simetrías del estilo español, he sospechado que diferimos insalvablemente de España; esas dos líneas del Quijote han bastado para convencerme del error; son como el símbolo tranquilo y secreto de nuestra afinidad. Profundamente lo confirma una noche de la literatura argentina: esa desesperada noche en la que un sargento de la policía rural gritó que no iba a consentir el delito de que se matara un valiente, y se puso a pelear contra sus soldados, junto al desertor Martín Fierro." Borges, "Nuestro pobre individualismo," 658. The English translation in the text is from Borges, "Our Poor Individualism," 309–10.

8. Nicolás Shumway, *The Invention of Argentina* (Berkeley: University of California Press, 1991), 265.

9. Ibid., 266.

10. Estaba el gaucho en su pago
con toda seguridá,
pero aura . . . ¡barbaridá!
la cosa anda tan fruncida,
que gasta el pobre la vida
en juir de la autoridá

Pues si usté pisa en su rancho
y si el alcalde lo sabe
lo caza lo mesmo que ave
aunque su mujer aborte . . .
¡no hay tiempo que no se acabe
ni tiento que no se corte!

Y al punto dése por muerto
si el alcalde lo bolea,
pues ahí nomás se le apea
con una felpa de palos.
Y después dicen que es malo
el gaucho si los pelea.

(José Hernandez, *The Gaucho Martin Fierro,* bilingual edition, English version by C. E. Ward (Albany: State University of New York Press, 1976), 21)

11. Domingo Faustino Sarmiento, *Facundo* (Buenos Aires: Losada, 1938).

12. Juan Bautista Alberdi, *Bases y puntos de partida para la organización política de la República Argentina* (San Miguel de Tucumán: Editorial Top Graph, 2002).

13. Alberdi wrote, "What name will you give, what name does a country covering two hundred thousand leagues of territory and a population of eight hundred thousand inhabitants deserve? A desert. What name will you give to the Constitution of this country? The Constitution of a desert. Well, that country is the Argentine Republic; and whichever its Constitution is, for many years it will not be but the Constitution of a desert. But, what is the Constitution that best suits a desert? The one useful for making it disappear" (ibid., 145–46).

14. Sarmiento wrote, "The moral progress, the culture of neglected intelligence in the Arab or Tartar tribe, is here, not only neglected but impossible. Where shall a school for the children to attend lessons be located when they live spread out ten leagues away from one another in all directions?" (op. cit., 39).

15. Sarmiento wrote, "In all other respects, the result of the fusion of these three families [the Spanish, the natives, and the Africans] is a homogeneous whole, characterized by its love for idleness and industrial incompetence" (op. cit., 34).

16. Alberdi explained, "What there is, is little and poor. It is better to raise the number of our population and, what is more, to change its condition in a way favorable to progress. . . . With three million of Christian and Catholic natives you will certainly not make a republic. You will neither make it with four million people from mainland Spain, for the pure Spanish is incapable of making a republic whether there or here. If we are to make up our population for our system of government, if it is easier for us to make the population for the system proclaimed than the system for the population, it is necessary to encourage the Anglo-Saxon population on our soil. The Anglo-Saxon population is identified with vapor, commerce and liberty, and it will be impossible for us to settle these things among us without the active cooperation of this race of progress and civilization" (op. cit., 144).

17. Alberdi wrote, "Here lies the purpose of today's constitutions: they must be prone to organize and build the great practical means to get the emancipated America out of the state of darkness and subordination in which [it] now is. . . . We must constitute ourselves today, if we are allowed to put it in these words, to have iron roads, to see our rivers navigated, to see our States opulent and rich. . . . Our contracts or constitutional pacts in South America must be some kind of mercantile contracts of corporations, especially formed to populate these deserts which we ostentatiously call Republics" (op. cit., 28).

18. Sarmiento wrote, "There is no encouragement; the example disappears; the

need of expressing oneself with dignity that is felt in the cities is not felt there in isolation and solitude. The necessary privations are justified by the natural laziness, and the frugality of pleasures brings about the exteriorization of barbarism. Society has completely disappeared; the isolated and concentrated feudal family is all that remains; and without a society, every type of government becomes impossible; the municipality does not exist, the police power cannot be exercised and civil justice does not have the means to catch the criminals" (op. cit., 38).

19. See Tulio Halperín Donghi, *Una Nación para el Desierto Argentino* (Buenos Aires: Editores de América Latina, 1997), 115.

20. See ibid., 116.

21. Alberdi wrote,

> Thus, the providential purpose of that law of expansion is the indefinite improvement of the human race, by means of the mixing of races, the communication of ideas and beliefs, and by maintaining a balance between populations and supplies. Unfortunately, its implementation found in South America an obstacle in the system of exclusion of its first conquerors. . . . The obstacles and prohibitions of the colonial system prevented European people—who went to North America, colonized by a country with a better economic sense—to populate it in a great and fruitful scale; this being one of the main reasons for its superiority over us. . . . We thus find ourselves before the requirements of a law that demands for civilization the territory we keep deserted because of the backward state of development. . . .
>
> European socialism is the sign of an imbalance that will sooner or later have in this continent its violent rejection, if our precaution does not use from today the means needed for that law to be peacefully executed and in the benefit of both worlds. . . . Europe, just as America, suffers from the violation exercised on the natural course of things. The population that we here vitally need is there overabundant to the point of illness. Will those societies reach a fundamental chaos regarding property issues when we have, within reach, one-fifth of the inhabited world? (op. cit., 1–2)

22. Jorge Luis Borges, "Domingo F. Sarmiento. Facundo," in *Prólogos. Con un prólogo de prólogos,* in *Obras Completas IV* (Buenos Aires: Emecé, 2007), 154.

23. Hernandez, op. cit., 21.

24. Simone Weil, "Electra," in *La fuente griega* (Madrid: Trotta, 2005), 66.

25. "El criminal salió de la guarida para pelearlos, Cruz lo entrevió, terrible, la crecida melena y la barba gris parecían comerle la cara, un motivo notorio me vela referir la pelea. Básteme recordar que el desertor malhirió o mató a varios de los hombres de Cruz. Éste, mientras combatía en la oscuridad (mientras su cuerpo combatía en la oscuridad), empezó a comprender. Comprendió que un destino no es mejor que otro, pero que todo hombre debe acatar el que lleva adentro. Comprendió que las jinetas y el uniforme ya lo estorbaban. Comprendió su íntimo destino de lobo, no de perro gregario; comprendió que el otro era él. Amanecía en la desaforada llanura; Cruz arrojó por tierra el kepis, gritó que no iba a consentir el

delito de que se matara un valiente y se puso a pelear contra los soldados, junto al desertor Martín Fierro" (Jorge Luis Borges, "Biografía de Tadeo Isidoro Cruz," in *El Aleph,* in *Obras Completas,* vol. 1 (Buenos Aires: Emecé, 1974), 563, trans. Andrew Hurley as "A Biography of Tadeo Isidoro Cruz" in *Collected Fictions,* Penguin Classics Deluxe Edition (New York: Penguin, 1998), 214).

26. Nora Avaro, "La Enumeración," in *Sarmiento-Hernández-Borges-Arlt. Los Clásicos Argentinos* (Rosario: Editorial Municipal de Rosario, 2005).

27. "Yo les he consentido a estos infelices que me alzaran la mano, porque lo que estoy buscando es un hombre. . . . Quiero encontrarlo pa que me enseñe a mi, que soy naides, lo que es un hombre de coraje y de vista" (Jorge Luis Borges, "Hombre de la Esquina Rosada," in *Historia Universal de la Infamia,* in *Obras Completas* (Buenos Aires: Emecé, 1974), 331, trans. Andrew Hurley as "Man on Pink Corner" in *Collected Fictions,* 47–48).

28. "De asco no te carneo . . . y alzó, para castigarlo, la mano. Entonces la Lujanera se le prendió y le echó los brazos al cuello y lo miró con esos ojos y le dijo con ira: —Dejálo a ése, que nos hizo creer que era un hombre" (ibid., 331).

29. ". . . en eso cae un desconocido y lo llama como desesperado para pelear y le infiere esa puñalada y que ella jura que no sabe quién es y que no es Rosendo. ¿Quién le iba a creer?" (ibid., 333).

30. "Entonces, Borges, volví a sacar el cuchillo corto y filoso que yo sabía cargar aquí, en el chaleco, junto al sobaco izquierdo, y le pegué otra revisada despacio, y estaba como nuevo, inocente, y no quedaba ni un rastrito de sangre" (ibid., 334).

31. "¿Dónde estará (repito) el malevaje / Que fundó en polvorientos callejones / De tierra o en perdidas poblaciones / La secta del cuchillo y el coraje?" (Jorge Luis Borges, "Tango," in *El otro, el mismo,* in *Obras Completas* [Buenos Aires: Emecé, 1974], 888).

32. ". . . la guerra servía, como la mujer, para que se probaran los hombres" (Jorge Luis Borges, "La otra muerte," in *El Aleph,* in *Obras Completas* [Buenos Aires: Emecé, 1974], 888).

33. "¿Cuál es la tradición argentina? Creo que podemos contestar fácilmente y que no hay problema en esa pregunta. Creo que nuestra tradición es toda la cultura occidental, y creo también que tenemos derecho a esa tradición, mayor que el que pueden tener los habitantes de una u otra nación occidental" (Jorge Luis Borges, "El Escritor Argentino y la Tradición," in *Discusión,* in *Obras Completas* [Buenos Aires: Emecé, 1974], 272, trans. James E. Irby as "The Argentine Writer and Tradition," in *Labyrinths* [New York: New Directions, 1964], 183–84).

34. Borges, "Domingo F. Sarmiento. Facundo," 154.

35. Josefina Ludmer, "Borges contra la ley," http://www.udesa.edu.ar/files/Events/archivos/JLudmer-Borges.pdf.

36. Ibid.

37. "Aquí interviene Borges para violar el texto sagrado. En 'El fin' Martín Fierro se separa de sus propios consejos, reniega de sí mismo, viola la ley que transmitió a sus hijos, asume la antigua justicia, y saca el cuchillo. Pero el negro se tiende en una puñalada final y venga por fin a su hermano mayor: en 1953, el negro hace justicia: una justicia oral, familiar. Allí Borges da otra vuelta a La vuelta, o le inventa un verdadero fin que no es más que otro principio, porque el negro que mata al viejo

Martín Fierro para vengar a su hermano mayor se transforma en el mismo Martín Fierro de La ida: había matado un hombre, se había 'desgraciado,' y no tenía destino sobre la tierra. Borges viola y cierra el clásico y lo hace retornar a su punto de partida, a la Ida del negro, al Martín Fierro de un negro" (Ludmer, op. cit.).

38. Compare Martin Fierro's action upon killing the Negro's brother ("Limpié el facón en los pastos . . .") (Hernandez, op. cit., 94) and the final phrase of the narrator of "Hombre de la Esquina Rosada": ". . . y no quedaba ni un rastrito de sangre" (Borges, "Man on Pink Corner," 52).

39. "Limpió el facón ensangrentado en el pasto y volvió a las casas con lentitud, sin mirar para atrás. Cumplida su tarea de justiciero, ahora era nadie. Mejor dicho era el otro: no tenía destino sobre la tierra y había matado a un hombre" (Borges, "El Fin," in *Ficciones,* in *Obras Completas* (Buenos Aires: Emecé, 521).

40. ". . . los argentinos, los sudamericanos en general . . . podemos manejar todos los temas europeos, manejarlos sin supersticiones, con una irreverencia que puede tener, y ya tiene, consecuencias afortunadas" (Borges, "El Escritor Argentino y la Tradición," 273, trans. Irby in *Labyrinths,* 184).

41. See Ludmer, op. cit.

42. Jorge Luis Borges, "Pierre Menard, autor del Quijote," in *Ficciones,* in *Obras Completas* (Buenos Aires: Emecé, 1974), 446, trans. Andrew Hurley as "Pierre Menard, Author of the *Quixote*" in *Collected Fictions,* 91.

43. "Veamos qué hace con el canon literario de la lengua: el Quijote de Cervantes. Los clásicos son el punto de partida de la literatura de Borges porque el texto clásico funciona siempre como ley a transgredir en su escritura. Esto ya se ve en su primer texto de ficción, 'Pierre Menard autor del Quijote' donde le cambia el autor, o le inventa otro autor, al clásico. En el título mismo hay, entonces, un delito contra el derecho de autor, contra el mismo Miguel de Cervantes. Y en el relato se cuenta otro delito contra el Quijote: un plagio de dos capítulos realizado por un francés a comienzos del siglo XX. En otros términos, 'Pierre Menard, autor del Quijote,' una falsa atribución y un plagio, es un doble ataque al texto clásico desde el punto de vista del derecho: contra los derechos de autor y contra el carácter inviolable del texto. Borges piensa o escribe a partir del clásico de la lengua para violarlo en tanto título y texto. Y con esto debuta en la ficción en 1939.

. . . Dos problemas, entonces, en la escritura de Borges: por un lado el tratamiento del canon literario, del texto clásico que hay que atacar, tergiversar, plagiar, cambiarle de autor, cambiarle el sentido y el final. Y por el otro lado el tratamiento del canon jurídico o de la ley escrita que hay que atacar para ejercer la venganza: la ley pierde siempre. Como pierde Narciso Laprida, 'hombre de cánones y de leyes,' en el 'Poema conjetural'" (Ludmer, op. cit.).

44. . . . Yo, que estudié las leyes y los cánones,
yo, Francisco Narciso de Laprida,
cuya voz declaró la independencia
de estas crueles provincias, derrotado,
de sangre y de sudor manchado el rostro,
sin esperanza ni temor, perdido,
huyo hacia el Sur por arrabales últimos.
. . . .

Yo que anhelé ser otro, ser un hombre
de sentencias, de libros, de dictámenes
a cielo abierto yaceré entre ciénagas;
pero me endiosa el pecho inexplicable
un júbilo secreto. Al fin me encuentro
con mi destino sudamericano . . .

(Jorge Luis Borges, "Poema conjetural," in *El otro, el mismo,* in *Obras completas* (Buenos Aires: Emecé, 1974), 867, trans. Anthony Kerrigan as "Conjectural Poem" in *A Personal Anthology* (New York: Grove Press, 1967), 192)

45. Simone Weil, *The* Iliad *or The Poem of Force* (Wallingford: Pendle Hill Pamphlet 91, 2003), 34.

46. Borges, "Pierre Menard, autor del Quijote," trans. Hurley in *Collected Fictions,* 91.

47. "El texto de Cervantes y el de Menard son verbalmente idénticos, pero el segundo es casi infinitamente más rico. (Más ambiguo, dirán sus detractores; pero la ambigüedad es una riqueza.)

Es una revelación cotejar el *Don Quijote* de Menard con el de Cervantes. Éste, por ejemplo, escribió (Don Quijote, primera parte, noveno capítulo):

> . . . *la verdad, cuya madre es la historia, émula del tiempo, depósito de las acciones, testigo de lo pasado, ejemplo y aviso de lo presente, advertencia de lo por venir.*

Redactada en el siglo diecisiete, redactada por el 'ingenio lego' Cervantes, esa enumeración es un mero elogio retórico de la historia. Menard, en cambio, escribe:

> . . . *la verdad, cuya madre es la historia, émula del tiempo, depósito de las acciones, testigo de lo pasado, ejemplo y aviso de lo presente, advertencia de lo por venir.*

La historia, *madre* de la verdad; la idea es asombrosa. Menard, contemporáneo de William James, no define la historia como una indagación de la realidad sino como su origen. La verdad histórica, para él, no es lo que sucedió; es lo que juzgamos que sucedió. Las cláusulas finales—*ejemplo y aviso de lo presente, advertencia de lo por venir*—son descaradamente pragmáticas.

También es vívido el contraste de los estilos. El estilo arcaizante de Menard—extranjero al fin—adolece de alguna afectación. No así el del precursor, que maneja con desenfado el español corriente de su época" (Borges, "Pierre Menard, autor del Quijote," trans. Andrew Hurley as "Pierre Menard, Author of the *Quixote*" in *Collected Fictions,* 94).

48. Trans. Ian Johnston at http://records.viu.ca-Johnstoi/aeschylus/aeschylus_eumenides.htm.

49. See Anthony Kronman, *The Lost Lawyer* (Cambridge: Harvard University Press, 1996), chap. 2.

50. -Ya sabía yo, señor, que podía contar con usted.

El otro, con voz áspera, replicó:

-Y yo con vos, moreno. Una porción de días te hice esperar, pero aquí he venido.

Hubo un silencio. Al fin el negro respondió:
-Me estoy acostumbrando a esperar. He esperado siete años.
El otro explicó sin apuro:
-Más de siete años pasé yo sin ver a mis hijos. Los encontré ese día y no quise mostrarme como un hombre que anda a las puñaladas.
(Borges, "El Fin," trans. Andrew Hurley as "The End" in *Collected Fictions,* 169)

51. -Ya me hice cargo -dijo el negro. Espero que los dejó con salud.
El forastero, que se había sentado en el mostrador, se rió de buena gana. Pidió una caña y la paladeó sin concluirla.
-Les di buenos consejos -declaró-, que nunca están de más y no cuestan nada. Les dije, entre otras cosas, que el hombre no debe derramar la sangre del hombre.
Un lento acorde precedió la respuesta del negro:
-Hizo bien. Así no se parecerán a nosotros.
(ibid.)

52. See n. 37.

53. "Sucedió entonces lo que nadie quiere entender. En ese botarate provocador me vi como en un espejo y me dio vergüenza. No sentí miedo; acaso de haberlo sentido, salgo a pelear. Me quedé como si tal cosa. El otro, con la cara ya muy arrimada a la mía gritó para que todos lo oyeran:
—Lo que pasa es que no sos más que un cobarde.
—Así será—le dije-. No tengo miedo de pasar por cobarde. Podés agregar, si te halaga, que me has llamado hijo de mala madre y que me he dejado escupir. Ahora ¿estás más tranquilo?
La Lujanera me sacó el cuchillo que yo sabía cargar en la sisa y me lo puso, como fula, en la mano. Para rematarla, me dijo:
—Rosendo, creo que lo estás precisando.
Lo solté y salí sin apuro. La gente me abrió cancha, asombrada. Qué podía importarme lo que pensaran.
Para zafarme de esa vida me corría a la República Oriental, donde me puse de carrero. Desde mi vuelta me he afincado aquí. San Telmo ha sido siempre un barrio de orden" (Jorge Luis Borges, "Historia de Rosendo Juárez," in *Informede Brodie,* in *Obras Completas* (Buenos Aires: Emecé, 1974, 1038), trans. Andrew Hurley as "The Story from Rosendo Juárez," in *Collected Fictions,* 363).

54. Plato, *Protagoras,* trans. Stanley Lombardo and Karen Bell (Indianapolis and Cambridge: Hackett Publishing, 1992), 17.

Moral Disagreement in a Culture of Certainty

Howard Lesnick

In this essay, Howard Lesnick addresses a common and disturbing feature of our contemporary culture of political argument: namely, the use of triumphalist or dismissive characterizations to avoid responding to arguments on the merits—characterizations that in their own way work as manifestations of what Simone Weil calls the "empire of force." As Lesnick says, three such terms, themselves somewhat related, are in common use: liberal, secularist, *and* relativist, *each of which is a word that can be used to close a conversation, working as an epithet that justifies a refusal to respond on the merits. (One might say, for example, "I do not have to attend or respond to what you say because you are a liberal." The reader can probably think of other examples.) Lesnick's main concern here is with the last of these terms. He asks in particular how one who is not a relativist can intelligibly and forcibly respond to claims that he is.*

Much is at stake here, including the question whether we live in a world in which we can hope or expect that arguments will be responded to in their own terms, rather than dismissed with an inaccurate and conclusory characterization. At stake is also the quality of our own thought and expression, and in particular whether we can learn to carry on conversation in ways that respect our own (and others') uncertainties as well as our (and their) convictions.

Lesnick begins with a quotation from A Man for All Seasons *that suggests how deeply the question runs: into our own sense of belief and conviction, indeed into our own sense of what it means to make up one's mind, to have a view of one's own, in the first place.*

> *The Duke of Norfolk:* All right—we're at war with the Pope!
> The Pope's a Prince, isn't he?
> *Sir Thomas More:* He is.
> *Norfolk:* And a bad one?

> *More:* Bad enough. But the theory is that he's also the Vicar of God, the descendant of St. Peter, our only link with Christ.
> *Norfolk* (*Sneering*): A tenuous link.
> *More:* Oh, tenuous indeed.
> *Norfolk:* Does this make sense? You'll forfeit all you've got—which includes the respect of your country—for a theory?
> *More* (*Hotly*): The Apostolic Succession of the Pope is—(*Stops; interested*) Why, it's a theory, yes; you can't see it; can't touch it; it's a theory. But what matters to me is not whether it's true or not but that I believe it to be true, or rather, not that I *believe* it, but that *I* believe it.
>
> —ROBERT BOLT, *A Man for All Seasons*

> Nothing can count as a reason for holding a belief except another belief.
>
> —DONALD DAVIDSON

The unholy trinity of much public discourse today is liberalism, secularism, and relativism. Like a (very small) deck of cards, they are often thought to support one another, to engender one another, at times even to stand in for one another semantically. Whether as three or as one, they are widely viewed as the root cause of much of our social malaise. Let me start with expressions of the evils of the first two isms, chosen almost at random.

> Liberalism . . . seems unable to arrest the barbarism of modern culture; indeed, contemporary liberalism is implicated in many of the most corrosive moral and intellectual trends of our time.[1]

> The general climate of society . . . shows a radical loss of the sense of the transcendent, a devaluation of the religious dimension of human experience, and a great disregard for spiritual values. As a consequence of this general social impoverishment caused by secularism, life both personal and social is more and more guided by practical atheism, which leaves unchecked the worst human tendencies and thus delivers people to the other great vices of these societies: individualism, utilitarianism, hedonism, materialism, and consumerism.[2]

I find sadly apt the description of our culture as "corrosive," in some ways even "barbaric," and as widely characterized by "individualism, utilitarianism, hedonism, materialism, and consumerism." I also deeply deplore the "radical loss of the sense of the transcendent" in contemporary society. I find seriously problematic, however, the tendentious attribution of such social evils to the influence of relativism, liberalism, and secularism, especially because this claim obscures the fact that the political outlook of many of the severest critics of liberalism and secularism often legitimates that very catalogue of social ills. To me, the terms *liberalism* and *secularism* are too protean for words, and I will not here address their responsibility for prevalent social evils. I offer instead a critique of anti-relativism.

ANTI-RELATIVISM

Let me start by saying that my aim is not to defend something called "relativism." Indeed, it is only because I reject relativism, as I do, that I can contend that the widespread use of the charge of relativism to allow one to avoid engaging with claims to a different "knowledge" of the truth regarding a moral issue is not simply annoying but wrongful—a form of rhetorical immorality, if you will. The wrong is compounded when, as too often is the case, the charge sweeps all whose moral sensibilities differ into the same derisively labeled trash pail. My aversion is strengthened by the belief that the attempt to defend a position on anti-relativist grounds is not infrequently bound up with a repellent indifference to the human suffering the position casually overlooks or seeks to justify. In this I am following Clifford Geertz, who (so far as I am aware) coined the term *anti-anti-relativism.* With him, my effort is "to counter a view rather than to defend the view it claims to be counter to."[3]

The anti-relativist might object at the outset that I am misconceiving his claim, which is not a specific moral position—a single ethical assertion, such as, divorce is a wrongful act (whether always or only in specified circumstances)—but the view that what might be termed a "culture of relativism" in contemporary society creates a generalized aura of lassitude about the truth of many moral scruples, such that people come to take a "live and let live" attitude toward a whole range of conduct previously thought freighted with (negative) moral significance. That fog dispelled, the immorality of such conduct once again will appear plain.

The claim so articulated simply assumes the correctness of the panoply of "moral scruples" that previously reigned unchallenged. The critique attacked here as relativist is in fact often based not on lassitude but on an assertedly long-overdue emergence of a more penetrating morality, recognizing and seeking to work free of the pervasive immorality of (formerly) prevailing moral norms: to stay with the example, it is not divorce but imprisoning people (usually women) in oppressive marriages on morally insufficient grounds that is wrongful. Expressing the emancipatory claim in relativist terms is indeed at times an unfortunate way of making what is in truth a profoundly content-laden moral objection.[4] But the countercharge against relativism nonetheless serves to reaffirm the traditional moral position without engaging seriously with the morality-grounded concerns of its critics. That it may result in diverting attention from the need for such an engagement is hardly a defense. Whether the conflict in moral norms is posed as a matter of the general cultural environment or of specific moral questions, my contention is that the issue is evaded by framing it as the infirmity of relativism.

Objecting to the misuse of questioning the soundness of relativism does not, of course, warrant ruling objections to relativism out of bounds, and I will later say why I do reject it as a metaethical stance. The focus on relativism is a distraction from recognition of the significance of conflicts in justified beliefs about a moral question; what is condemned as a "culture of relativism" may in fact be (less ringingly) a culture of conflicting justified beliefs, concededly complicating our moral environment, but, all things considered, constituting an enrichment, or at the least a potential enrichment, of it.

RELATIVISM

The primary question I will consider has arisen out of settings as inconspicuous as was Geertz's own venue—the 1983 annual meeting of the American Anthropological Association—and as unprecedently public as was the prelude to the 2005 conclave of the Roman Catholic College of Cardinals, where, in his last published statement prior to being elected pope, Cardinal Joseph Ratzinger, with a substantial percentage of the people of the world attending closely, condemned a perceived "dictatorship of relativism."

> Relativism, which is letting oneself be tossed and "swept along by every wind of teaching," looks like the only standard (acceptable) to

today's standards. We are moving toward a dictatorship of relativism which does not recognize anything as for certain and which has as its highest goal one's own ego and one's own desires.[5]

Geertz devoted much of his critique to a demonstration of the rhetorical excesses of anti-relativists in anthropology ("Anti Anti-Relativism," 266–68). I prefer to look here at the appropriateness of relativism as a target in moral debate. What is "relativism"? There is, of course, a variousness in the beliefs of self-described relativists, but it will serve for present purposes to note two variants. The first, emphasizing what morality is thought to be relative to, is well summarized by Judge Richard Posner.

> There are no *interesting* moral universals. There are tautological ones, such as "murder is wrong" where "murder" means "wrongful killing." . . . But what counts as murder . . . varies enormously from society to society. There are a handful of rudimentary principles of social cooperation . . . that may be common to all human societies. But they are too abstract to be criterial. Meaningful moral realism is therefore out, and a form (not every form) of moral relativism is in. Relativism in turn invites an *adaptationist* conception of morality, in which morality is judged—nonmorally, in the way a hammer might be judged well or poorly adapted to its goal of hammering nails into wood or plaster—by its contribution to the survival, or other ultimate goals, of a society or some group within it. . . . [M]oral progress is in the eye of the beholder.[6]

This approach sees morality as a matter of convention and function, a description of social practices and utilities, lacking any basis for noninstrumental evaluation. A stronger version of relativism as to morality asserts that when one says that a certain practice is "wrong" (or "right," in the moral sense; "immoral" or "moral"), he or she can only be telling you something about the speaker. Morality, David Hume asserted, "is more properly felt than judg'd\ of."[7] To a relativist (Hume was not), the feeling cannot be evidence of a truth existing independently of it, to which it points, because there is no "truth to which it points"; there exists only a "taste," "preference," or condemnatory practice of the evaluator. On this view, as my former colleague, Michael Moore, put it, "the only thing to be said about watermelons or concentration camps is that some people like them and some people don't."[8]

It is necessary to be careful about taking the content or meaning of a disputed way of thinking from one who is opposed to it. Moore's bon mot has to be understood in context. Of course, it is not literally the "only" thing a relativist (professed or otherwise) would say. What a relativist would not do is ground a negative judgment about concentration camps in a commitment to a "mind-independent" truth.

Ratzinger's "definition" of relativism, however, is pure invective; few (if any) relativists think that all positions are equal or regard "one's own desires" as unquestionable; it is only that one's values or goals cannot be evaluated by an external standard of truth, for no such external standard exists. Whether that is a distinction without a difference is a fair question, which I will address in context; the answer should not, however, be taken for granted.

In a more extended treatment, I attempt to untangle the relations between relativism and secular thinking and between relativism and liberalism, describing those relations unaffected by any presumptive condemnation or embrace of any of them.[9] To me, the core of the matter is this: to attack secularism or liberalism as promoting relativism or to attack relativism as grounded in either one engages with neither them nor relativism. Even if, in the process, it did not mistake the source (or the consequence) of a moral stance that it means to dispute, it would be rhetorically objectionable, for it displaces attention from the content of that stance.

The truth, of course, is that both secular and relativist thinking share, to a substantial degree, a common cause—a market economy—which at the same time legitimates the very "individualism, utilitarianism, hedonism, materialism, and consumerism" (Rico, *John Paul II,* 205) that many anti-relativists selectively deplore. Craig Gay, examining the "recent evangelical debate over capitalism," puts the matter thus:

> The market economy has institutionalized . . . a particular kind of rationality . . . The cost-profit calculus powerfully propels the logic of enterprise, . . . rationalizing man's tools and philosophies, his medical practice, his picture of the cosmos, his outlook on life, everything in fact including his concepts of beauty and justice and his spiritual ambitions.
>
> . . . Modern secularization and decadence are not entirely attributable to "secular humanism." Indeed, the nineteenth-century cultural pattern to which many of those on the evangelical right would have us return—a pattern in which capitalism was more firmly bounded by

> the constraints of family, church, and community—was at least in part destroyed by capitalism itself.[10]

Yet far too many self-professed anti-relativists are quick to defend the ethic of a market economy, directing their ire elsewhere.[11]

As for the asserted linking of liberalism and relativism I believe that much of it proceeds from an unacknowledged conflation of relativism and pluralism. The similarities are real, yet the differences are fundamental. As I understand it, pluralism asserts that although objective criteria support (at least some of) our ethical choices, the beliefs of one person or group, however strongly held, do not justify insisting that others who believe the contrary nonetheless live by them. Pluralism is an approach to determining how a society should respond to the fact that there is a great (although not limitless) diversity of moral norms among people of goodwill. To the extent that pluralism speaks to us as individuals, it affects our opinions and beliefs, not by altering their content or the assurance with which we hold them, but by ameliorating the intensity and fervor with which we assert them and the stance that we take toward those whose moral sense differs from our own.

There are some who regard the pluralism of civil society as at best a regrettable necessity, perhaps hopefully a temporary one, until enough of their fellow citizens come to see the rightness of their views that there is the political will needed to act on them. However, pluralism as a philosophical stance—and here it may well be intertwined with political liberalism—is rooted in the belief that as humans, we are created (and this word can be understood in religious or secular terms) with the capacity and the desire to seek, to discern, and to follow the good, but that in all of those capacities and desires, we are limited, in no way more than in our capacity to know that we have accurately found the Truth. This belief grounds a genuine acceptance, which is neither grudging nor resigned, of the diversity of moral insight. In this way, it may supply what Lawrence Hinman terms a "middle ground" between relativism and realism (which he terms "absolutism"), one that "incorporates insights from both."

> From relativism, it retains the sensitivity to the contextuality of our moral beliefs and the recognition that moral disagreement and conflict are permanent features of the moral landscape. From absolutism, it retains the commitment to the relevance of reasoned dis-

course in the moral life and the belief that some moral positions are better than others.[12]

It would be naive to suggest that those who scornfully dismiss relativism would, on pondering the ways in which pluralism differs from it, find pluralism attractive. I do think that their continuing critique would necessarily focus more authentically on the matters genuinely at issue, which I will explore in the succeeding sections of this essay.

TRUTH AND CERTAINTY

The fundamental failing of anti-relativism—by which I mean the attempt to support a moral claim by attacking as "relativist" the stance attributed to one not sharing that claim—is that it ignores the fact that any assertion of a truth about morality raises but does not answer the question how one knows it. Jeffrey Stout has made the point well, in my judgment.

> I claim that positing a transcendent Moral Law (or the like) does not help explain what it is for a moral proposition to be true. Nor, I claim, does such a posit help as a criterion for judging the truth of moral propositions. [However,] neither of these claims . . . implies that there are no moral truths.[13]

To speak as Stout does is to insist that a claim of the truth of a moral matter engages the distinction between there being a truth of a matter (which exists independent of what anyone believes regarding it) and the justification for believing the truth of the assertion made regarding its content. The existence of such a distinction is certainly open to challenge, but it should not be elided, whether by one who doubts the reality of a mind-independent truth or by one who is certain that he or she knows what the content of that truth is.

The distinction is challenged frontally by many relativists. Denying the existence of "a transcendent Moral Law," they draw their inspiration from John Dewey, to whom both belief and knowledge describe the same condition, which he termed "warranted assertibility" and described as "the institution of conditions which remove need for doubt."

> *Belief* may be so understood as to be a fitting designation for the outcome of inquiry. . . . The word *knowledge* is also a suitable term to designate the objective and close of inquiry. . . . That which satisfactorily terminates inquiry is, by definition, knowledge; it is knowledge because it *is* the appropriate close of inquiry. . . . The term "warranted assertion" is preferred to the terms *belief* and *knowledge*. It is free from the ambiguity of these latter terms.[14]

What Dewey regarded as removing an ambiguity creates it. It is true that relativists would not define knowledge, as most philosophers ordinarily do, as belief that is true as well as justified, because such usage suggests that the word *true* has a meaning that goes beyond "justification" or "warrant." Since relativists deny that suggestion, they naturally will deem the standard definition question-begging. However, by giving *truth* a meaning that effectively conflates it with justification, they are also begging the question (although assuming a different answer).

It seems clearer to retain the verbal distinction, while allowing relativists to maintain their objection on the merits to the metaphysical existence of truth so defined, rather than to define the issue away. Preserving the distinction between belief and knowledge permits us readily to understand one another across that critical boundary, without necessarily crossing it, in either direction. For a nonrelativist to assert that a specific moral norm is "true" is most usefully understood as a claim about (an instance of) the content of reality and is a coherent statement to one who believes that no such reality exists, as well as to one who believes to the contrary.

If "knowledge" denotes truth, its existence cannot be verified—I may know, but do I know (or only believe) that I know; if I do (know that I know), do I know (or only believe) that I know that I know; and so on—but it can be believed with greater or lesser justification. The assertion that one "knows" is a functional claim, asserting that the extent of persisting uncertainty is of no existential or decisional significance. Conceptually, the claim of "truth" may be faulted as analogous to taking a last step to disregard or overpower (rather than respect or transcend) Zeno's paradox. If, for example, having begun in Philadelphia, I successively travel one-half of the distance to Ann Arbor one hundred times, it is "true" that I am not yet there, but I may nonetheless have compelling reason to act as if I am and no reason to act as if I am not. Indeed, in most circumstances, to say that I am not yet there would simply be a bit of pedantry, even though neither inductively nor deductively can the gap remaining be bridged.

The millions of people who would join Job in insisting, "I know that my Redeemer liveth" (Job 19:25), have taken that "last step" as their first, by reason of religious faith. Faith may ground certainty, as may love (and perhaps even hope), where reason cannot. Martha Nussbaum, writing of "love's knowledge," terms that condition "cataleptic": "The cataleptic impression is said to have the power," she writes, "just through its own felt quality, to drag us to assent, to convince us that things could not be otherwise."[15] One may then be speaking loosely of "certainty" yet have warrant for the avowal.

But certainty is necessarily a condition that describes the stance toward reality taken by the person believing (or knowing). It cannot be a statement about the world external to the speaker, for no one has unmediated access to reality or unmediated access to anyone else's assertion of such access.[16] Even Euclid never "looked on beauty bare."[17]

To the believer claiming certainty, whether grounded in faith, love, or reason, it will not appear so, and for him or her to speak as if nothing has been said about "reality bare" is to belie that certainty. It cannot be inherently improper to refuse to do so. Yet, there is a boundary, I suggest, the crossing of which is not justified by certainty of belief. I will use the term *triumphalism* to describe that which lies across that boundary, and now turn to it.

TRIUMPHALISM

To me, the essence of triumphalism—whether in religion, nationalism, or any other profound source of values[18]—is to move beyond holding a set of beliefs as "known," as to be true and certain, to maintaining that such certainty suffices to delegitimate any claim that the contrary belief of another may be justified. That is just the difference that Robert Bolt's Sir Thomas More (as quoted in an epigraph to this essay) realized and, after a momentary spontaneous lapse, respected regarding his commitment to the truth of the papal claim to the authority given by Jesus to St. Peter. More would not take an oath avowing that which contradicted his actual belief. It was the fact of his belief, not the truth of its foundation (although he believed it to be true), that was dispositive.

Thomas More was confronting a dissonance between his speech (the oath) and his beliefs. Typically, the conflict is between one's sense of the certainty of the truth of one's beliefs and the fact that others question that truth (and what may follow from it). Clifford Geertz has described felicitously the reason why conversation in that context is challenging. He writes of "the collection of notions a people has of how reality is at base put together" as its world view and of the "general style of . . . the way they do things and like to see things done" as its ethos. He describes "the office of religious symbols" as to "render the world view believable and the ethos justifiable . . . by invoking each in support of the other." He observes:

> Seen from outside the religious perspective, this sort of hanging a picture from a nail driven into its frame appears as a kind of sleight of hand. Seen from inside, it appears as a simple fact.
>
> . . . Religious beliefs . . . are regarded as being not conclusions from experience . . . but as being prior to it. For those who hold them, religious beliefs are not inductive, they are paradigmatic; the world . . . provides not evidences for their truth but illustrations of it. They are a light cast upon human life from somewhere outside it.[19]

What to the believer is obvious, to the skeptic is simple question-begging. What the one sees in the other as obduracy (or worse), the other sees in the one as triumphalism (or worse). The willingness to entertain the possibility that one's fundamental avowals are in error is to one a fateful step on a dark and slippery road to apostasy; the unwillingness to take that step is to the other a mark of subjection (nascent or full-blown) to "tyranny over the mind."[20]

Alvin Plantinga, defending the ethical permissibility of believing that his religion is true and that other beliefs, when contrary to it, are false, observes:

> I must concede that there are a variety of ways in which I can be and have been intellectually arrogant and egotistic; I have certainly fallen into this vice in the past and no doubt am not free of it now. But am I really arrogant and egotistic just by virtue of believing what I know others don't believe, where I can't show them that I am right?[21]

The problem, however, is deeper than the presence or absence of such ethically dubious personality traits as arrogance or egotism. Some—not all, but some—religious people regard their faith as primarily concerning the truth of certain propositions about the nature of reality, including the authority of religious texts or institutions to express or propound such truths and their moral implications. Part of that set of beliefs is often a felt obligation to be exceedingly wary of attempts to be persuaded to violate one or more of the norms of their faith.[22] It is also true that for many believers, the matter is not one of conscious will, for they do not regard their assent as a voluntary decision. Paul Griffiths has described the experience of such people this way:

> There is a long (and usually complicated) story to be told about why I find myself involuntarily moved to assent to these claims at a particular time. Usually, the story will involve reference to habits, skills, and knowledge I've gained in the past, but in all cases the upshot is the same: I find myself irresistibly moved to assent. . . . I cannot deliberate and then decide whether to believe it or not. When I find myself assenting to some claim (believing it, taking it as true), then, my assent typically does not involve some choice or deliberation. It is simply given to me.[23]

Nonreligious people should therefore be cautious about dismissing as triumphalist or impositional the reluctance or unwillingness of some (again, not all, but some) religious believers to find legitimacy or (in some sense) validity in other religions, to acknowledge that others may have justification for holding their understanding of the Truth, or to engage in "dialogue" about matters of belief (or morality grounded in belief) with those who disagree.[24] All other things being equal, openness to dialogue across difference is, in my judgment, a good, but it is not inherently a universal moral imperative, and all else is not always equal. The matter turns on the specifics of the individual actor's motivation, intention, and—especially—actions. Imposition is a serious wrong; a triumphalist attitude alone may best be thought of as simply a source of interpersonal incompatibility.

However, triumphalist attitudes tend to leach into actions. Indeed, the expression of an attitude is itself an action, in the practical sense that it can "pinch" those who do not share its wellsprings. This, I believe, is the core of the problem of the appropriateness of certain forms of public prayer. What to the devout may be simply a legitimate expression of deep-seated feelings of gratitude toward or dependency on the One "from whom all blessings flow" cannot help, when expressed by a large percentage of the like-minded, but constrain the freedom of those who differ.[25]

More broadly, "certain" believers need to realize that their certainty, like the belief to which it relates, is "theirs," not only in the sense that it is an aspect of their identity, but in the sense that it cannot escape its boundary in the self: as a statement about the world, it may well be true, but its truth (like all such truths) is not verifiable. Donald Davidson's dictum (a portion of which is quoted in an epigraph to this essay) seems on point to me: "What distinguishes a coherence theory [which Davidson espouses] is simply the claim that nothing can count as a reason for holding a belief except another belief."[26] At the same time—and for the same reason—the "justification" that others may have for their conflicting beliefs does not contradict the believers' own certainty, since justification makes no truth claim. The two incompatible beliefs may therefore reside, compatibly though uncomfortably, alongside one another.

A special complexity arises because of the need to consider the proper reach of the principle that members of a religious community may claim the right, free of adverse judgment from those who are not members, to attempt to keep "the faithful" faithful. I grew up feeling quite aggrieved by what I regarded as the efforts of the Roman Catholic Church to induce the polity to adopt its views regarding such matters as the censorship of movies, restrictions on the sale of contraceptives, and the availability of several varieties of medical intervention in life-threatening emergencies. I now see those past efforts not so much as aimed at me and other non-Catholics than as primarily reflecting the Church's concern for the moral environment of its communicants, increasingly attracted by the blandishments of a society responsive to other voices on moral issues. Whether and how a religious leader is obliged to keep in mind and make clear what his intended audience is and to take responsibility for the wider scope of his predictable audience[27] is a singularly elusive question.

However, the questions of the appropriateness and justification of such efforts, as well as the actors' responsibilities for adverse consequences on the quality of public life, are not exhausted by the issue of entitlement. Today, when examples such as censorship of movies and access to birth control are no longer at center stage, the issue remains. The adversarial manner in which Pope John Paul II engaged what he called the "culture of death"[28] perhaps reflected a concern with the moral climate of contemporary society (one shared by many Protestants, Jews, and Muslims, as well as not a few nonbelievers) because of its effect on the practices of Roman Catholics. However, he described his teachings as embodying moral norms accessible through reason, therefore binding on all persons.[29] Although to that extent he spoke outside of the "certainty" of revelation, all who differed were denounced as "relativists," whatever their objections to the morality of his "culture of life" and regardless of the secular or religious grounding of those objections.

The reflexive move from a judgment of immorality to the espousal of regulation or prohibition by the secular law is an especially problematic move. Being "certain" of the truth of one's beliefs, rejecting the thought of "dialogue" with those who differ, refusing to entertain the possibility that they might be justified in their beliefs—each of these might be justified as an authentic, conscientiously held point of view. Invoking the power of the state to constrain or even place at risk the lives of others for their failure to see the world that way is quite another step. This is a large and complex area, and there would be no utility in my cataloguing my own evaluations of specific morally grounded overtures of public policy. I mean here only to claim validity for a genuine caution and respect for difference in those seeking to see public law adopt their understanding of moral truth. It is one thing to oppose the decriminalization of abortion, quite another broadly to encourage pharmacists (including those working in areas lacking a plenitude of consumer choices) to refuse to fill prescriptions for birth control or morning-after pills, on the ground that they are illicit methods of contraception or "abortifacients."[30]

Moreover, it is far from clear whether and how far the institutional interest in keeping the "flock" from straying justifiably applies to a communicant's participation in public life. Examples are strongly worded pastoral admonitions, whether coming from a Catholic prelate or an Orthodox rabbi, to vote a certain way in public elections, and selective applications of internal sanctions to highly visible members of its faith community who hold or are seeking public office.[31] The rapidity and scope of the changes in prevailing norms of morality in so many aspects of public and private life—too rapid and broad-ranging for some, too slow and limited for others—have produced vast areas of resentment and anger, further poisoning the atmosphere and making nearly everyone feel unheard and disentitled. In the context of that maelstrom, an attempt to unravel the multiple threads that should properly be brought to bear on more-or-less public discourse may seem simply naive. The narrow question I am considering here is whether one may justly complain of any input into public policy, not that it is religiously motivated, but that the attempt to gain support for a contested moral position by attacking relativism may be a demagogic diversion of attention from the merits of the question or a triumphalist constriction of the possibility of conscientious disagreement regarding them.

The contours of a frontier that I have sought to describe are less substantive than attitudinal. They reflect the concerns I have expressed: the use of anti-relativism as a rhetorical diversion of the discourse and, the practice (which I have termed *triumphalism*) of going beyond the assertion of a commitment to the certain truth of a moral belief, to scornful dismissal of the possibility that others may be justified in believing otherwise. Whether such cautions have a greater capacity than substantive ones to penetrate the maelstrom is not altogether clear.

MORAL REALISM

I want now to turn from claims to know the truth of a moral matter to issues raised by one making no such highly confident claim but still asserting a justified belief about a disputed moral claim. Both a relativist and a realist may speak in a similar way of justified belief, yet they differ in that the former can assert that two inconsistent beliefs may each be true for one of two belief holders, while the realist's assertion would be that both beliefs may be justified but that no more than one can be true. Justified belief is an epistemological concept, while knowledge (in the sense that seems most useful to me) denotes truth, a metaphysical concept, therefore not verifiable. Without attempting here a developed expression of the conditions that constitute justification for belief, suffice it to say that I find persuasive the approach suggested by John Rawls's notion of "considered judgment in reflective equilibrium."[32] What I understand by that state is that the belief in question has a stabilizing and resonating coherence with my overall understanding of the world and my place in it, specifically with my overall moral judgments.

In considering the bases on which I believe (and believe myself justified in believing) that moral realism is true, two factors bear noting initially. First, my own (like others') beliefs as to the right and wrong of a matter tend to be bound up in an underlying conviction that those beliefs are actually true. A person asserting that a certain act is right (or wrong) does not ordinarily appear simply to be telling us something about himself or herself or about his or her affinity group. Second, while awareness of the variousness of moral norms and their evolution across time and cultures may (as an empirical matter) be the cause of relativist beliefs, it does not logically imply relativism. Indeed, despite the salience of such an awareness, I think it less significant than the existence of a startling amount of moral agreement.[33]

Beyond that, exploration of the bases of change and divergence of beliefs themselves actually supports realist premises. It places the question in context to think about the issue as it arises in the scientific realm. John Searle notes that the occurrence of "scientific revolutions" supports, rather than undermines, belief in mind-independent truth: "We would not bother to change our account from classical physics to relativity physics except on the presupposition that there is a way the universe really is, and we are trying to get as close as we can to stating how it is."[34] In the moral arena, Richard Shweder and Jeffrey Stout have persuasively undermined reliance on two classic situations proffered as counterexamples of the reality of moral truth. Their analyses are powerful, and the lessons they draw are of general import.

Shweder considers Richard Posner's claim that the context in which infanticide and slavery were practiced in the ancient world made them morally appropriate and that such a realization implies the truth of relativism. Posner reasoned:

> Infanticide is abhorred in our culture, but routine in societies that lack the resources to feed all children that are born. Slavery is routine when the victors in war cannot afford to feed or free their captives, so that the alternative to slavery is death. . . . It is provincial to say that "we are right about slavery, . . . and the Greeks wrong," so different was slavery in the ancient world from racial enslavement, as practiced, for example, in the United States until the end of the Civil War, and so different were the material conditions that nurtured these different forms of slavery. . . . The inhabitants of an infanticidal or slave society would say with equal plausibility that infanticide or slavery is presumptively good, though they might allow that the presumption could be rebutted in peaceable, wealthy, technologically complex societies.[35]

Far from seeing these culture-specific differences as probative of the truth of relativism, Shweder draws from Posner's explanations just the opposite lesson.

> Judge Posner constructs and interprets both infanticide and slavery . . . as cases that are intelligible as morally valid practices . . . by representing each practice as a means to a universally recognized moral good—namely the reduction of physical harm (to already born children and to the slaves themselves, respectively). . . .
>
> Posner's argument is potentially persuasive because he is able to direct our attention to the moral integrity of local contexts; and those local contexts become morally intelligible precisely because he can presuppose and thus trade on our common sense revelation of a base set of moral truths.
>
> The correctness of a moral judgment may well be relative to circumstances. Nevertheless, implicit in Posner's argument is the idea that . . . with an informed understanding of the local scene any rational person should be able to recognize those practices, in those instances and under those circumstances, as local instantiations of some universal moral ideal. (Shweder, "Moral Realism," 88–89)

Stout considers Sartre's famous account of the young man who had to choose between supporting his aged mother and joining the French Resistance, which Sartre characterizes as "supporting the conclusion that moral judgments express unreasoned choices" (quoted in Stout, "Ethics after Babel," 46). Stout observes:

> Sartre is able to paint the dilemma in considerable detail, and each detail is itself a sample of the moral knowledge that Sartre is trying to deny us. In showing or saying that one consideration balances another he reveals his own recognition of the nature and force of the various considerations, and appeals to our own recognition of their nature and force. Dilemmas of this kind show us, sometimes quite vividly and poignantly, where our moral uncertainties, and thus our probable areas of moral disagreement, are. But they don't show that there's no such thing as moral truth or justified moral belief. In fact . . . they trade on the assumption that certain moral beliefs are justified and true in making their point. ("Ethics after Babel," 46–47)

How far Stout's argument carries one implicates the question whether moral discernment "runs out," as it were, so that as to some highly specific questions there is no "right answer." I consider that question briefly later.

In considering the weight of these factors, it is important to realize that much of the resistance to the acceptance of moral realism is supported by the attachment to it of the baggage of several thoughts or qualities that (rightly) seem dubious but are plainly separable. I here address five examples of this practice:

(i) To speak of moral truths as "existing" is not to assert that, in Thomas Nagel's words, "they must be real objects of some other kind."[36] Interestingly enough, the same mistaken assumption is made, by believers and skeptics alike, about the necessary meaning of an avowal of the existence of "God." Gordon Kaufman writes of the need to "de-reify" God-language.

> Devotion to the "creator/lord" today should be understood as consisting in the attempt to live in rapport with the movements of life and history that provide the actual context of our human existence; it is to attempt to be in tune with what we discern as the nature of things.[37]

Writing out of the tradition of Reconstructionist Judaism, Rabbi Harold Kushner observes that "God is not an entity out in space somewhere." The question of God's existence, he maintains, need not be thought of as one "about the population of Heaven."[38] One may reject these theological views and yet recognize that the traditional assumption confuses the familiar and the essential, whether the question arises with respect to religious or philosophical language.

(ii) John Finnis is perhaps the best-known contemporary philosopher who espouses a morality of "exceptionless norms."[39] (The classic expression of such an approach is Kant's assertion of an obligation to tell the truth to a would-be murderer who has asked one for the whereabouts of his or her intended victim).[40] While one holding such a view of morality would probably be a realist, it is neither logically nor empirically true that moral realism entails or even inherently tends toward such an avowal. The existence of mind-independent truth is a different matter from the question of its content, and recognition that a moral judgment should be nuanced, qualified, or context-specific makes its truth more difficult to discern and articulate and multiplies points of potential disagreement, but it does not introduce a subjectivity that was not otherwise warranted. One may say that Kant is right in asserting a broad deontological justification for the immorality of lying, and nonetheless dispute his application of it to the instance stated. Insisting on drawing the line at telling the truth to would-be murderers applies, rather than eliminates, an asserted distinction between right and wrong.

(iii) A realist metaphysics is not inconsistent with uncertainty about the correctness of particularized moral judgments. Indeed, the conception of justification for belief inherently implies the possible existence of circumstances in which the complexity or subtlety of the factors that bear on a moral question varies. The limits of the evaluator's access to knowledge of some of those factors make uncertainty in application wholly predictable and wholly appropriate. If I may be forgiven an egregious mix of metaphors, that we "see through a glass, darkly" does not imply that "there is no there there." Jeffrey Stout puts the matter more elegantly: "We should not confuse doubting that there is a single best thing to do in a given case with doubting that there is a moral truth with respect to that case" ("Ethics after Babel," 47).

This question is presented, although not resolved, if one rejects (in the case at hand or in general) blanket condemnation (à la Finnis) of a given act regardless of considerations of justification. Abortion is of course the premier case in point. To one who finds the act of intentionally inducing an abortion to be illicit without regard to any further considerations—whether from the moment of conception, the end of the possibility of twinning, the fortieth day of pregnancy, the onset of viability, or any other assertedly critical moment in fetal development—the issue of uncertainty does not arise (except, at times, with respect to those facts). That one such as myself deems such views morally infirm does not imply that every instance of "abortion on demand" is a morally acceptable "choice." I believe that the factors bearing on a proper moral judgment are not only various and subtle but are often not fully accessible to anyone but the mother, especially so to outsiders to her family. I am certain that many abortions lack, and that many have, moral acceptability, but I also believe, no less strongly, that even a careful appraisal of the relevant factors will often not enable an outsider to judge the matter very confidently. The barriers to epistemic confidence are formidable, and for that reason alone, legal barriers or other coercive responses are, in my judgment, morally unjustified. Abortion to one side, I believe that epistemic modesty in judging the moral universe of others is often morally appropriate and that its absence is a morally hazardous trait, but whether I am right or wrong about that, epistemic modesty is not inconsistent with a realist view of morality.

(iv) The polar concern is equally misplaced. Moral realism does not warrant or justifiably lead to excessive certainty about moral judgments. Realists about moral questions—setting aside for the moment judgments based on revelation—have in principle no lesser capacity than relativists to recognize the tentativeness of their moral beliefs. Katharine Bartlett has wisely described an outlook that a sensible moral realist would find wholly apt, one of "an ideal of self-critical commitment whereby I act, but consider the truths upon which I act subject to further refinement, amendment, and correction." She goes on:

> Some "truths" . . . seem to confirm the view that truth does exist (it must; these things are true) if only I could find it. . . . The problem is the human inclination to make this list of "truths" too long, to be too uncritical of its contents, and to defend it too harshly and dogmatically. Positionality [the word Bartlett coined to describe her approach] reconciles the existence of reliable, experience-based grounds for assertions of truth . . . with the need to question and improve these grounds.[41]

It is here that religiously grounded morality presents a conceptually more challenging context. To the "certain" believer, certainty does not inhere only in questions of the sort that Geertz calls "world views," how reality is put together. Those views accredit, with like certainty, epistemological premises about the truth of moral principles, however "uncritically" embraced or many in number. (Examples are the many moral precepts contained in the 613 *mitzvot* (incumbent obligations) of Orthodox Judaism or the 2,865 paragraphs of the Roman Catholic catechism.) A believer asked to accept the "justification" for contrary beliefs will experience the request as demanding more than simple humility. Yet the one seeking to engage a moral question from a different faith tradition, a different understanding of a single public community, or from a skeptical stance toward all faith-based claims cannot be expected to find sufficient reason to put aside Bartlett's admonition against speaking "harshly and dogmatically." I do not know a way out of this impasse.

(v) Finally, moral realism is not inconsistent with a commitment to pluralism in social policy. It unnecessarily gives credence to the rhetoric of anti-relativism to assert a relativist morality—"it's all relative" or "it's just your opinion"—in responding to a moral claim one rejects when the response in actuality would be that the claim either has no moral valence or is in fact immoral.[42] Anti-anti-relativism can therefore properly espouse a (limited) form of anti-relativism of its own, but without the rhetorical fervor that often accompanies objections to relativism. Our society is quick to treat the assertion that another is in error as on (or over) the edge of a required "tolerance" for "diverse viewpoints."[43] To disagree is not intolerance (although one can be intolerant in disagreement). To say that you are wrong is not to attempt to silence you (although it might be expressed in such a way or lead to such an attempt). To respond to a moral avowal by shifting the focus from challenging its correctness to making a relativist claim is the converse of the failing of the anti-relativist. If a red herring is thrown into your fishing pail—a fortiori, if you find that you have thrown one in yourself—do not proceed to examine it; throw it overboard.

CONCLUSION

> To meet a human being is a major challenge to mind and heart. . . . To meet a human being is an opportunity to sense the image of God, *the presence* of God. According to a rabbinical interpretation, the Lord said to Moses: "Wherever you see the trace of man there I stand before you. . . ." When engaged in a conversation with a person of different religious commitment I discover that we disagree in matters sacred to us, does the image of God I face disappear? Does God cease to stand before me?
>
> —Abraham Joshua Heschel[44]

In considering the destructive force of conclusory or triumphalist dismissal of opposing positions with the label *relativism,* I seek much more than eliminating a diversion from the conversation. Greater acknowledgment of the fact that important controversies in contemporary society are a product of a diversity of justifiably held discernments of moral truth can prompt efforts to enhance

apprehension of the need to articulate the epistemological bases of one's beliefs,

self-awareness about expressions that cross the frontier between justified belief and certainty,

thoughtful discernment and disclosure of the premises that are believed to ground certainty, open to the possibility that incompatible beliefs (though strongly believed to be in error) may nonetheless be justified, and resistance against the temptation to caricature opposing positions and to demonize those who hold them.

To the extent that all that happens, disagreement will surely persist and perhaps will not even be lessened in extent. It would be naive to presume otherwise. However, it is not beyond hope to look toward a lessening of its intensity and hostility and a greater recognition of the compatibility between a proper continuing assertion of what one believes to be the Truth and a genuine (yet bounded) receptivity to pluralism in the setting of social policy.[45]

NOTES

This essay appears in expanded form as "The Rhetoric of Anti-Relativism in a Culture of Certainty," 55 *Buffalo L. Rev.* 887 (2007).

1. Matthew Berke, "A Jewish Appreciation of Catholic Social Thought," in Kenneth L. Grasso, Gerard V. Bradley, Robert P. Hunt, eds., *Catholicism, Liberalism and Communitarianism: The Catholic Intellectual Tradition and the Moral Foundations of Democracy* 235, 237 (1995).

2. Herminio Rico, *John Paul II and the Legacy of "Dignitatis Humanae"* 205 (2002) (attributing this view to Pope John Paul II).

3. Clifford Geertz, "Anti Anti-Relativism," 86 *Am. Anthropologist* 263 (1984), reprinted in Michael Krausz, ed., *Relativism: Interpretation and Confrontation* 12 (1989).

4. Robert P. George notes, "The claim that morals laws are unjust is inescapably a moral claim" (*Making Men Moral: Civil Liberties and Public Morality* 3 (1993)).

5. Joseph Ratzinger, "Homily at the Votive Mass of the Election of a New Pope," 34 *Origins* 719 (28 April 2005). The quoted passage is from Ephesians 4:14.

6. Richard A. Posner, *The Problematics of Moral and Legal Theory* 6 (1999).

7. David Hume, *A Treatise of Human Nature,* book 3, part 1, section 1, p. 470 (L. A. Selby-Bigge, ed., 1986).

8. Michael Moore, "Moral Reality," 1982 *Wis. L. Rev.* 1061, 1064.

9. "The Rhetoric of Anti-Relativism in a Culture of Certainty," 55 *Buffalo L. Rev.* 887 (2007).

10. Craig M. Gay, *With Liberty and Justice for Whom? The Recent Evangelical Debate over Capitalism* 233–34 (1991). See also, to like effect, H. Jefferson Powell, "The Earthly Peace of the Liberal Republic," in Michael McConnell, Robert F. Cochran Jr., and Angela C. Carmella, eds., *Christian Perspectives on Legal Thought* 71, 85 (2001); David Hollenbach, "Afterword: A Community of Freedom," in R. Bruce Douglass and David Hollenbach, eds., *Catholicism and Liberalism: Contributions to American Public Philosophy* 327–32 (1994).

11. See, e.g., Todd Whitmore's critique of Michael Novak's failure to recognize that "the seemingly unending quest for more and more of ever more specialized and refined items in a consumer society is a spiritual and moral malady" (Todd David Whitmore, "John Paul II, Michael Novak, and the Distance Between

Them," 21 *J. Soc'y Christian Ethics* 215, 224 (2001)). See also, for a perhaps trivial, but telling, example, Richard John Neuhaus's "A Word for Commercializing Christmas" (*First Things,* December 1993, 76), in which he warns readers to be "braced for this year's round of campaigning against the commercialization of Christmas" and complains that in such efforts, "advertisers and merchants are demonized, and their legitimate economic vocations are demeaned."

12. Lawrence Hinman, *Ethics: A Pluralistic Approach to Moral Theory* 48 (1994).

13. Jeffrey Stout, *Ethics after Babel: The Languages of Morals and Their Discontents* 35 (2001). Simon Blackburn notes that "you can admit the authority of truth without immediately supposing you possess it" (*Truth: A Guide* 29 (2005)). Yes, and you can proclaim the authority of truth without establishing that you possess it.

14. John Dewey, *Logic: The Theory of Inquiry* 7–9 (1938).

15. Martha C. Nussbaum, "Love's Knowledge," in *Love's Knowledge: Essays in Philosophy and Literature* 261, 265 (1990).

16. Access to another's claim is necessarily mediated by belief in the truth of the other's access. Robert Bellah felicitously asserts, "there is no truth that truths itself" (Robert N. Bellah, "At Home and Not At Home: Religious Pluralism and Religious Truth," *Christian Century,* 19 April 1995, 425). David Luban terms revelation "esoteric," in the sense that "to rely on it is to have faith in the prophets who communicate the revelation" ("A Theological Argument against Theopolitics," 16 *Institute for Philosophy and Public Policy,* Report 13 (1996)). Jeff Powell describes the opposition of seventeenth-century British Protestants to any exposition of scripture that "went beyond the text [as], of necessity, a 'human invention,' 'which a discreet Man may do well; but 'tis his Scripture, not the Holy Ghost['s]'" (H. Jefferson Powell, "The Original Understanding of Original Intent," 98 *Harv. L. Rev.* 885, 889–90 (1985), quoting John Selden, *Table-Talk: Being the Discourse of John Selden Esq.* 25, 45 (1699)).

17. Edna St. Vincent Millay may have led us to understate the matter, I am suggesting, when she began a sonnet, "Euclid alone has looked on beauty bare." *The Selected Poetry of Edna St. Vincent Millay,* ed. Nancy Milford 155 (New York: Modern Library, 2001).

18. The primary example of the merging of nationalist and religious grounds is Israel, as its renewed existence (after 1900 years) and continued survival is understood by many Jews (and Christians). Certain varieties of "American exceptionalism" fit this model, usually (although perhaps not necessarily) through a religious foundation, which sees this country as in some unexplained way the special object of providential care. I will not address the phenomenon of nationalist triumphalism, whether religiously based or not.

19. Clifford Geertz, *Islam Observed: Religious Development in Morocco and Indonesia* 97–98 (1968).

20. On the wall of the Jefferson Memorial in Washington, D.C., is inscribed, "I have sworn eternal hostility to every form of tyranny over the mind of man."

21. Alvin Plantinga, "Pluralism: A Defense of Religious Exclusivism," in Thomas D. Senor, ed., *The Rationality of Belief and the Plurality of Faith* 191, 200 (1995).

22. For some (not all) such people, more is at stake than the outcome of a disagreement, more or less friendly, about a matter of metaphysics, ethics, or public policy. In the friendly disputant's expressions may be heard the voice of Satan. Of

course, holding the belief that the beliefs of another person (or worse, a person who holds to such beliefs) are the work of the devil is a moral hazard and might lead the believer into seriously wrongful speech or conduct. Wariness is therefore an appropriate response; a preemptive dismissal is not. (The one so believing will assert the defense of truth as justification, which the other will regard as compounding the felony. That this leads to an indefinite regress is a problem, but that observation is not a solution to the problem).

23. Paul J. Griffiths, *Problems of Religious Diversity* 26 (2001).

24. For a clear and (in my judgment) fair-minded introduction to the variety of views about the stance that Christian traditions and individuals should take toward other religions—a subject that has produced a voluminous literature—see Paul F. Knitter, *No Other Name? A Critical Survey of Christian Attitudes toward the World Religions* (1985).

25. Cf. Marvin E. Frankel, "Religion in Public Life—Reasons for Minimal Access," 60 *Geo. Wash. L. Rev.* 633, 639 (1992). Judge Frankel asks, "Why . . . the proliferation of committees and public officials insisting that creches be placed . . . on the public squares?" He answers: "The reason . . . is exactly to show others who's boss. This is Christian country. If you don't like it, as you presumably don't, you know what you can do."

26. Donald Davidson, "A Coherence Theory of Knowledge and Truth," in *Subjective, Intersubjective, Objective* 137, 141 (2001).

27. Pope Benedict, on the eve of his election to the office of pope, made the statement I quoted (and have quarreled with) earlier in this essay in a homily during a mass, a central moment in a deeply private religious service. Yet his words were, predictably, soon transmitted throughout the world—learned of by millions of Catholics, to be sure, but millions of non-Catholics as well. Similarly, an essay of his titled "Relativism: The Central Problem for Faith Today" (1996), was first delivered to a gathering of Roman Catholic bishops but (forseeably) has been widely read.

28. E.g., *Evangelium Vitae* [The gospel of life] (1995), no. 28: "[W]e are facing an enormous and dramatic clash between good and evil, death and life, the 'culture of death' and the "culture of life.'" *Evangelium Vitae* is available online at http://www.vatican.va/holy_father/john_paul_ii/encyclicals/documents/hf_jpii_enc_25031995_evangelium-vitae_en.html. For a measured description and appraisal, see James F. Childress, "Moral Rhetoric and Moral Reasoning: Some Reflections on *Evangelium Vitae*," in Kevin Wm. Wildes and Alan C. Mitchell, *Choosing Life: A Dialogue on "Evangelium Vitae"* 21, 28–32 (1997) (analyzing the pope's "metaphor of war, enemy, conspiracy, and so forth" (31)).

29. E.g., *Evangelium Vitae*, no. 2:

> The Church knows that this Gospel of life, which she has received from her Lord, has a profound and persuasive echo in the heart of every person—believer and non-believer alike. . . . [E]very person sincerely open to truth and goodness can, by the light of reason and the hidden action of grace, come to recognize in the natural law written in the heart . . . the sacred value of human life . . . , and can affirm the right of every human being to have this primary good respected to the highest degree. Upon the

recognition of this right, every human community and the political community itself are founded.

30. A number of scholars writing out of the Roman Catholic tradition have expressed measured reflections on the emergent approach of the Vatican. Herminio Rico's study *John Paul II and the Legacy of "Dignitatis Humanae"* is a carefully nuanced, sympathetic, yet critical account of Pope John Paul's preference for "the seeking of direct political influence" over "the patient formation of consciences and, through that change, achieving the transformation of the social consensus" (Rico, supra n. 2, at 169–76 (the quoted words are at 175)). David Hollenbach grounds in the work of John Courtney Murray an eloquent case for "intellectual humility" in engaging with the "full array of intellectual currents in culture" today (David Hollenbach, *The Global Face of Public Faith: Politics, Human Rights, and Christian Ethics* 142 (2003)). "The virture of society," he maintains, "is built from the bottom up, not mandated from the top down and it is built by citizens who take responsibility for their own lives and for the well-being of society through active participation in public life." He continues, "A fundamental element of this social well-being is a robust commitment to the freedom of one's fellow-citizens" (139).

For additional thoughtful analyses from within the Catholic tradition, see Todd David Whitmore, "What Would John Courtney Murray Say? On Abortion and Euthanasia," *Commonweal,* 7 October 1994, 16; M. Cathleen Kaveny, "The Limits of Ordinary Virtue: The Limits of the Criminal Law in Implementing *Evangelium Vitae,*" in Wildes and Mitchell, supra n. 27, at 46. Writing from an Evangelical Protestant perspective, David Skeel and William Stuntz have developed a sophisticated case for great restraint in moving from moral to legal prohibitions, in "Christianity and the (Modest) Rule of Law," 8 *U. Penn. J. Const. L.* 809 (2006).

31. For a sensitive and careful approach to this question from a Roman Catholic perspective, see Amelia J. Uelmen, "The Spirituality of Communion: A Resource for Dialogue with Catholics in Public Life," 43 *Cath. Law.* 289, 305–8 (2004). The difficulty is compounded for members of religious traditions whose leaders do not simply counsel their communicants on public issues but whose theology makes the counsel binding on their actions.

32. John Rawls, *A Theory of Justice* 29 (1971).

33. For excellent examples of articulation of the presence of an important core of intercultural agreement on the fundamental norms of morality, see Sissela Bok, *Common Values* 13–18 (1995); Richard Shweder, "Moral Realism without the Ethnocentrism: Is It Just a List of Empty Truisms?" in Andras Sajo, ed., *Human Rights with Modesty: The Problem of Universalism* 65 (2004).

34. John Searle, "Relativity and Realism: Shweder on a Which? Hunt," 6 *Anthropological Theory* 112, 113 (2006).

35. Quoted in Richard Shweder, supra n. 33, at 75–76.

36. Thomas Nagel, *The View From Nowhere* 144 (1986).

37. Gordon D. Kaufman, "Reconstructing the Concept of God: De-reifying the Anthropomorphisms," in Sarah Coakley and David A. Pailin, eds., *The Making and Remaking of Christian Doctrine* 96, 102 (1993).

38. Harold Kushner, *When Children Ask about God* 60 (1976).

39. John Finnis, *Moral Absolutes: Tradition, Revision, and Truth* 1 (1991).

40. Immanuel Kant, "On a Supposed Right to Lie Because of Philanthropic Concerns," in *Grounding for the Metaphysics of Morals* 64 (James W. Ellington, trans., 1785; reprint, 1993).

41. Katharine T. Bartlett, "Feminist Legal Methods," 103 *Harv. L. Rev.* 829, 883–84 (1990).

42. An example of the former is, in my judgment, an objection to homosexual sex. Whatever the undeniable moral significance of much sexual activity, I see no basis for regarding the sex of one's partner as a morally salient factor. An example of the latter (a morally grounded position that is itself immoral) is the exclusion of homosexuals from access to various benefits available to heterosexuals in analogous relationships.

Of course, these examples are highly contestable; suffice it to say that I believe that homosexual sex is not per se immoral, whether the contrary belief is justified or not, and that seeking to bring about a legal response based on moral condemnation of homosexuality is an immoral act. For some "pointing" discussions (all religiously grounded), see Jeffrey Stout, "How Charity Transcends the Culture Wars," 31 *J. Relig. Ethics* 169 (2003); John B. Cobb Jr, "Being Christian about Homosexuality," in Walter Wink, ed., *Homosexuality and Christian Faith* 89 (1999); Richard B. Hays, *The Moral Vision of the New Testament* 400 (1996). However, this is not the place to argue the correctness of my beliefs, for their truth or falsity has nothing to do with relativism, whether dragged into the debate by one side or the other.

43. For two eloquent and troubled accounts of this phenomenon among students, see Kay Haugaard, "The Lottery Revisited—A Case of Too Much Tolerance?" *Chronicle of Higher Education,* 27 June 1997, B4; Robert L. Simon, "Suspending Moral Judgment: The Paralysis of 'Absolutophobia,'" id., B5 ("Discussion of moral issues need not consist of two fanatics asserting conflicting principles they regard as self-evident; it can involve dialogue, the consideration of the points raised by others, and an admission of fallibility on all sides").

44. Abraham Joshua Heschel, "No Religion Is an Island," in *No Religion Is an Island: Abraham Joshua Heschel and Interreligious Dialogue* 7–8 (Harold Kasimov and Roger Sherwin, eds., 1991).

45. In *The Common Good and Christian Ethics* (2002), David Hollenbach has written a marvelously rich, sophisticated, thought-provoking—and heartening—study of the contours, possibilities, and importance of what he terms "intellectual solidarity" in a "community of freedom."

The Resilience of Law

Joseph Vining

One of the striking developments in academic law in the past half century is the reconception of law as one of the social sciences. The idea at work in this movement, as Joseph Vining says in this essay, is not that the law should use the findings of other disciplines for its own purposes and in its own way, but that in some deep way law itself—legal thinking, legal life—can and ought to proceed on the premises of social science, indeed of science itself. This is in one sense obviously impossible: a scientific rule is a prediction of future events based upon prior experience; a legal rule is the expression of a mind speaking to other minds—to other persons—seeking to affect their behavior by shaping their sense of the meaning as well as the consequences of what they do. Law works by an appeal from mind to mind.

Yet in academic law, as in the culture more generally, the image of science as the paradigm of thought, including legal thought, has enormous presence and force. The inherent dehumanization of this kind of thought—the erasure of the human person, the voice, the mind, the elimination of human value and hope—threatens both law and democracy at their core. Vining's deep claim is that even in the face of these forces of dehumanization and trivialization law retains a life and vigor, a resilience, upon which we can found our hopes and seek to build.

After my first year in law school and a summer at a New York law firm, which I loved, I was home for a bit before returning to my second year. It was 1962. My father, an economist who had studied under Frank Knight and Oskar Lange at Chicago in the 1940s, came into my room with the manuscript of a book he was working on. Its title was *On Appraising the Performance of an Economic System: What an Economic System Is, and the Norms Implied in Observers' Adverse Reactions to the Outcome of Its Working.* This was going to be my legacy, he said. If he did not finish it, he hoped I would.

The book's argument was that an economic system was in fact a system of legislated rules, within the bounds of which economic actors made their decisions, responding of course to incentives and disincentives and others' actions under these conditions. It was a "mechanism," the behavior of which, in the sense of outcomes of its overall action over time, was to be described statistically. What the economist participating in the legislative process was to do was to determine and set out for legislators considering a change in a rule what the statistical consequence of the change would be, with respect to one or another parameter such as income inequality or employment in which legislators were interested because they were dissatisfied. For clarity he proposed a notation: "The modifiable operating mechanism, the thing for which *economic system* is the name . . . , I shall denote by $\{\theta,S\}$." The *S* represented the collection of statistical mechanisms that depended upon the θ, and "the θ," he said, "is to represent a set of constraining and prescriptive rules," that part of the thing that is "directly" modifiable, a "system" of "statutory law and administrative rule." To be useful or even relevant, economists were to start with the set of rules that could be so denoted by the abstract symbol θ.

I read into the manuscript and eventually came to my father and said I could not help him. I could not help him because my sense of a "law" or a collection of "laws" was so very different. Law, I had already seen, was expressed in words spoken by responsible human beings to one another, who were listening to one another, and it was reexpressed and respoken over time. The meaning and effect of a "piece" of human law in the world, its very existence beyond the shadow existence a "dead letter" has, depended upon its authority, which came from constant mutual work with it. Laws might have systematic qualities but law was alive in a way rules that make a system are not. Law could die as well as live. There is a world of difference, I might have said if I had been older, between the authoritative and the authoritarian.

My father took the manuscript away. The problem I had was too central, the difference between us unbridgeable. He published the book twenty years later,[1] two years before I published *The Authoritative and the Authoritarian*,[2] and in one of those strange encounters of life, indeed as something of a sign of what has happened, his editor at Cambridge University Press came to where I was working, to head up the University of Michigan Press.

The gulf between human law and rules that can be represented by an abstract symbol remains as large today. My father's work was a chapter in the history of those who were involved in economics waking up to law, which was then in time followed by those in law waking up to economics. If they were academic lawyers—rather than practitioners, judges, or prosecutors and attorneys general carrying on the everyday work of law—larger and larger numbers of them entered a period of trying to accede to the claims of economics upon our thought, and beyond economics, the claims of social science, and beyond social science, the claims of scientific thought generally. The last were claims to a total occupation of the mind that grew so much over this same period, connected, I think, to twentieth-century experimentation with totalisms of various other kinds.

James Buchanan, whose *Calculus of Consent*[3] appeared in 1962, the same year as my conversation with my father, and who received the 1986 Nobel Prize in Economics for "public choice theory," speaks of the "economic theory of politics" involving "the extension of *homo economicus* to behavior under observed institutional rules." He treats my father's work as its precursor in several ways, principally in "initiating what was to become a centrally important component . . . , the stress on rules as contrasted with the then universal stress on policy alternatives within rules."[4] Like "public choice theory," "mechanism design theory" in current economics also has evident affinities with what *On Appraising the Performance of an Economic System* was seeking to achieve in its focus on law.[5] I do not think my father, in his work, participated in the elimination of public value and the melding of the premises of social science with those of natural science that is encapsulated in Buchanan's phrase *homo economicus.* My father's choosers and modifiers of rules legislatively or administratively still acted on behalf of a larger entity. But he was first of all a statistician. He repeatedly presented the true form of a rule as the rule of an ordinary game and was enamored of game theory which was then new.[6] He was himself a "player," to use that term for a successful academic lawyer heard commonly in law schools now—he was devoted to football. He thought of mathematics as the ultimately serious form of thought—hence the abstract symbol θ precisely denoting the "set" of rules. While he might have demurred in life, he would have understood in his professional capacity how the geneticist and Nobelist François Jacob could say in his *Logic of Life,* published contemporaneously with *On Appraising the Performance of an Economic System,* that there is "no longer a difference in nature between the living and the inanimate worlds," that "statistical analysis and the theory of probability have supplied the rules for the logic of the whole world," and that "large numbers are studied not so much because it is impossible to investigate the individual units, but mainly because their behavior is of no interest at all."[7]

So, despite my father walking out of the room with his manuscript in 1962, that manuscript was a legacy to me. The fundamental premises of its thought began to appear in academic law about the time I entered it. It was not just economics in the form celebrated by Buchanan's Nobel Prize. It was the turn toward social science more generally and, despite doubts going back to its beginning, the turn of social science to the natural sciences. Into law—the most linguistic of disciplines, person speaking to person, individuals listening and speaking on behalf of persons—was imported the view that the discipline of law was a branch of social science. The American Academy of Arts and Sciences makes it such today, and academic lawyers post their online papers on the Social Science Research Network.

The public treatment of human language in academic law reflects these developments in an important way. In 1961, Paul Freund, a name still known in constitutional law, gave a little talk to my first-year moot court club to introduce us to the world of law. He would say "a few things about words, and then a few words about things." His theme was the problem, for law, of writing dictionaries on the assumption that the difference between the "statistical" norm and the "normative" norm could be eliminated—the problem this presented for nuance in expression, the problem of the "impoverishment of language." Freund noted that law "lived by metaphor, advanced by simile." It "created," really, in its "overarching concepts." Speaking of the development of number theory in mathematics, which he viewed as analogous but not the same, he said to us "the legal achievement is no less a grand and important thing." A generation later, in 2006, I listened to a younger colleague give a talk on a public occasion in which he implied everyone knew that "there was no sharp line between language and law." I inwardly nodded. Then he went on, "and no sharp line between language and logic, or between logic and mathematics."

This ultimate turn, to mathematics, indicates how far the fact we are speaking together can disappear from view. There are Vicos and Collingwoods still arguing, and Alfred Marshall's introduction to *The Principles of Economics* is still there to be read,[8] but social science cannot escape its connection to the natural sciences and the premises or commitments of the natural scientist today. Most social scientists would not want to escape them. As the recent report of the quite representative commission setting up the new Life Sciences Initiative at the University of Michigan observed,

> Closely allied to the life sciences are the social sciences, which, though distinctive in their definition, are in fact concerned with a particular level of analysis in living organisms (usually humans). Indeed the boundaries between neuroscience (a life science) and psychology (a social science) are rather indistinct and are becoming increasingly more so. . . . [T]he laws of physics and chemistry should, in principle, be able to explain and predict biological phenomena in a precise manner. Understanding these aspects of the life sciences in the terms of mathematical modeling and theoretical applications of universal laws and principles is one of our greatest challenges for the next century.[9]

In light of these premises of the natural scientist, so fruitful in exploration of what we may call the world of force and its "mechanisms"—to use my father's word—finding a place for human purpose is an effort, to say the least. It is a long step from a working-day "methodological naturalism" to denying or to thinking one must deny the real existence of purpose even in the evening. But the step is taken, to an "ontological naturalism" declared and taught. A proper attention to the way things are, to which the development of statistical techniques and analysis can contribute, is joined to a cosmic impossibility of an ought and the way things might be. We see all around how easily this happens. Then with the departure of purpose goes value, beyond "preference" which is the leaning of a system. And with the departure of value, the distinctively legal meaning of "norm" in "legal norm" is stripped away, as Paul Freund feared even in 1961.

But purpose and value are everywhere in the discipline of law. They always have been, they are now, and they signal the first and immediate difference between law and social science, the nature of a "legal rule." Different in the most basic way is what goes by the name "rule" in social science, what must be ultimately its character, from what goes by the name "rule" in law, this somewhat static form turning in the mind toward a more energetic form in the domestic and international hope for the "rule of law." Of course it is a proper question and it is asked by lawyers themselves: why can't a "legal rule" become like a "rule" conceived within the terms of social science; why indeed is that not an ideal by the law's own lights, something graspable, predictable, "objectively" existing apart from the intentions, good faith, assent, and meaning of individuals and persons—like a rule of chess? Much of the answer, I think, is that life is not a game, despite what we all sometimes say about life.

Life is not a game and law is not, however much contest is brought into law as a device in inquiry and reflection. Insofar as we are persons acting in positions that are not ours alone, that connect us to other individuals and that are defined by public value, there is an authenticity sought that is completely foreign to what we call "gaming." Games that are "play" are relief and time-out from life, which is serious, painful, often tragic, as real as can be. Sometimes we have to turn from the relief games give and, cliché though it is, say to ourselves, our friends, our children, "This is for real, not a game." Games can be good. They can be an entry into playfulness and its creativity. There may be an aesthetic experience in games, a dance in them. But games, as games, are empty, and their emptiness is a source of their relief and pleasure, the unconflicted joy in the exercise of capacities that they allow. It makes no difference what the outcome is, really. The end of the game, as game, is only a prelude to the beginning of another.

This difference in present character and ultimate ideal between legal rules and scientific rules is wrapped up with the centrality of authority in law, a phenomenon from which a social scientist would backpedal as if his or her very identity as scientist depended on distance from it. Listen to the distinguished contemporary neuroscientist Jean-Pierre Changeux, turning to the question whether the ordering of society might be "elevated" to the rank of a science. Changeaux speaks of the "task of devising precise rules of conduct," "the various prescriptions that regulate behavior at a given moment of the history of a society," that "entire set of rules of interactions among the individual members of a social group." He observes, as did the commission on the Life Sciences Initiative at Michigan which I quoted earlier, that ultimately those "precise rules," those "prescriptions that regulate behavior," "that entire set of rules of interaction," must be translatable into "hierarchical and parallel sets of neurons [that] contribute to the cognitive functions that jointly construct a code of right action," and must be understood in terms of natural selection, not just as the grounding of work in biology, but as a total theory of the world. "Darwinian variations of social representations," Changeux says, working from the unstated premises of many today in his and in related fields—by "Darwinian variations," he means differences in "social representations" thrown up by chance on the model of genetic mutation—are "propagated from one brain to another, selected at the level of the community, and finally retained in the minds of lawmakers."[10]

What is critical in law is nowhere to be seen in this or any formulation like it, including that with which I began this essay—my father's "$\{\theta,S\}$," "an operating, working modifiable mechanism . . . the modifiable component of which is a system of constraining and prescriptive law and rule."[11] Implicit even in references to "precise rules of conduct" and "the entire set of rules of interactions among members of a social group," emanating from the neural structures of "lawmakers," is the order that might be given after someone says, "But that would be illegal," whether referring to taking a baby from her mother or drilling for oil in the Arctic wilderness; the order that might be given after saying, "Yes, that is legitimate," again whether referring to taking a baby from her mother or drilling for oil;[12] or, indeed, the order implicit in opinions issued through an appellate hierarchy on how to structure ongoing thinking and argument. Orders are implicit, but what is forgotten, and forgotten throughout discussion of law in social scientific terms translatable into basic science, is the correlative of an order, obedience.[13] Never reached is why others out there obey, repeating the order in their own voice and words with their own sense of it, and implementing it or responding to it in good faith—not so much why they should obey, but why they do obey, pay attention, and continue to pay attention when there are so often so many reasons not to, when so much is at stake. What is forgotten, in short, is authority, the premise and the object of legal thinking, legal argument, and legal conclusion, kept untouched by modernity's challenges to authority elsewhere, and not only kept but expanded with expanded claims for law, the "rule" of law, "law" expanding around the world.[14]

One reason for forgetting the presence of authority in law—and the inevitable issuing of orders and question of obedience—is the historical association of the development of scientific and social scientific work with struggles for freedom of thought accompanying the political struggles of the last few centuries, freedom of thought that, in an ironic turn, total theorists in the sciences today are so strenuously trying to limit. But more basic in the forgetting is the erasure of the individual in scientific and social scientific thought, both the individual facing a claim of authority, listening and himself or herself judging while listening, and the individual contemplated and protected in and by law. Neither is the person really there in scientific and social scientific thought, the individual person or the corporate or institutional person, other than as a linguistic shorthand for a system. Nor is there living value that makes claims on us. Authority, person, value, individual—none are there, ultimately, in social science. All are there at the center of law.

After the experience of the twentieth century, its struggles and its horrors, the erasure of the individual is the most glaring. Units of one kind or another of course figure in any professional thought and discussion. It is widely said today that as interacting units you and I are "adaptive systems." Someone using this term in professional scientific discourse would add, if pushed, "and nothing more," an addition critical to the difference between such professional thought and legal thought. Pictured in this way, a human being at any particular point in the course of life is a snapshot of the particular and changing outcome of two factors interacting over time: internal system and external system, nature and nurture, genetic endowment and environment. In 2007, journalists sought out expert commentary on why a man waiting for the subway with his two daughters leapt to press down between the tracks and save the life of a man who had suffered a seizure and fallen in front of an oncoming train. What was offered was that he had within him an "impulse" that was "followed spontaneously, either by virtue of genetic disposition or childhood/cultural training."[15] These were the two sources of what this human unit was.

But this is not the way we think about the individual—not me thinking, not you I imagine, not even those who speak in these terms. The word for the unique product of the action and interaction of the two factors, internal system and external system, is in fact not "individual" but "phenotype." The way we do think about the individual is reflected in law and legal thought and includes something more than internal and external system, something "in" the individual—you, me, the scientist and social scientist too—which holds all of us back from vivisecting each other, which almost holds us back from torture.[16] That is something real in social scientists' minds and hearts and lives. It is real in law and legal thought, in which they themselves participate, not least when they are facing an order or asked to carry one out. Its reality, its presence, is alone enough to keep law from being a social science or ever becoming a social science.[17]

It is almost embarrassing to make these points, they are so obvious, so unoriginal. Making them is like looking up and saying there is a sun in the sky. But they do need to be made, and made more explicitly than they have been. I have painted law as proceeding rather on its own, too important to be affected at its core by what has happened in academic law over the last half century. But of course law has been affected. That is why it is better to think of law, with all it presupposes and makes real in human life and thought, as "resilient" rather than impervious.

Particularly striking, I think, has been the attempt to fit the law of the central private institution of our time, the business corporation, to the premises of social science. Twentieth-century corporate law developed along lines analogous to the development of public administrative law, with the focus on the decision being made on behalf of the corporate body, and the questions being the authority of the decision maker, the enforcement of the decision if challenged, and the values and considerations procedural and substantive taken into account by the decision maker, or not taken into account.[18] In the 1970s and 1980s a push began to replace this analysis—which assumed that profit in a competitive market was the primary but not exclusive consideration if the corporation was a business corporation—with analysis on the assumption that the legal standard for decisions on behalf of business corporations was "maximization" of profit. The very notion of maximization was drawn from Western microeconomic theory and from biology, where "maximization" describes what must be done to survive in evolutionary competition or competition in a "perfect market." In terms of the process of decision making, what began to be taught in law schools as well as business schools was that "business" thinking was supposed to be wholly calculating and manipulative, with no place in it for any genuine concern for effects on employees, retirees, the surrounding community, the nation, or the world.

This push, coincident with the movement of James Buchanan's *homo economicus* into the academic picture of legislative drafting, administrative regulation, and judicial decision making, reached the American Law Institute in the 1980s and early 1990s. It was proposed that the institute state that the purpose of the business corporation should be "long-term maximization" of corporate profit and shareholder gain. This was rejected as a reading of the law, judicial or statutory. The reason was explicit, that it referred to "maximization" which, the council of the institute observed, would eliminate any authentic consideration of public value. In the institute's statement of what a "business purpose" was in corporate law, "maximization" of profit was replaced by "conduct of business activities with a view to enhancing" profit.[19]

But the teaching of maximization in its economic and biological sense continued even after the Enron case laid bare just what was being taught. The response of the law, that in the "name" of which individuals speak, was to move during this same period to the application of the criminal law to the corporate entity itself—criminal law, in which the attitude toward public value described by "maximization" precisely fits the standard formulation of what makes action or inaction criminal, the element of *mens rea,* the criminal mind. As an example, causing death (a fact) becomes murder (a crime) as a result of "extreme indifference to the value of human life."[20] That development in corporate criminality, state and federal, substantively and in sentencing, legislatively and administratively, reintroduces taking into account values for their own sake in decisions made on behalf of a business corporation. It has been fought in turn, and the struggle continues today. The struggle points up not only the effect of the effort to push economic premises into legal thought, but law's resilience: here it is living value, pushed out at one point, that can be seen reentering analysis at another point.

On a larger canvas, there has been an attempt to introduce into legal thought generally a form of "cost-benefit" analysis that excludes all else, in line with the totalizing thought called "scientific" so frequently today. There is, as is said, "nothing sacred," nothing that is just not done, nothing that is not touched. It shows in the reopening of the question of torture.[21] "What does that mean, 'outrages upon personal dignity'?" the U.S. president asked in the struggle over the criminality of violations of the Geneva Conventions. "That's a statement that is wide open to interpretation," he continued. "And what I am proposing is that there be clarity in the law so that our professionals will have no doubt that what they are doing is legal. . . . They don't want to be tried as war criminals. They don't want to break the law."[22] What the president was reflecting is a view of law very much affected by its identification with social science. There are large implications—this is one of them—of the absence there of person, purpose, value, individual, all folded into the term "human dignity" found in the various conventions against inhumane treatment of human beings. Person, purpose, value, individual are mocked, and not just in discussions of torture, as being vague, too "imprecise" to affect "rational" decision making—"rational," of course, only in the sense defined by the deliberately limited presuppositions of social science.

It should not be overlooked that the current biological view of the living world may well have grown out of economics, rather than the reverse.

The axiomatic hostility to what modern biology calls "vitalism" mirrors the cynicism—the moral stance—of a view of the human as intrinsically alone, ruthlessly self-seeking for a self that is axiomatically limited. The denial of the humane in the human is not everywhere in biology and economics, but it is prominent enough; and with and through these disciplines there has been imported into thought and discussion in law the dichotomy seen in both, between the "selfish" and the "altruistic," with the selfish the undeniably basic and with the altruistic an illusion eventually to be understood in a way consistent with the selfish. Not for nothing is the widespread popularity in academic discussion of the "prisoner's dilemma." Its imagery, imprisonment and threat from others of pain or death, fits an underlying vision of what it is to be human—utterly alone in the world and knowing that one is utterly alone in the world.

But again this is not the view of law, which over time has more and more protected the humane in the human. The individual contains the whole world, but is not alone. The individual is connected with others through participation in the life of living value, to which legal language makes constant reference, participation indeed in the creation of living value. As Alasdair MacIntyre has recently shown so well in his *Dependent Rational Animals,*[23] there is no such dichotomy of the selfish and altruistic in the real world, which is the world of law, where we are all dependent or disabled at some point in our lives, receiving from those whom we cannot repay and giving to those who cannot repay us, unpredictably and disproportionately in both the giving and the receiving. In this connection too I might note as another example of law's resilience that the acknowledgment of the full range of living value, which developed during the first three-quarters of the twentieth century in the law of standing and the very conception of who a legal person can be, still stands despite pressure on it from biological and economic thinking. The decoupling of the common law of judicial jurisdiction from "property" and "contract," the abandonment of the so-called legal interest test of an earlier time, remains undisturbed by the presence of *homo economicus* in academic teaching and discussion.[24]

The attempt to challenge the absolute prohibition in law of the torture of human beings is emblematic, as is the attempt to reconceive the nature of the legal persons we call business corporations. The language and the way of thinking shown in this challenge and this reconception are case studies in the implications of identifying law with social science. But there is a canvas larger still that may include the question of torture. On it can be projected not only the implications of the pressure on law from this identification but law's resilience under this pressure: the pushing back, which the mind can feel, of the individual, the person, purpose, responsibility, living value.

Before us is a prospect of a kind different from the movement into law of biological thinking and such social scientific thinking that blends into it—economic, psychological, sociological, historicist. We are faced in law with the achievements of biological science within its own sphere and with developments in technology that permit manipulation in light of its achievements. The very real possibility now of the creation of forms of being that are hybrids of humans and animals, the circumvention of the breeding barrier that has heretofore identified an individual as of one or another kind, or species, raises the old question of slavery in a new context. And as Kazuo Ishiguro has explored quietly and effectively,[25] the possibility of beings genetically engineered for organ donation also raises that old question of the association of property with human flesh. What is human, what is less than human, law and lawyers will be asked, what or who is an individual in the sense in which we speak of individuals in law, what or who is a person, what material forms of being human or almost human can be bought and sold and exploited, and, yes, treated as animal? In addition to this—the question of slavery—the genetic engineering of individuals, the possibility of human clones, and the selecting of embryos "in" or "out" in human reproductive technology all raise the eugenic question again in a twenty-first-century context.

Slavery and eugenics—one would have thought the one was resolved by the late nineteenth century and the other by the mid-twentieth. The struggle with them is before us still. If anyone is dubious about the seriousness of the conflict when biological and eugenic thinking come to the front of the legal mind, I suggest reading or reading again the Supreme Court's decision on race and slavery in *Dred Scott,* that creatures with traces of African blood in them could never reach a position of full human dignity and responsibility. There were two dissents, with Justice McLean's dissent pointing away from the biological and eugenic in a clear statement not so much of law as of law's difference, a statement of what law can comprehend that is simply not comprehensible within the framework being pressed upon it: "A slave is not a mere chattel. He bears the impress of his Maker, and is amenable to the laws of God and man; and he is destined to an endless existence."[26] Or read the Court's decision in *Buck v. Bell* on eugenics, that the poor, the less clever in calculating, the delinquent were less than fully human and should not contribute to the future material of the human form of being. This was the 1927 Court of Holmes, Stone, Brandeis, and Taft. There was one dissent without opinion.[27] It may be notable that this sole dissent was by the only member of the Catholic Church on the Court, Justice Butler, who went to Mass every morning, and that the church's teaching was pointing by 1927 toward the universal human dignity latent in law's distinctive recognition of the individual.[28]

Dred Scott was overruled by John Brown, Harriet Beecher Stowe, a war, and a century of internal legal development, but we are not certainly away from it yet. *Buck v. Bell* has been reviled but never overruled or repudiated. The questions of slavery and eugenics persist, as questions. How then can it be thought law will stay resilient under these pressures and in face of such enormous demands as these, when the very grounding of the human may be shifting underfoot?

Law will stay resilient because the individual at home in law is the bedrock, prior to any discussion of history or process, or presently existing system, or scientific conclusion—in fact, prior to any discussion of "the individual." Though some individual waves his wand at us again and again, we are not changed from the individuals we are into products or statistical notions. Beyond that bedrock—our actual presence to one another—I should say there is some assurance in the fact that law, with its presuppositions and, more than presupposition, its ontology, is the one thing other than food that we cannot do without. Social scientists, too, cannot do without it.

Among the particulars that might be noted as we look forward, the worldwide development of human rights law,[29] anticipated and perhaps in some way affected by the evidence of the lonely dissents in *Dred Scott* and *Buck v. Bell,* is founded on a vision of the individual and of the nature of value that social science cannot share, and insofar as domestic law is pressed by that mode of thought, international law can reach back and recall. Even while law in general was being identified in teaching and discussion with social science in general, international law emerging from the revelatory horrors of "our" century was making implausible the identification of "legal rules" that live in human minds and speech with rules that can be conceived in the terms of social science. Indeed the development of the web of international conventions on genocide, on torture, on human experimentation, on inhumane treatment, on behalf of the disabled, on behalf of women and children has been loosening our own law from the positivism that began to affect it and thinking about it, at least in academic law, in the nineteenth and early twentieth centuries, before the fifty years past that are our concern here.

One of these international developments, proceeding from the midcentury Nuremberg Trials, has been especially important in protecting the understanding of the human individual as something more than the product of genetic and environmental systems. These are the legal limitations on experimentation on human individuals, that arena where the legal vision of the human being and the scientific and social scientific vision explicitly confront one another. Such experimentation in the United States had its own eugenic and authoritarian cast—its subjects disproportionately children, the poor, the military, or those who had some forebears who had suffered slavery—and it was not pulled back substantially until the 1970s and 1980s.

I would add as important also the developing conception in law of the sentient beings we call animals, the other part of the hybrids I have mentioned. This development is another reason to believe that commitments to living value, to the individual, and to a dimension of reality that sustains and attracts what we might call law's eschatological thrust have been fundamentally unaffected. It too has its international side. Legally recognizing interests that are not proxies of human interests and acknowledging a shared sentience and special human responsibility for its protection has something of an a fortiori effect. In many ways the treatment of animals was the horror in the revelatory events of the twentieth century, as human beings were treated as animals so systematically and so cruelly, and when it comes to our own behavior toward each other we should eventually be able to exclaim, "Why, you would not do this to an animal!" Pulling the treatment of animals toward the treatment or the "legitimate" treatment of human beings, rather than the treatment of human beings toward the treatment of animals, is a working out of something within law, pushed not only by law's restlessness with incoherence but also by law's eschatological thrust, the pointing to a whole from the partial, which can be seen whenever the word "justice" is mentioned in the same breath as the word "law." In secular terms, that might be thought "Hegelian" or "Platonic," though Hegel had contempt for the American experiment, and there is the possibility Plato might have. I prefer to think in terms of John Noonan's articulation of the way an inner logic of a human institution works itself out over long periods of time, on slavery, on torture, and on the ownership and exploitation of women and children.[30]

To be sure, whenever the border between human and animal is opened to any extent, there can be migration in both directions across it. Hearing the "cry of animals" as human cries are heard can reverse and can become hearing human cries as the cries of animals. An essay by a neurologist featured in the *Chronicle of Higher Education* a few years ago proposed that human language and literature "grow out of a biological system for attempting to fill needs," and the piece argued for "reuniting language with the screams and cries of animal communication, looking at it as a secretion of one of the spongiest organs in the body."[31] But I think the movement across today's more porous border between human and animal is rather in the other direction, as the evolutionary biologist Simon Conway Morris has so eloquently argued.[32]

Mention of a view of language as "a secretion of one of the spongiest organs in the body" leads me to two final indications of the essential health of the legal mind. One is the growing sophistication about the nature of human language and its constitutive action in law. I was exposed to a precursor of it studying under Lon Fuller in the 1960s.[33] But a full focus on the importance of language began at about the same time as the development of "public choice theory" and similar schools of thought in economics and their movement in various ways into academic law. That full focus is the work of James Boyd White, in volume after volume.[34] White has made clear that the sounds made by isolated competitors contending with one another, or the sounds made in advertising or political manipulation, are not the language of a person and not language with the force of law, but the sounds of force and force alone. I emphasize "alone" because they fit a vision of the human world, indeed the universe itself, in which there are ultimately only forces (as Oliver Wendell Holmes once said). This is not the world of law. Because of White and his work, it can be said with confidence that when Steven Pinker or Herbert Simon and the disciplines with which they are associated speak of language, its origins, mechanisms, and meaning, they are not talking about human language, or about the language of law, but about something else, in rather the same way that so many who set out to study the idea of God are not thinking about God, but about something else.[35]

There is, secondly, a new openness of mind among figures prominent in discussion of organized human life. The representative figure outside law may be Jürgen Habermas, whose grappling with the issues raised by our new capacities for manipulation of the material substrate of the human has led him to acknowledge the sometime dependence of secular discussion on a dimension of reality that is not secular—in his words, "to the reasonable attitude of keeping one's distance from religion without closing one's mind to the perspective it offers," or "keeping a distance . . . from a religious tradition whose normative substance we nevertheless feed on," or acknowledging "moral feelings which only religious language has as yet been able to give a sufficiently differentiated expression."[36]

This openness, which can be seen more widely in arriving at consensus at each stage in the expansion of universal human rights, is beginning to be matched within law by an increasingly explicit acknowledgment of an uninterrupted ontological commitment in law to a dimension of reality that, whether or not it is or is called religious, has no place in scientific work or social science. Perhaps it can never have and should not have a place, given the power of the scientific method in understanding and possibly freeing us to some degree from the blind systems of the world with which and within which we live. The representative figure I would point to in this connection is Steven Douglas Smith, whose work and contributions to law's self-understanding have also been developing alongside the movements with which I began.[37] Habermas and those who work with his work, White and those who work with his, Smith and those who work with his, other examples from this volume—all these are not going to go away. If law and the legal mind were a rough tough animal, they are nourishing its bones and sinew. There is, both within law, even in academic law, and outside law, even in academic social science and social theory, increasing awareness that the human which the humanist insists is "all we have got" includes an open dimension to which there is really no limit.

This should not be surprising. The world of the active mathematician is not accessible to many, even though the operation and application of mathematics may be. But it is a familiar thing to hear that mathematicians who call themselves realists acknowledge a dimension of reality that transcends the here and now of our developing physical existence. They say—and invite us to accept—that natural selection as a "theory of everything" does not reach and cannot explain mathematics, which is not, in itself, reducible to the organization of neural tissue, but is real in a realm of its own. Lawyers and all those actively participating in law who are realistic about their thought and action acknowledge a dimension of human experience of reality that is not at all the same as that of realist mathematicians but, like theirs, lies both beneath and beyond the realities admitted by the rules and presuppositions of the natural and social sciences.

Law will be tough enough in the future. We can speculate why it has not been tougher in the past. There are tensions within law, as there are in your and my own thought, and there always have been. Identification of law with social science can have been an effort to escape them. Social science and science behind it perhaps need not have pressed so. They might just have offered themselves, for there is a constant pull toward the authoritarian, the meaningless, the automatic, away from responsibility, away from facing grief for what we ourselves do. Work in law even has an element of the frightening in it, which must be handled in some way. Just as there is biblical awe, dread, and fear, so too can it be positively frightening to think that what is necessary to authenticity of any kind at any level—and necessary therefore to authority and therefore to law—runs straight up to a transcendent dimension of the universe. This is a problem the social scientist of our time, thinking as a social scientist, does not have. But the lawyer does.

NOTES

1. Rutledge Vining, *On Appraising the Performance of an Economic System: What an Economic System Is, and the Norms Implied in Observers' Adverse Reactions to the Outcome of Its Working* (Cambridge: Cambridge University Press, 1984). For the material previously quoted, see 6, 9, 16 n. 8, 23, 26.

2. Joseph Vining, *The Authoritative and the Authoritarian* (Chicago: University of Chicago Press, 1986; paperback ed., 1988).

3. James M. Buchanan and Gordon Tullock, *The Calculus of Consent: Logical Foundations of Constitutional Democracy* (Ann Arbor: University of Michigan Press, 1962).

4. James M. Buchanan, *Better than Plowing, and Other Personal Essays* (Chicago: University of Chicago Press, 1992), at 13, 79, 94, 95–96, 98, 103. See also *The Calculus of Consent* (1962), supra n. 3, at 346 n. 7; Gordan Tullock, "Theoretical Forerunners," appendix 2 to *The Calculus of Consent,* at 339 ("The work of Rutledge Vining had a major effect on both of us, largely through his emphasis on the necessity of separating consideration of what 'rules of the game' were most satisfactory from the consideration of the strategy to be followed under a given set of 'rules'"), 326, 359 n. 3 ("Game theory studies the behavior of individuals in a 'game' with given rules. Economics does the same, but the end or purpose of the investigation in economics is to choose between alternative sets of rules. . . . As many economists will already have guessed, I am indebted to Professor Rutledge Vining for this point.").

Rutledge Vining was known sometimes as an "institutionalist" in economics. See Malcolm Rutherford, "Chicago Economics and Institutionalism," http://web.uvic.ca/~rutherfo/Chicago4.pdf, at 20–21.

5. See Leonid Hurwicz and Stanley Reiter, *Designing Economic Mechanisms* (Cambridge: Cambridge University Press, 2006); Roger B. Myerson, "Fundamental Theory of Institutions: A Lecture in Honor of Leo Hurwicz," http://home.uchicago.edu/~rmyerson/research/hurwicz.pdf.

6. See John von Neumann and Oskar Morgenstern, *Theory of Games and Economic Behavior* (Princeton: Princeton University Press, 1944).

7. François Jacob, *The Logic of Life: A History of Heredity,* trans. Betty S. Spillmann (London: Penguin, 1982), at 245, 196.

8. Alfred Marshall, *Principles of Economics,* 8th ed. (London: Macmillan, 1920) (reprinted 1982), at 1–11. "Economics" in the large has its fields and schools, and an interest in "economics" can and does ground sensitive inquiries into human experience in community and with institutional life. Indeed, there can be an internal dispute about the nature of the connection between "economics" and science and mathematics, as there can be disputes about the meaning of "science" or "mathematics" among scientists or mathematicians mutually recognizing one another as such. This was in part the subject of *On Appraising the Performance of an Economic System* (supra n. 1), e.g., at 23: "If there is to be a science whose subject is the economic system—a cumulation of knowledge about how a thing of this sort works . . ." In this regard, it was not only experience of a year in law school and a summer of practice that stood between me and my father in 1962. Looking forward to graduate study and law school four years before our conversation about his book, I had written on law as a science of the human by contrast with the biological sciences, which had been my principal subject up to that time.

9. *Report of the President's Commission on the Life Sciences* (University of Michigan, 1999), at ix, 5, 61.

10. Jean-Pierre Changeux and Alain Connes, *Conversations on Mind, Matter, and Mathematics,* ed. and trans. M. B. DeBevoise (Princeton: Princeton University Press, 1995), at 210–12, 216, 219, 231.

11. *On Appraising the Performance of an Economic System,* supra n. 1, at 7, 12. See also 16 n. 8, 23.

12. An example at the international level would be orders given with respect to enriching uranium into material suitable for nuclear warfare. Consider the words used and the reach for the force in them, the "force of law," in Iran's 2007 statement to the UN Security Council when Iran rejected calls for suspension of its uranium enrichment program: "The world must know—and it does—that even the harshest political and economic sanctions or other threats are far too weak to coerce the Iranian nation to retreat from their legal and legitimate demands" (Alexandra Olson, "Penalty to Iran: Assets Frozen: UN Ban on Arms Exports Is Among Sanctions Iran Rejects," Associated Press, 25 March 2007).

13. H. Jefferson Powell's essay in this volume, "Law as a Tool," addresses the authority of statutes, particularly their authority for those enforcing and administering them.

14. A. W. Brian Simpson is known for his work on legal method and the nature

of the "rule of law," and on the difference between a "legal rule" and rules presupposed in the "economic analysis of law." See, e.g., his essay in this volume, "Anti-Social Behaviour Orders in the United Kingdom." In his comments in 2005–6 on H. L. A. Hart's still much-discussed *The Concept of Law* (Oxford: Clarendon, 1961), he picks up the absence of authority in the "concept" proposed by Hart (A. W. B. Simpson, "Stag Hunter and Mole," *Times Literary Supplement*, 11 February 2005, at 7; "Herbert Hart Elucidated," 104 *Michigan Law Review* 1437, 1457 (2006)).

What is necessary to the "existence" of a legal "system" is authority, and in practice and fact the availability of willing executioners is not the source of it. Hart's *Concept of Law* appeared (not entirely coincidentally, I think) at almost the same time as Buchanan's *Calculus of Consent* and the filial conversation with which I begin. The distance of *The Concept of Law* from the reality of law was noted by those of us who read it as law students then, when it was new and before it became a text central to academic discussion.

15. Cara Buckley, "Why Our Hero Leapt onto the Tracks and We Might Not," *New York Times* 7 January 2007, sec. 4, at 3.

16. Or—even with regard to a past or future slave who is not a legal person—it might hold "us" back from accepting, as a justification for working to death, that it is cheaper to purchase a replacement than to provide adequate food, medical care, and rest.

17. Science in the sense of "knowledge" could disavow precision as an ideal, but certainly the "precise rules" sought in all scientific inquiries that hope ultimately to link their conclusions to mathematics—and to what Eugene Wigner famously called the "miracle" of mathematics, its "unreasonable effectiveness"—require units of reference that can be "defined." Units of reference in law cannot be corralled so. They are living, they spill over any boundaries set for them. Any statement of law, including a statement of law implicitly or explicitly defining a legal unit of reference, can be and regularly is challenged; and the conclusion of the challenge becomes simply one more statement of law.

18. A brief review of the development of corporate law and practice in the first half of the twentieth century can be found in Adolf A. Berle Jr., *The Twentieth Century Capitalist Revolution* (New York: Harcourt Brace, 1954), at 164–69.

19. This history is detailed in my "China, Business Law, and Finance—Accession to the World Trade Organization," 2001/2 Manuscripts of Public Lectures, Sir Edward Youde Memorial Visiting Professorship Scheme (2003), http://www.sfaa.gov.hk/doc/en/scholar/seym/Prof_Joseph_Vinings_report.doc.

20. E.g., American Law Institute, *Model Penal Code,* Official Draft, 1962, § 210.2(1)(b).

21. Prominent academic lawyers have been involved in reopening the question of torture. See James Boyd White's essay "Law, Economics, and Torture" in this volume. See also, e.g., Philippe Sands, "Extraordinary Rendition: Complicity and Its Consequences" (lecture, JUSTICE, London, 15 May 2006), at paragraphs 10–17; Richard A. Posner, *Not a Suicide Pact: The Constitution in a Time of National Emergency* (New York: Oxford University Press, 2006), at 82–87. Of course, the reopening is occurring in more than legal discussion. See "Can Torture Ever Be Justified?" *Bulletin of the American Academy of Arts and Sciences,* Summer 2004, 3–4; Michael Ig-

natieff, *The Lesser Evil: Political Ethics in an Age of Terror* (Princeton: Princeton University Press, 2004); and essays in *Torture: A Collection,* ed. Sanford Levinson (New York: Oxford University Press, 2004). But in all discussion today the law's impact, "legitimacy," must be faced.

22. Jim Rutenberg and Sheryl Gay Stolberg, "Bush Says G.O.P. Rebels Are Putting Nation at Risk: Excerpt from Bush's Remarks," *New York Times,* 16 September 2006.

23. Alasdair MacIntyre, *Dependent Rational Animals: Why Human Beings Need the Virtues* (Chicago: Open Court, 2001).

24. I explored this decoupling in *Legal Identity: The Coming of Age of Public Law* (New Haven: Yale University Press, 1978). For examples and summary of development since, see Animal Legal Defense Fund v. Glickman, 154 F.3d 426 (D.C. Cir., en banc, 1998); Massachusetts v. Environmental Protection Agency, 127 S. Ct. 1438 (2007).

25. Kazuo Ishiguro, *Never Let Me Go* (New York: Alfred A. Knopf, 2005).

26. Dred Scott v. Sandford, 60 U.S. 393, 550 (1857).

27. Buck v. Bell, 274 U.S. 200 (1927). The well-known opinion ("Three generations of imbeciles are enough") was by Justice Holmes.

28. The human eugenics movement and evolutionary biology stated in terms of high and low emerged at the same time in the mid-nineteenth century. It is intriguing that the human eugenics movement, looking to the elimination of categories of human beings, also emerged at the same time as enslavement was being taken away as an optional course of action after perceiving a human being as of a lesser kind.

The question or problem is often set out and discussed today, how to "explain" religious experience or human dignity in terms of our current perception of organic evolution and its mechanisms. This becomes something of an academic exercise. The pressing question is rather the reverse, how to explain our current perception of organic evolution, our admiration for it, fascination with it, and persuasion to it, while staying realistic and acknowledging our actual presence to one another, the mutual recognition of individual, person, and spirit on which we build any kind of belief about the world.

29. For a beautiful introduction to human rights law and its early history, see Mary Ann Glendon, *A World Made New: Eleanor Roosevelt and the Universal Declaration of Human Rights* (New York: Random House, 2001). On the significance of international developments for human self-understanding, and on the human future they may make possible, see Philip Allott, *Eunomia: New Order for a New World,* 2d ed. (Oxford: Oxford University Press, 2001), and *The Health of Nations: Society and Law beyond the State* (Cambridge: Cambridge University Press, 2002). On the individual, human experimentation, and eugenic practices, see also, e.g., Charter of Fundamental Rights of the European Union, preamble and chap. 1 (Dignity), available at http://www.eucharter.org/.

30. See John T. Noonan's essay "Conscience and the Constitution" in this volume and his *A Church That Can and Cannot Change* (Notre Dame, IN: University of Notre Dame Press, 2005).

31. Alice Weaver Flaherty, "Writing Like Crazy: A Word on the Brain," *Chronicle of Higher Education (Chronicle Review)* 50, no. 13 (21 November 2003), at B6.

32. See, e.g., Simon Conway Morris, *Life's Solution* (Cambridge: Cambridge University Press, 2003), and his Gifford Lectures for 2007, *What Organic Evolution Tells Us about Our Place in the Universe, Not Least in Terms of Religious Perspectives and Natural Theology* (forthcoming).

33. See *Rediscovering Fuller: Essays on Implicit Law and Institutional Design,* ed. W. Witteveen and W. van der Burg (Amsterdam: Amsterdam University Press, 1999), and my chapter in that collection, "Fuller and Language," at 453.

34. See, e.g., James Boyd White, *The Legal Imagination* (Boston: Little, Brown, 1973); *Justice as Translation* (Chicago: University of Chicago Press, 1990); *Living Speech* (Princeton: Princeton University Press, 2006).

35. In this connection too, a classic work on computers and language should be noted: *Computer Power and Human Reason* (New York: W. H. Freeman, 1976) by Joseph Weizenbaum, a pioneer in computer programming.

36. Jürgen Habermas, *The Future of Human Nature* (Oxford: Blackwell, 2003), at 113, 108, 114. I have tried to explore this openness further in "Legal Commitments and Religious Commitments," 44 *San Diego Law Review* 69 (2007), and "The Mystery of the Individual in Modern Law," 52 *Villanova Law Review* 1 (2007).

37. See, e.g., Steven Douglas Smith, *Law's Quandary* (Harvard: Harvard University Press, 2004). As well as the implicit and increasingly explicit, there is overt acknowledgment with an unbroken history. See, e.g., Patrick McKinley Brennan, "A Quandary in Law? A (Qualified) Catholic Denial," 44 *San Diego Law Review* 97 (2007), and "Locating Authority in Law," chap. 9 in *Civilizing Authority: Society, State, and Church,* ed. P. M. Brennan (Lanham, MD: Lexington Books, 2007), at 161.

Justice Jackson's Republic and Ours

Barry Sullivan

Over the past few decades it has been repeatedly said by lawyers and judges that the form of thought and expression we know as the judicial opinion has been changing in deep, disturbing, but obscure ways. Somehow the expectations that were once appropriate to the work of courts, especially the Supreme Court, are frustrated and blocked. What has in fact been happening? How has our conception of the law been changing? What can now be done about it?

In this essay, Barry Sullivan addresses these large questions by focusing on two opinions: first, the important opinion by Justice Jackson in the Steel Seizure Case, *with an eye both to what that opinion originally meant, in the legal and political culture in which it was issued, and to its present-day reception and interpretation; second, the opinion of Justice O'Connor in the recent* Hamdi *case (the "enemy combatant" case). Sullivan is asking how opinions used to be written and read; how they are written and read today; and what this means about the changes in the nature of legal thought, argument, and judgment that both practitioners and teachers have noticed. Much is at stake here, including the fundamental nature of law as both an intellectual and a political activity.*

In December 1950, President Truman declared a state of "national emergency" because of the undeclared war in Korea. In April 1952, while the war continued, the president authorized the secretary of commerce to seize most of the nation's steel mills to ensure the continued availability of steel. In *Youngstown Sheet & Tube Co. v. Sawyer,*[1] as every high school student used to know, the Supreme Court held that the president exceeded his authority when he issued that order. The vote was six to three. There were either seven or eight opinions in the case, depending on how one counts Justice Frankfurter's two submissions, but it is Justice Jackson's opinion that most of us remember. That in itself is curious because Justice Jackson did not write the opinion for the Court, and no other justice expressly joined in Justice Jackson's opinion. Yet Justice Jackson's opinion is an extraordinary example of judicial opinion writing for several reasons: the strength of its reasoning, the felicity of its expression, the integrity of its voice, and the depth of its practical understanding of the intersection of law and politics. Paradoxically, it is also a very personal opinion, although it concerns the most profoundly public of subjects: the degree to which the courts, in our democratic society, can and should act to protect legislative authority and individual rights against claims of executive convenience or necessity.

What we usually remember about Justice Jackson's opinion is the three-part scheme that he used to illustrate his understanding of the complex constitutional relationships that exist among the three branches of government—a scheme that encompasses all three branches but focuses particularly on the degree of solidarity between the political branches.

> 1. When the President acts pursuant to an express or implied authorization of Congress, his authority is at its maximum, for it includes all that he possesses in his own right plus all that Congress can delegate. In these circumstances, and in these only, may he be said (for what it may be worth), to personify the federal sovereignty. If his act is held unconstitutional under these circumstances, it usually means that the Federal Government as an undivided whole lacks power. A seizure executed by the President pursuant to an Act of Congress would be supported by the strongest of presumptions and the widest latitude of judicial interpretation, and the burden of persuasion would rest heavily upon any who might attack it.
>
> 2. When the President acts in absence of either a congressional grant or denial of authority, he can only rely upon his own independent powers, but there is a zone of twilight in which he and Congress may have concurrent authority, or in which its distribution is uncertain. Therefore, congressional inertia, indifference or quiescence may sometimes, at least as a practical matter, enable, if not invite, measures on independent presidential responsibility. In this area, any actual test of power is likely to depend on the imperatives of events and contemporary imponderables rather than on abstract theories of law.
>
> 3. When the President takes measures incompatible with the expressed or implied will of Congress, his power is at its lowest ebb, for then he can rely only upon his own constitutional powers minus any constitutional powers of Congress over the matter. Courts can sustain exclusive Presidential control in such a case only by disabling the Congress from acting upon the subject. Presidential claim to a power

> at once so conclusive and preclusive must be scrutinized with caution, for what is at stake is the equilibrium established by our constitutional system.[2]

Fifty-five years later, Justice Jackson's three-part test is ubiquitous. As presidents have asserted increasingly broader authority, courts repeatedly have invoked Justice Jackson's test to measure the constitutionality of executive actions. For example, in the two most important decisions to emerge thus far from the "War on Terror"—*Hamdi v. Rumsfeld*[3] and *Hamdan v. Rumsfeld*[4]—Justice Jackson's test was invoked countless times in a variety of opinions. Even when the Court did not specifically mention it, the test hovered ghostlike above the rhetoric of the opinions, implicitly framing the terms on which the issues were to be resolved. Does the Force Act[5] authorize the president's classification of prisoners as "enemy combatants" subject to indefinite detention, without judicial review? Does the Force Act authorize the president's use of military tribunals to determine the guilt or innocence of persons so classified? To what extent, and with what degree of specificity, has Congress spoken?

At bottom, however, one wonders whether the Court's seemingly admiring use of Justice Jackson's test is truly consistent with the spirit and intent of his opinion. Justice Jackson's opinion haunts the Court's consideration of these questions, but the voice it projects is something of a distorted echo. After all, it is not the opinion as a whole that is analyzed and applied or implicitly relied upon. It is only the three-part test, in decontextualized form, which provides the template. And it is often a simplistic form of the test—one that exceeds Justice Jackson's intention by seeming to assume that nothing is forbidden to the president and Congress acting together, notwithstanding the care with which Justice Jackson reserved the point that some actions may lie beyond the power of the national government. Justice Jackson's test also represents only a small part of his own opinion—one that comes at the beginning and attempts to synthesize the Court's somewhat confusing and inconsistent precedents.[6] Justice Jackson himself immediately characterized the test as oversimplified but helpful as a beginning. Most important, the opinion embodies a style of judging that is both foreign to current styles of adjudication and inconsistent with the use made of Justice Jackson's test in recent cases.

The Court in *Hamdan,* for example, recently held that the president was not authorized by existing law to try enemy combatants before special military commissions (and pursuant to special rules) expressly created for that purpose.[7] The disagreements among the justices were complex and defy brief summary. Justice Stevens spoke for a majority of the Court on most issues, but two parts of his opinion commanded only a plurality.[8] Justice Kennedy delivered a separate opinion endorsed by a different plurality. The Stevens and Kennedy opinions are both lengthy, detailed, and complicated. Justice Breyer, who wrote for the same plurality as Justice Kennedy, purported to sum up the Court's holding (those parts of Justice Stevens's opinion that commanded five votes) in a single page. He wrote:

> The dissenters . . . suggest that [today's decision] undermines our Nation's ability to "preven[t] future attacks" of the grievous sort that we have already suffered. . . . That claim leads me to state briefly what I believe the majority sets forth both explicitly and implicitly at greater length. The Court's conclusion ultimately rests upon a single ground: Congress has not issued the Executive a "blank check." *Cf. Hamdi v. Rumsfeld,* 542 U.S. 507, 536 (2004) (plurality opinion). Indeed, Congress has denied the President the legislative authority to create military commissions of the kind at issue here. Nothing prevents the President from returning to Congress to seek the authority he believes necessary.[9]

Notably, Justice Stevens did not endorse this abridged version of his opinion.[10]

Justice Breyer's opinion is striking, not only for its brevity and simplicity, but for its black-letter quality and for its similarity to an advisory opinion. Technically, Justice Breyer makes no promises to the president. He simply says that, "Nothing prevents the President from returning to Congress to seek the authority he believes necessary." But one need not read very much into the opinion to find an expectation that all that the president needs to do to win the Court's approval is to win Congress's approval first. In other words, the important thing is for the president and Congress to work through this problem together; whatever specific provisions they agree on will be agreeable to the Court. Read in this way, Justice Breyer's opinion seems predicated on a simplified view of the constitutional problem—one that focuses only on its interbranch dimension and ignores the constraints placed on the national government by the Bill of Rights and the institution of federalism.

What interests me about Justice Jackson's test and its current popularity is the opportunity those subjects present for thinking about the activity of judging and how the conditions of that activity (and our notions of it) may have changed in the past half century. Many things touching on the judicial role have changed in that time. On the one hand, at least in courts without control over their dockets, we have seen an explosion of litigation that has led to a certain "bureaucratization of justice," as Judge Wade McCree once called it.[11] Since 1981, when Judge McCree delivered that judgment, the explosion has continued. On the other hand, we also have seen the caseload of the Supreme Court of the United States fall dramatically during the same period,[12] which undoubtedly has had an effect on the Court's case-handling and opinion-writing techniques. In 1981, of course, another great change in legal practice was only beginning to be felt. That was the emergence of electronic databases as the primary tool of legal research—a development that has transformed the way in which lawyers are trained to conceptualize and accomplish legal research projects.[13] Moreover, while the volume of new case law produced each year seemed astronomical in 1981, it was nothing then compared to what it is today. That, too, has had a profound effect on the way legal opinions are researched and written. More subtle, perhaps, are changes in the method of judicial selection and confirmation and differences in the backgrounds of the justices. In 1952, for example, the Court included a number of former cabinet officers, senators, and congressmen, and all had been selected in a manner far different from that which exists today. Finally, and most important, is our current preoccupation with theories of interpretation and adjudication. If nothing else, three-quarters of a century of concern about judicial activism has led to an increased self-consciousness and circumspection on the part of judges.[14] We all believe in judicial restraint now, but what, precisely, do we believe in, and what are the consequences of that belief for our public life?

Justice Jackson and Justice Frankfurter were perceived in their time as conservatives with respect to the nature of the judicial role. Yet they seem freewheeling and wide-eyed radicals in some respects today. In a memorial tribute to Justice Jackson, Justice Frankfurter acknowledged both the objective reality of law and its dependence on individual minds.

> The duty of Justices is not to express their personal will and wisdom. Their undertaking is to try to triumph over the bent of their own preferences and to transcend, through habituated exercise of the

> imagination, the limits of their direct experience. But since the designed or the inevitable ambiguity of language makes the pronouncement of law not a mechanical but a judgmatical process, ascertainment of what the Constitution and the laws of the United States require partly depends on the personalities of the Bench.[15]

In truth, Justices Frankfurter and Jackson approached their cases in a highly individualistic and engaged way, bringing their own intellectual and life experiences to bear on the issues they faced in a way that seems almost embarrassing by today's standards—or at least contrary to prevailing styles of constitutional interpretation. But it is precisely in that individualistic approach, undertaken with understanding, modesty, and restraint, that the basis for the moral and intellectual excellence of their work is to be found.

These observations bring me to the primary focus of this essay, which is to consider the context and qualities of Justice Jackson's opinion in *Youngstown* and to compare that opinion with Justice O'Connor's plurality opinion in *Hamdi*. In a penultimate section, I will suggest some questions that someone with Justice Jackson's approach might raise with respect to *Hamdi*. I will then close by offering some modest observations about the state of our republican government.

YOUNGSTOWN

In *Youngstown*, the Supreme Court held that the president lacked the power to seize the steel mills. That the Court would reach that result did not seem a foregone conclusion in 1952. The decisions in *Curtiss-Wright Export Corp.*[16] and *Waterman Steamship*[17] provided substantial support for a broad view of the president's authority, both as commander in chief and as the nation's voice in foreign affairs; the Court and the country had both acquiesced in President Roosevelt's assertions of broad presidential power during the economic crisis of the 1930s and in the Second World War;[18] the signs of the times favored a somewhat modest view of judicial power after the perceived excesses of the "old Court" in reviewing the work of the political branches;[19] and, not insignificantly (from the standpoint of legal realists), all of the sitting justices in 1952 had been appointed by either President Roosevelt or President Truman. Indeed, several had performed valuable service in advancing President Roosevelt's ambitious view of presidential power during the Great Depression and in the war against fascism. Among other things, Justice Jackson, as attorney general, had formulated the legal theory to support the president's assertion of broad authority with respect to the Lend-Lease program.[20] Finally, as Justice Frankfurter noted, "It is not a pleasant judicial duty to find that the President has exceeded his powers and still less so when his purposes were dictated by concern for the Nation's well being, in the assured conviction that he acted to avert danger."[21]

The *Youngstown* Court was not unanimous in reaching the result it did, nor was the majority able to speak with one voice. The vote was six to three. Justice Black delivered the opinion of the Court, which consisted of himself and Justices Frankfurter, Jackson, Burton, and Douglas, with Justice Clark concurring in the judgment. Chief Justice Vinson dissented in an opinion joined by Justices Reed and Minton. But the box score tells little about the respective views of the justices, particularly those in the majority.

Justice Black, as the senior justice in the majority, assigned the majority opinion to himself, but in the end, every justice who joined his opinion also wrote separately. For Justice Black, the president's action constituted "lawmaking," which Article I of the U.S. Constitution assigns to Congress, not the president: "The President's order does not direct that a congressional policy be executed in a manner prescribed by Congress—it directs that a presidential policy be executed in a manner prescribed by the President."[22] Justice Frankfurter's main concurrence eschewed any general delimiting of the president's powers as inappropriate to the judicial function, but it rejected the president's position on the ground that Congress had withheld the very authority the president claimed.[23] The variety of points of view within the majority was not lost on the dissent. The Chief Justice acidly observed:

> The diversity of views expressed in the six opinions of the majority, the lack of reference to authoritative precedent, the repeated reliance upon prior dissenting opinions, the complete disregard of the uncontroverted facts showing the gravity of the emergency, and the temporary nature of the taking all serve to demonstrate how far afield one must go to affirm the order of the District Court.[24]

It is worthwhile to focus on Justice Jackson's opinion in *Youngstown* and on the singularity of the voice of that opinion. This, of course, is an opinion in the grand style. It points to prior authorities, but it is not weighed down by them. To use a biblical formulation, the opinion speaks with its own authority.[25] Moreover, Justice Jackson's voice is both dispassionate and personally engaged; theoretically sophisticated and profoundly distrustful of theory; the voice of a citizen and statesman as much as a judge; the voice of a man of action as well as an intellectual. The richness, complexity, and engagement of this voice are made obvious from the first words of the opinion.

> That comprehensive and undefined presidential powers hold both practical advantages and grave dangers for the country will impress anyone who has served as legal adviser to a President in time of transition and public anxiety. While an interval of detached reflection may temper teachings of that experience, they probably are a more realistic influence on my views than the conventional materials of judicial decision which seem unduly to accentuate doctrine and legal fiction. . . .
>
> A judge, like an executive adviser, may be surprised at the poverty of really useful and unambiguous authority applicable to concrete problems of executive power as they actually present themselves. Just what our forefathers did envision, or would have envisioned had they foreseen modern conditions, must be divined from materials almost as enigmatic as the dreams Joseph was called upon to interpret for Pharaoh. . . . And court decisions are indecisive because of the judicial practice of dealing with the largest questions in the most narrow way.
>
> The actual art of governing under our Constitution does not and cannot conform to judicial definitions of the power of any of its branches based on isolated clauses or even single Articles torn from context. While the Constitution diffuses power the better to secure liberty, it also contemplates that practice will integrate the dispersed powers into a workable government. . . . Presidential powers are not fixed but fluctuate, depending upon their disjunction or conjunction with those of Congress.[26]

It is then that Justice Jackson states his famous test. Significantly, as I mentioned earlier, he sees the test as helpful but "over-simplified" and meant only as a "begin[ning]."[27] At all events, neither of the test's first two groupings is met; this is not a case in which Congress and the president have acted in concert, nor has Congress left open the field. If the president has the power he claims, it must be because he can meet "the severe tests under the third grouping," that is, "where it can be supported only by any remainder of executive power after subtraction of such powers as Congress may have over the subject."[28] Thus, as Justice Jackson noted, "we can sustain the President only by holding that seizure of such strike-bound industries is within his domain and beyond control by Congress."[29]

But that was not possible on any of the four grounds urged by the government. First, Justice Jackson rejected the view that the "vesting clause" of Article II of the Constitution, which grants "[t]he executive Power" of the national government to the president, constituted by its own operation an exclusive "grant in bulk of all conceivable executive power." The account of prerogative powers contained in the Declaration of Independence led him "to doubt that [the framers] were creating their new Executive in [the] image [of George III]."[30] Second, Justice Jackson found the government's reliance on the commander-in-chief clause equally unavailing. That clause cannot provide "support for any Presidential action, internal or external, involving use of force, [on the theory] that it vests power to do anything, anywhere, that can be done with an army or navy."[31] Indeed, the Constitution "certainly lays upon Congress primary responsibility for supplying the Armed Forces," as well as for "the raising of revenues and their appropriation."[32] Most important, Justice Jackson stated, "No penance would ever expiate the sin against free government of holding that a President can escape control of executive powers by law through assuming his military role."[33] Third, Justice Jackson found no support for the government's position in the general constitutional direction that the president "shall take Care that the Laws be faithfully executed." That is to be matched against the due process clause: "One gives a governmental authority that reaches so far as there is law, the other gives a private right that authority shall go no farther."[34] Finally, Justice Jackson rejected the contention that the seizure of the steel mills could be supported "upon nebulous, inherent powers never expressly granted but said to have accrued to the office from the customs and claims of preceding administrations."[35] Justice Jackson acknowledged that the "claim of inherent and unrestricted presidential powers has long been a persuasive dialectical weapon in political controversy"[36] but not a compelling basis for answering a constitutional question.

Two important points need to be made here. First, Justice Jackson's personal engagement with these issues is made obvious from the first sentence of his opinion, in which he alludes to his service as presidential advisor in a time of crisis.[37] The extent of that engagement is further demonstrated by the following statement:

> While it is not surprising that counsel should grasp support from such unadjudicated claims of power [historical instances in which broad powers were claimed but not passed upon by the courts], a judge cannot accept self-serving press statements of the attorney for one of the interested parties as authority in answering a constitutional question, even if the advocate was himself.[38]

Although Justice Jackson's opinion does not explain what he means by the reference to "the advocate" being "himself," the meaning of that statement is clear from the briefs and oral argument.

Of course, the government made extravagant arguments with respect to the sweep of executive power at every stage of *Youngstown,* as John W. Davis pointed out to great effect in his brief for the steel industry.[39] Thus, Davis quoted the following colloquy between the trial judge and government counsel:

> The Court: So you contend the Executive has unlimited power in time of emergency?
> Mr. Baldridge: He has the power to take such action as is necessary to meet the emergency.
> The Court: If the emergency is great, it is unlimited, is it?
> Mr. Baldridge: I suppose if you carry it to its logical conclusion, that is true. But I do want to point out that there are two limitations on the Executive power. One is the ballot box and the other is impeachment.
> The Court: Then, as I understand it, you claim that in time of emergency the Executive has this great power.
> Mr. Baldridge: That is correct.
> The Court: And that the Executive determines the emergencies and the Courts cannot even review whether it is an emergency.
> Mr. Baldridge: That is correct.
> The Court: So, when the sovereign people adopted the Constitution, it enumerated the powers set up in the Constitution but limited the powers of the Congress and limited the powers of the Judiciary, but it did not limit the powers of the Executive. Is that what you say?
> Mr. Baldridge: That is the way we read Article II of the Constitution. . . . It is our position that the President is accountable only

> to the country, and that the decisions of the President are conclusive.[40]

To justify these points in the Supreme Court, the government found itself relying on historical practice, the "unadjudicated claims of power" to which Justice Jackson referred, as well as case law. In its brief, the government recited twelve instances in which President Roosevelt, without congressional authorization, had issued executive orders "taking possession of various companies when it appeared that a work stoppage would seriously impede operations."[41]

The government's brief states, "The first seizure occurred as much as six months prior to Pearl Harbor, and a total of three plants were seized before our entry into the War."[42] Significantly, the government explained, "This first seizure, of the North American Aviation Plant, was justified by then Attorney General Jackson as an act within the 'duty constitutionally and inherently rested upon the President to exert his civil and military, as well as his moral, authority to keep the defense efforts of the United States a going concern.'"[43] Solicitor General Perlman continued in the same vein at oral argument. Grounding his argument on historical examples,[44] the solicitor general eventually reached the Roosevelt administration.

> The first seizure made by President Franklin D. Roosevelt, during his Administration, was that of the plants of the North American Aviation Company. . . . There was no war at the time and there was no statutory authority for that seizure. But the President, in the light of the existence of threats to the nation, . . . did seize those plants and exercised the authority that was vested in him without any specific statutory authorization, and on the powers vested in him by the Constitution, under all of the sections that I have read, and under his duty, the duty that had been vested in him time and again by Congress to carry out the previous Acts of Congress and the various Acts that Congress had passed.[45]

This argument provoked a sharp response from Justice Jackson: "Are you not taking a good deal for granted when you take that as a precedent here? Looking back at the matter, if I remember rightly, North American was under direct contract with the United States, and they were subject to control, to that extent, by the United States."[46] The solicitor general indicated that he thought that was correct, which led Justice Jackson to observe: "The Government owned the materials, the goods, and had control of the plants, and the whole thing, in a measure, was in the hands of the Government. There is no Government property here."[47] Again, the solicitor general conceded the point.

Justice Jackson continued: "I do not believe that unless you amend those points you can make that stand as a precedent for this. I looked it up because I wondered how much of this was laid at my door." The solicitor general responded, "Your Honor, we lay a lot of it at your door." "Perhaps rightly," Justice Jackson acknowledged. After a brief interruption by the solicitor general, however, Justice Jackson continued by stating: "I claimed everything, of course, like every other Attorney General does. It was a custom that did not leave the Department of Justice when I did."[48] The solicitor general then quoted at length from Justice Jackson's statement as attorney general, but Justice Jackson objected that the quotation had been truncated, leaving out an observation he deemed important, namely, that the "situation of North American plants more nearly resembles insurrection."[49] The solicitor general responded:

> That is right, Your Honor, but the part we have reproduced in our brief we think correctly explains the Constitutional powers of the President in the absence of any statutory provisions, and what Your Honor said with respect to the seizure of North American Aviation by the President more clearly states the Constitutional power vested in him. I think you will find that to be so, Your Honor.[50]

In a sense, Justice Jackson responded to this point in his opinion, when he stated, "Nothing in my experience convinces me that such risks [of placing in the hands of the executive the sole responsibility for deciding whether to invoke emergency powers] are warranted by any real necessity, although such powers would, of course, be an executive convenience."[51] But the chief justice returned to the issue in his dissent: "President Roosevelt ordered the seizure of the plant 'pursuant to the powers vested in (him) by the Constitution and laws of the United States, as President of the United States of America and Commander in Chief of the Army and Navy of the United States.' The Attorney General (Jackson) vigorously proclaimed that the President had the moral duty to keep this Nation's defense effort a 'going concern.' His ringing moral justification was coupled with a legal justification equally well stated."[52]

The foregoing discussion demonstrates the depth of Justice Jackson's personal engagement with these issues. The second central point I want to make is that it would be difficult to overstate the importance that Justice Jackson attributes to the problem presented in this case. The theory of American government depends on a balance between Congress and the president, and the potential consequences for liberty could be catastrophic if that balance were significantly upset.[53] But the conditions of modern society and the amount of practical power that the president has make it difficult for Congress to hold its own, even if it has the will to do so and even if the Court has the will, as here, to lend Congress its support when necessary.[54] This problem is vexing in itself, but all the more so if the president has the inherent power to declare and administer an "emergency." Moreover, neither the existence of will on the part of Congress nor the existence of will on the part of the Court is something to be taken for granted.

Justice Jackson had no doubt about either the purposes of the founders or their wisdom. The nation and the states may have been plagued by the absence of an effective executive under the Articles of Confederation and the first wave of state constitutions, and the Constitutional Convention of 1787 may well have seen the weakness of the executive as a central problem to be solved. But the founders certainly did not intend to replicate the British monarchy when they designed the presidential office. As Justice Jackson noted, none of the government's arguments to the contrary is persuasive. Even the prosecution of war requires the participation of both political branches: The president "has no monopoly of 'war powers,' whatever they are. While Congress cannot deprive the President of the command of the army and navy, only Congress can provide him an army or navy to command."[55] Moreover, the president's claim to broad, unchecked "emergency powers" is unsupported by the express language of the Constitution, which provides for only one such "emergency power"—the suspension of habeas corpus—which appears in Article I, not Article II.[56] Justice Jackson maintained that the founders' failure to provide for other emergency powers was not accidental: "They knew what emergencies were, knew the pressures they engender for authoritative action, knew, too, how they afford a ready pretext for usurpation. We may also suspect that they suspected that emergency powers would tend to kindle emergencies."[57]

Of course, some other constitutions do provide for emergency powers, and Justice Jackson thought the experiences of countries under such constitutions might be instructive.[58] It was no coincidence that the justice, so lately occupied by Nuremberg, should begin with Germany; the Weimar Constitution empowered the president, acting unilaterally and without legislative approval, "to suspend any or all individual rights if public safety and order were seriously disturbed or endangered."[59] Justice Jackson noted that "This proved a temptation to every government, whatever its shade of opinion, and in 13 years suspension of rights was invoked on more than 250 occasions." The last of these occasions was when "Hitler persuaded President Von Hindenburg to suspend all such rights, and they were never restored."[60] Other countries, where the constitution required parliamentary approval of emergency measures, had not fared so poorly. According to Justice Jackson, then-recent experience might be "inconclusive as to the wisdom of lodging emergency powers somewhere in a modern government," but it suggested that "emergency powers are consistent with free government only when their control is lodged elsewhere than in the Executive who exercises them."[61]

The opinion ends on a somber note.

> I cannot be brought to believe that this country will suffer if the Court refuses further to aggrandize the presidential office, already so potent and so relatively immune from judicial review, at the expense of Congress.
>
> But I have no illusion that any decision by this Court can keep power in the hands of Congress if it is not wise and timely in meeting its problems. . . . If not good law, there was worldly wisdom attributed to Napoleon that "The tools belong to the man who can use them." We may say that power to legislate for emergencies belongs in the hands of Congress, but only Congress itself can prevent power from slipping through its fingers.
>
> The executive action we have here originates in the individual will of the President and represents an exercise of authority without law. . . . With all its defects, delays, and inconveniences, men have discovered no technique for long preserving free government except that the Executive be under the law, and that the law be made by parliamentary deliberations.
>
> Such institutions may be destined to pass away. But it is the duty of the Court to be last, not first, to give them up.[62]

In other words, the Court has done what it can in this case, but the question remains whether that is enough. After all, the Court has said that the power belongs to Congress, but will Congress have the will or the fortitude to insist on it? If it has the will and the fortitude, will it have the cunning and the perseverance to be successful? It is not easy to challenge the president's authority, particularly in time of war or national emergency, when much is at stake, the president has the best interests of the country at heart, and the president presumptively has superior access to important information.

Indeed, would the Court be willing to stand up to the president on another occasion? As Justices Clark and Frankfurter both observed, that is not an assignment to volunteer for. Justice Jackson made a similar point in *The Supreme Court in the American System of Government,* when he noted that the great distinguishing feature of our system of government, as opposed to "those governments abroad which have been subverted by dictatorship," is that the Supreme Court "can interpose judicial authority between political forces and those whose liberty they would override." At the same time, however, he emphasized that our judiciary also has certain "jurisdictional, procedural, and political shortcomings," which limit its capacity and its will to use that authority and which therefore "counsel against leaving the protection of liberty wholly to the judiciary, while heedlessly allowing the elected branches to be constituted without regard to their members' attitudes towards liberty."[63]

The Court's consciousness of its own infirmities, Justice Jackson suggested, "may explain its apparent yielding to expediency, especially during war time."[64] Certainly Justice Jackson had seen that "yielding to expediency" in *Korematsu v. United States,*[65] in which the Court upheld the criminal conviction of a Japanese American who had failed to comply with a military order requiring all persons of Japanese descent to leave their home districts. Justice Jackson was one of three dissenters. In his dissent, Justice Jackson observed that the Court's willingness to endorse this scheme was "a far more subtle blow to liberty" than the scheme itself.[66] Thus, he wrote:

> The very essence of the military job is to marshal physical force, to remove every obstacle to its effectiveness, to give it every strategic advantage. Defense measures will not, and often should not, be held within the limits that bind civil authority in peace. No court can require such a commander in such circumstances to act as a reasonable man; he may be unreasonably cautious and exacting. Perhaps he

> should be. But a commander in temporarily focusing the life of a community on defense is carrying out a military program; he is not making law in the sense the courts know the term. . . .
>
> But if we cannot confine military expedients by the Constitution, neither would I distort the Constitution to approve all that the military may deem expedient. This is what the Court appears to be doing, whether consciously or not. I cannot say, from any evidence before me, that the orders of General DeWitt were not reasonably expedient military precautions, nor could I say that they were. But even if they were permissible military procedures, I deny that it follows that they are constitutional. If, as the Court holds, it does follow, then we may as well say that any military order will be constitutional and have done with it.
>
> The limitations under which courts always will labor in examining the necessity for a military order are illustrated by this case. How does the Court know that these orders have a reasonable basis in necessity? No evidence whatever on that subject has been taken by this or any other court. . . . So the Court, having no real evidence before it, has no choice but to accept General DeWitt's own unsworn, self-serving statement, untested by any cross-examination, that what he did was reasonable. . . .
>
> [O]nce a judicial opinion rationalizes such an order to show that it conforms to the Constitution, or rather rationalizes the Constitution to show that the Constitution sanctions such an order, the Court for all time has validated the principle. . . . Every repetition imbeds that principle more deeply in our law and thinking and expands it to new purposes. . . . A military commander may overstep the bounds of constitutionality, and it is an incident. But if we review and approve, that passing incident becomes the doctrine of the Constitution. There it has a generative power of its own, and all that it creates will be in its own image.[67]

Justice Jackson was clear that "the existence of a military power resting on force so vagrant, so centralized, so necessarily heedless of the individual is an inherent threat to liberty." On the other hand, the Court's performance in *Korematsu* caused Justice Jackson to conclude that people should not be led "to rely on this Court for a review that seems to me wholly delusive."[68] Thus, he turned again to the responsibility of the people in a democratic society: "If the people ever let command of the war power fall into irresponsible and unscrupulous hands, the courts wield no power equal to its restraint."[69] While Justice Jackson undoubtedly contemplated a larger role for the courts in *Youngstown* than he had in *Korematsu,* the basic point remained the same.

HAMDI

Fifty-two years later, the Court was again presented with a case involving extravagant claims about the scope of the president's powers as commander in chief and the nation's organ in the field of foreign affairs.[70] In *Hamdi v. Rumsfeld,*[71] the Court was asked to decide whether the president was constitutionally and legally authorized to detain a U.S. citizen within the United States based solely on the president's determination that the citizen was an "enemy combatant." Significantly, the term *enemy combatant* had no recognized definition, but the Court found no need to consider the due process implications of that fact.[72] In any event, the Court split dramatically on the issues it did address, and the distribution of votes and rationales is difficult to summarize in short compass. Justice O'Connor wrote a plurality opinion, in which she, the chief justice, Justice Kennedy, and Justice Breyer took the view that Congress, by passing the Force Act (which it did within days after the attacks of September 11, 2001), impliedly authorized the president to seize and detain "enemy combatants." But they also determined that U.S. citizens so seized and thereafter held within the United States were entitled, under the due process clause, to a "meaningful opportunity to contest the factual basis for that detention before a neutral decision maker."[73]

When the *Hamdi* decision was announced, Justice O'Connor's opinion was justly praised for its rejection of the administration's most extravagant position, that is, that the president's classification of a U.S. citizen as an "enemy combatant" was conclusive, not subject to any further review, and a proper basis for indefinite detention. According to Justice O'Connor, a citizen so held was constitutionally entitled to an independent review of that determination. But that required answering the next question, namely, what kind of review was required: "Even in cases in which the detention of enemy combatants is legally authorized, there remains the question of what process is constitutionally due to a citizen who disputes his enemy-combatant status."[74]

Justice O'Connor first rejected the government's argument that the "undisputed" fact of Hamdi's capture in a combat zone was, by itself, a sufficient legal basis for his classification as an "enemy combatant." In her view, the fact of his apprehension in a combat area could not obviate the need for further factual inquiry. Justice O'Connor dispatched the idea that there was any basis for saying that Hamdi, who had not been allowed access to counsel until after the petition for review in the Supreme Court had been filed on his behalf, and had been denied any opportunity whatsoever to tell his side of the story, had made any "concessions."[75] Justice O'Connor also rejected the government's second argument, that is, that "the extraordinary constitutional interests at stake" (by which she meant those of the government, not the individual) required the courts to "assume the accuracy of the Government's articulated basis for Hamdi's detention, as set forth in the Mobbs Declaration, and assess only whether that articulated basis was a legitimate one."[76] But Justice O'Connor likewise rejected the district court's "apparent belief" that "the appropriate process would approach . . . that [which] accompanies a criminal trial."[77] She observed:

> Both of these positions highlight legitimate concerns. And both emphasize the tension that often exists between the autonomy that the Government asserts is necessary in order to pursue effectively a particular goal and the process that a citizen contends he is due before he is deprived of a constitutional right. The ordering mechanism that we use for balancing such serious competing interests, and for determining the procedures that are necessary to ensure that a citizen is not "deprived of life, liberty, or property, without due process of law," . . . is the test that we articulated in *Mathews v. Eldridge,* 424 U.S. 319 (1976). . . . *Mathews* [which involved eligibility for social security benefits] dictates that the process due in any given instance is determined by weighing "the private interest that will be affected by the official action" against the Government's asserted interest, "including the function involved" and the burdens the Government would face in providing greater process. . . . The *Mathews* calculus then contemplates a judicious balancing of these concerns, through an analysis of "the risk of an erroneous deprivation" of the private interest if the process were reduced and the "probable value, if any, of additional or substitute procedural safeguards."[78]

Justice O'Connor then purported to apply the *Mathews* test to Hamdi's case to determine what process is due in the circumstances. There is much uplifting language here and elsewhere in Justice O'Connor's opinion: "Whatever power the United States Constitution envisions for the

Executive in its exchanges with other nations or with enemy organizations in times of conflict, it most assuredly envisions a role for all three branches when individual liberties are at stake."[79] Justice O'Connor acknowledged both the importance of the individual's interest in liberty and the government's interest in protecting the nation.

> Striking the proper constitutional balance here is of great importance to the Nation during this period of ongoing combat. But it is equally vital that our calculus not give short shrift to the values that this country holds dear or to the privilege that is American citizenship. It is during our most challenging and uncertain moments that our Nation's commitment to due process is most severely tested; and it is in those times that we must preserve our commitment at home to the principles for which we fight abroad.[80]

Justice O'Connor then rejected both the procedural framework proposed by the government and "the process apparently envisioned by the District Court below."[81] According to Justice O'Connor, the risk of erroneous deprivation of liberty is too high under the government's proposal, and the additional safeguards suggested by the district court are unwarranted "in light of their limited 'probable value' and the burdens they may impose on the military in such cases."[82] Despite this language, there is little clarification of the real interests at stake, still less so of the weights that might reasonably be assigned to those interests or of the actual effects that might be expected to follow from the granting or withholding of any particular procedural protections. The Court did not emphasize the point, but a balancing test that pits the preservation of the nation against the liberty of one individual seems heavily weighted on one side of the scales.

Justice O'Connor focused on considerations she deemed less global. She was moved, for example, by the government's interest in autonomy, which she thought particularly important in this context. But the government (meaning the executive branch) is normally concerned about autonomy, if, by that, one means the government's interest in doing what it chooses to do, in accordance with its own view of the national interest, with minimal transparency and with as little interference as possible from Congress, the courts, and the public. More to the point, as Justice O'Connor recognized, are "the weighty and sensitive governmental interests in ensuring that those who have in fact fought with the enemy during a war do not return to battle against the United States."[83] In addition, the government has practical concerns about military officers being "unnecessarily and dangerously distracted by litigation half a world away" and with the conduct of discovery that would both "intrude on the sensitive secrets of national defense and result in the futile search for evidence buried under the rubble of war."[84] The government's interests also may include an interest in avoiding cumbersome and inefficient procedures in a large number of routine cases; but that consideration is not invoked here, and it probably could not be invoked, given the small class of persons to whom the rule would apply.

The individual's interest is straightforward: he would prefer not to be classified as an "enemy combatant" and possibly deprived of liberty for the rest of his life. Even assuming that some balancing of interests is appropriate or possible, however, it is far from self-evident as to how such incommensurable goods are to be balanced, as a practical matter, and Justice O'Connor's opinion sheds very little light on that issue. To be sure, the competing interests are nominally identified, but what weights they are to be given and how they are to be balanced remain to be seen. Nothing is quantified, even in the crudest terms, and the "judicious balancing of these concerns, through an analysis of 'the risk of an erroneous deprivation' of the private interest if the process were reduced and the 'probable value, if any, of additional or substitute safeguards,'" occurs, if at all, in only the most abstract and generalized sense.

Purporting to apply *Mathews,* but actually speaking only in the most conclusory terms, Justice O'Connor concluded that a citizen challenging his classification as an "enemy combatant" must be given notice of the factual basis for his classification and "a fair opportunity to rebut the Government's factual assertions before a neutral decisionmaker."[85] Similarly, due process requires that "the right to notice and an opportunity to be heard 'must be granted at a meaningful time and in a meaningful manner.'"[86] Justice O'Connor then proceeded to articulate the various ways in which customary procedures might "be tailored to alleviate their uncommon potential to burden the Executive at a time of ongoing military conflict."[87] Beyond her general statements about distracting military officers from their duties, possibly endangering sensitive information, and possibly having to search for evidence "under the rubble of war," Justice O'Connor's opinion did not attempt to demonstrate why this situation presented an "uncommon potential to burden the Executive." Nor did she attempt to evaluate the possible effects of her "tailoring" on the integrity and reliability of the fact-finding process, let alone on the rights of the accused. Justice O'Connor wrote:

> Hearsay, for example, may need to be accepted as the most reliable available evidence from the Government in such a proceeding. Likewise, the Constitution would not be offended by a presumption in favor of the Government's evidence, so long as that presumption remained a rebuttable one and fair opportunity for rebuttal were provided. Thus, once the Government puts forth credible evidence that the habeas petitioner meets the enemy-combatant criteria, the onus could shift to the petitioner to rebut that evidence with more persuasive evidence that he falls outside the criteria. . . . In the words of *Mathews,* process of this sort would sufficiently address the "risk of an erroneous deprivation" of a detainee's liberty interest while eliminating certain procedures that have questionable additional value in light of the burden on the Government.[88]

Justice O'Connor's claim is that the threats to military operations posed by a basic system of independent review are not so weighty as to trump a citizen's core rights to challenge meaningfully the government's case and to be heard by an impartial adjudicator.[89] In reality, however, those core rights are so cabined and redefined by the opinion as to be almost unrecognizable. Nonetheless, Justice O'Connor also expressly rejected the government's suggestion that judicial review should not deal with individual cases but should be limited to a review of the overall classification system. She rejected the idea that the government's classification of someone as an "enemy combatant" should be upheld if there is only "some evidence" to support it.[90] On the other hand, if the government were to provide an appropriate opportunity for a person designated as an "enemy combatant" to be heard by an "appropriately authorized and properly constituted military tribunal," the civilian courts presumably could apply a less rigorous standard of review than would be the case if the civilian courts were essentially considering the issues for the first time.[91] Justice O'Connor also suggested that "a habeas court in a case such as this might accept affidavit evidence like that contained in the Mobbs Declaration, so long as it also permits the alleged enemy combatant to present his own factual case to rebut the Government's in return."[92]

Finally, Justice O'Connor claimed to address the question whether an accused "enemy combatant" facing the prospect of indefinite detention has the right to consult an attorney, whether appointed or retained. Hamdi had been held incommunicado, without access to counsel, family, or anyone else, from the time he was turned over to the U.S. military by the Afghan Northern Alliance sometime in fall 2001 until December 2003, shortly before the Court granted certiorari.[93] Although a proceeding was brought on Hamdi's behalf, he was allowed no contact with those who brought the proceeding, and he had no input whatever into the conduct of that proceeding. Indeed, he was first allowed access to counsel (in a monitored meeting) only after a petition for certiorari had been filed on his behalf in the Supreme Court. When the government permitted Hamdi to have access to counsel, it did so as a matter of grace, accompanied by a firm assertion that Hamdi was not so entitled. The government intended to moot the issue in the Supreme Court, and the ploy worked. Justice O'Connor noted: "He unquestionably has the right to access to counsel in connection with the proceedings on remand. No further consideration of this issue is necessary at this stage of the case."[94] In other words, the government's limited concession relieved the Court of any need to decide whether Hamdi was entitled to consult counsel. The question was therefore left open as to whether the demands of military convenience—in addition to justifying the use of hearsay and the reversal of the burden of proof—might justify the withholding of legal advice to someone who faced the possibility of life imprisonment.

JACKSON AND O'CONNOR: AN IMAGINED INTERROGATION

Justice O'Connor's pronouncement that Hamdi was entitled to due process in connection with his designation as an "enemy combatant," together with her description of what procedures were due in the circumstances of the case, constitute the heart of her opinion. In this way, the Court declared what was to be done on remand in this case and what the executive and judicial branches presumably are to do in future cases. Justice O'Connor's resolution of these issues is to be contrasted with Justice Jackson's opinion in *Youngstown*. In both instances, we have opinions in constitutional cases that raise fundamental questions about executive power, the separation of powers, and individual rights. But the opinions themselves are entirely different. What Justice Jackson had to say in *Youngstown* was personal, practical, and transparent. It built on existing law but transformed that law as well.[95] The same cannot be said of Justice O'Connor's opinion in *Hamdi.* That opinion does not convey the same sense of personal engagement. Nor does it seem practical or transparent in the same way that Justice Jackson's opinion did. Indeed, the reader of Justice O'Connor's opinion is left with profound uncertainty as to what it means. In fairness, of course, the two opinions served different purposes: Justice O'Connor aspired to speak for a majority and succeeded in speaking for a plurality, but Justice Jackson spoke only for himself.

In any event, one can only begin to imagine how someone with Justice Jackson's approach to constitutional adjudication would respond to the *Hamdi* opinion. For example, Justice O'Connor goes to great lengths to demonstrate that the due process clause applies to persons the government wishes to classify as "enemy combatants," but she then recognizes that the government's need for "autonomy" and relief from "the burdens [that procedural requirements] may impose on the military in such cases" requires that the procedures be specially tailored to these circumstances. When the tailor has finished her work, the overcoat has become a fig leaf, but the fig leaf still answers to the name of an overcoat. What is the point of that? Is that style of constitutional decision making consistent with the purpose of constitutional law in a democratic society?

One may well imagine Justice Jackson, the old trial lawyer from Jamestown, New York, asking at the outset whether the government might not be obliged to define the term *enemy combatant.* As Justice O'Connor acknowledged, there is "a dispute" about the meaning of the term: it has no generally recognized meaning under either domestic law or the law of war (which traditionally has distinguished between "lawful combatants" and "unlawful combatants"), and the government seems to have chosen the term to avoid previous nomenclature and its legal implications.[96] But how can we tell whether someone meets the qualifications for treatment as an enemy combatant when the government declines to commit itself to a definition of general applicability?

The apparently easy application of the "what process is due" standard from *Mathews v. Eldridge* masks what really is at stake here: the possibility that a U.S. citizen may be imprisoned for life as a result of a military determination, based on an administrative dossier of possibly limited reliability, and susceptible to only limited judicial review.[97] But to be "meaningful," that analysis itself requires a rigorous policy analysis, starting from the ground up with hard facts. Applying it to generalities conveys an appearance of rigor where none in fact exists. Measuring Justice O'Connor's opinion by another standard from administrative law, we might wonder what findings she has actually made about relative burdens and benefits and, most important, where she would point us in aid of demonstrating a "rational connection between the facts found and the choice made."[98] Perhaps the problem is not that the use of *Mathews* trivializes what is at stake here, as Justice Thomas suggested in his dissent,[99] but that the determination of someone's status as an enemy combatant necessarily requires an application of the *Mathews* test more rigorous than the application it receives in Justice O'Connor's opinion.[100]

In the same vein, Justice Jackson undoubtedly would question whether Justice O'Connor had established that more traditional notions of due process necessarily would cast a substantial burden on the government, as opposed to a mere inconvenience. "It is fine," he might argue, "to talk about searching through rubble, losing control over secrets, and distracting the military from the war effort, but are those assertions not more poetry than reality? What is the evidence to support a real danger here? What is the evidence that shows the real costs here?" The old trial lawyer might also add that there is no reason to believe that Justice O'Connor's procedural "tailoring" is itself "tailored" to suit the problem. He might argue that the number of people we are talking about—U.S. citizens captured in a war zone and transported to the United States—will be very small in any case. How much burden could affording them a hearing be? How much of a burden could it be to have to prove their status according to traditional standards?[101]

The old trial lawyer might go on:

> Assuming you are right about the dangers and the costs, let's drill down a little and see how this system would work. The government can put in evidence like the Mobbs Declaration that the government submitted in *Hamdi*—which simply identifies the declarant as an employee of the Department of Defense who has reviewed records that show that Hamdi is an enemy combatant because he was fighting for the Taliban (then the legitimate government of Afghanistan), that Hamdi was apprehended on the battlefield by Afghan Northern Alliance forces, and that he was later turned over to the United States. Once someone in the government files a declaration like that, the burden shifts to Hamdi to refute that "evidence." But Hamdi is in the

brig in South Carolina, he is being held incommunicado, and he can consult with a lawyer only if the government grants him that privilege. In all likelihood, the evidence or witnesses he would need to refute those assertions would have been in Afghanistan at some point, but they could be anywhere in the world by the time he is afforded the opportunity to challenge the government's case.

It is bad enough that due process permits the government to brand someone as an "enemy combatant" with hearsay evidence, but requiring the individual to disprove the hearsay assertion—shifting the normal burden of proof—will make it impossible in most cases for anyone to prove his innocence. This scheme just cannot work in the way that our system of law and justice is supposed to work. This is a case like *Korematsu.* If this is the best that the Court can do, it might be better off not pretending to enforce the Constitution.

As a technical matter, I know that this is an administrative proceeding, not a criminal one. But this case is not about allocating public housing or social security benefits. If someone is branded an "enemy combatant," he can be held incommunicado for the duration of the conflict—which may be the rest of his life. When interests like that are at stake, our system of government has always insisted that the government prove its case, not that the individual carry the burden of showing the government made a mistake. The individual is presumed innocent, and the burden of proof rests with the government. That goes back to England, but also to Athens and Rome, and to the Hebrew Bible.[102]

How can we say so casually that "the Constitution would not be offended by a presumption in favor of the Government's evidence"? Cases are won and lost every day because of who has the benefit of a presumption or who must carry the burden of persuasion. We do not casually allocate those burdens and benefits. We do so only on policy grounds, after reflection; we consider such things as who has easiest access to the evidence. I don't see any analysis like that here. When someone has one hand tied behind his back, you don't tie the other one, too. How can someone held incommunicado muster a defense, especially if he does not even have the right to a lawyer?

There is another point, too. You talk about the government's interest. But the government's interest isn't just about winning. It's about seeing that justice is done. We've said before that the United States prevails whenever justice is done in its courts.[103] That's because our government, as Chief Justice Marshall said, is a government that is "emphatically, and truly, a government of the people."[104] A government of the people has as much interest in seeing that the innocent are not locked up as it has in seeing that the guilty are.

Like Justice O'Connor, Justice Jackson was capable of soaring phrases. But Justice Jackson's opinion in *Youngstown* is rooted and concrete; it attends to detail and acknowledges its consequences. It is ironic, of course, that Justice O'Connor and the other justices in *Hamdi* and *Hamdan* are so fond of quoting or following Justice Jackson's test in its decontextualized form, as if it were a touchstone or panacea. Such uses of the test are not consistent with Justice Jackson's view of the world or with his method of judging. They may skim the surface of his opinion, but their project was not his.

CONCLUSION

Justice Jackson recognized both the complexity and the moral quality of adjudication. Judging is not accounting, and it is not mechanical. It is creative in the best sense: human, personal, and engaged. For Justice Jackson, adjudication is nothing if not disciplined and restrained. But he also recognized that adjudication cannot suffer blinders; the materials with which judges necessarily work are subtle, unbounded, almost infinitely various, and often point in different directions. "There comes a point," Justice Frankfurter wrote, "where this Court should not be ignorant as judges of what we know as men."[105] Justice Jackson had no doubt that his view of adjudication demands much of judges. But just as he taught us to expect much of the courts, he taught us not to place all our hopes in them. Courts speak in terms of high principles, but courts, like other human beings and other human institutions, often temper their principles to suit the circumstances.

Like other human beings, judges sometimes betray their responsibilities and take advantage of the power that comes to them with their positions. Some will use that power to inflict their policy preferences on the rest of us; others will profit in more mercenary ways. Paradoxically, some judges will seek to preserve or aggrandize their power by not exercising it. Knowing that a different course might exact a cost to the judiciary itself, judges may be deaf to the voice of an unpopular group or cause. The balance is a delicate one; it requires that judges act with fortitude but also with understanding, modesty, and restraint. It requires wisdom, of course, and that, ultimately, is one reason why Justice Jackson counseled us not to place all our hopes in the courts. No nation can expect that the wisdom of its courts will supply the deficits of its other institutions, or of the people themselves.

It may be even less prudent to depend on the courts now than it was in Justice Jackson's time. Judges generally do not view their work in the same way that Justices Jackson and Frankfurter did. Among other things, critics of the courts often confuse the exercise of creativity, intellectual engagement, and moral responsibility with a lack of fidelity to the proper role of an unelected judiciary. Judges (or their clerks) often seek to deflect such criticism by writing in formulaic ways. To be sure, some questions can be answered in this way. The problem comes when even major constitutional decisions like *Hamdi* read as if constitutional adjudication were an essentially mechanical undertaking—a task to be accomplished by shuffling the beads of an abacus. Complexity is ignored, rather than confronted, and judges purport to decide difficult cases with tests and checklists that produce seemingly certain results. But that "certainty" is more apparent than real. It comes only after someone has somehow chosen the factors to be considered and assigned values to them, either explicitly or implicitly, in a particular case. The appropriateness of the mode of inquiry to the nature of the subject matter receives little attention. Ironically, the malleability of these tests may create an even greater temptation to idiosyncratic judgment than do more open-ended modes of inquiry, and it does so in a way that stifles frank discourse. Judges are more likely now than in Justice Jackson's day to think that their duty is to write in narrow ways about broad and transcendent issues, however they might think about them in the quiet of their studies.

As Justice Jackson reminds us, there are limits to what the Court can accomplish, even if the Court has the will to act. For example, the Court can ratify Congress's power, as it did in *Youngstown,* but it is up to Congress to find the wisdom and tenacity to use that power. Perhaps the Court can sometimes save Congress from the president, but the Court clearly cannot save Congress from itself. Nor can the Court save the people from themselves, and it is upon the people that liberty and democratic government ultimately depend.

We live in a time when great pressures have been put upon our system of government. Some of those pressures are external; others are the result of our own failings. Ironically, some are even the products of our success. To name just one, our very success in providing for a strong national defense has altered the alignment of the branches by further concentrating power in the executive. Of course, the president's power to commit the nation was not limited, even in Justice Jackson's day, to sending the navy halfway around the world and telling Congress to fund its return. But the implications of the president's power to commit the nation have increased dramatically in the past half century. With little or no congressional action, a president may commit the United States to military actions that set a practically irrevocable course and that may eventually exact costs that can be tallied up only in terms of thousands of lives, billions of dollars, and untold damage to the standing of the nation. This can be accomplished in consultation with a narrow group of advisors, and it may be done in a matter of hours, if not minutes. Moreover, even when actions cannot be so swiftly accomplished, the legitimate need for secrecy in matters of foreign and military affairs can easily be exploited to stifle debate on controversial policies until it is too late.

In the main, these are not problems for the Court. These are not problems that the Court can solve or likely will. But these problems are serious; they affect the very infrastructure of democracy. As Justice Jackson persistently reminded us, these problems are the people's problems. They are our problems, not the justices'. But we have become accustomed to tending our own fires. We have chosen to focus on our private lives and our private fortunes.[106] While there is reward in that, there is cost as well. In any event, it will not do, if Justice Jackson's republic is to be our own.

NOTES

1. 343 U.S. 579 (1952).
2. 343 U.S. at 635–38 (Jackson, J., concurring) (footnotes omitted).
3. 542 U.S. 507 (2004).
4. 126 S. Ct. 2749 (2006).
5. Authorization for the Use of Military Force, 115 Stat. 224 (2001).
6. See Youngstown, 343 U.S. at 635 n. 2, 637 n. 3, 638 n. 4 (Jackson, J., concurring).
7. Hamdan, a noncitizen, was "captured by militia forces and turned over to the U.S. military" (126 S. Ct. at 2759). He was detained at Guantanamo, without charges, for two and a half years, before being declared eligible for trial before a military tribunal established pursuant to presidential decree. He was eventually charged with one count of conspiracy "to commit . . . offenses triable by military commission" (id. at 2753). After the Supreme Court granted review, Congress enacted a statute that purported to divest the federal courts of jurisdiction over habeas corpus cases brought by Guantanamo detainees (id. at 2762–63). A majority of the Court found the statute inapplicable to Hamdan's case and rejected the

government's abstention arguments; they therefore proceeded to consider the merits of his contentions (id. at 2769). Congress subsequently enacted additional legislation to clarify its intent to withdraw jurisdiction over habeas petitions brought by prisoners held in Guantanamo, and that legislation was upheld by the District of Columbia Circuit. The Supreme Court initially denied review but subsequently reconsidered and granted the petition for certiorari. See Boumediene v. Bush, 476 F.3d 981 (D.C. Cir.), cert. denied, 127 S. Ct. 1478, cert. granted, 127 S. Ct. 3078 (2007).

8. Because the chief justice recused himself, the Court consisted of eight justices. With respect to most issues, Justice Stevens's opinion was joined by Justices Kennedy, Souter, Ginsburg, and Breyer. They "assume[d]" that the Force Act activated the president's war powers, including the authority to convene military commissions in appropriate circumstances, but they also held that "nothing in the text or legislative history of the [Force Act] even hint[s] that Congress intended to expand or alter the authorization set forth in Article 21 of the UCMJ" (126 S. Ct. at 2775). The Uniform Code of Military Justice authorizes the president to establish military commissions in accordance with the UCMJ and the law of war—requirements that the majority found not to have been met here (126 S. Ct. at 2789–91). All but Justice Kennedy also would have held that "conspiracy" was not an offense against the law of war and that the procedures established by the president did not satisfy Common Article 3 of the Geneva Conventions (id. at 2809). Justice Kennedy did not join in this part of the opinion, which he found unnecessary (id. at 2809). In his separate opinion, Justice Kennedy expressly framed the question in terms of Justice Jackson's three-part approach (id. at 2800).

9. Id. at 2799. Justice Breyer also noted: "Where, as here, no emergency prevents consultation with Congress, judicial insistence upon that consultation does not weaken our Nation's ability to deal with danger. To the contrary, that insistence strengthens the Nation's ability to determine—through democratic means—how best to do so. The Constitution places its faith in those democratic means. Our Court today simply does the same" (id. at 2799).

10. Three justices dissented. See id. at 2810 (Scalia, J., dissenting), 2823 (Thomas, J., dissenting), 2849 (Alito, J., dissenting). This is not the place to offer a sustained analysis of these opinions, but Justice Thomas's apparent characterization of adjudication as a "particular form of force against our enemies" is striking, to say the least. See id. at 2823.

11. Wade H. McCree Jr., "Bureaucratic Justice: An Early Warning," 129 *U. Pa. L. Rev.* 4 (1981).

12. In 1981, when Judge McCree was writing, the U.S. Supreme Court granted review in 210 cases annually; by 2005, the number had decreased to 78. See *Annual Report of the Director of the Administrative Office of the United States Courts* (Washington, DC: Government Printing Office, 1940).

13. Of course, many other changes in legal practice also have affected the litigation process in less immediate ways. See Barry Sullivan, "Professions of Law," 9 *Geo. J. Leg. Ethics* 1235 (1996).

14. See generally Barry Sullivan, "Constitutional Interpretation and Republican Government," 28 *Dublin U. L.J.* 221 (2006).

15. Felix Frankfurter, "Foreword," 55 *Colum L. Rev.* 435, 435 (1955). See also James Boyd White, "The Judicial Opinion and the Poem: Ways of Reading, Ways of Life," 82 *Mich. L. Rev.* 1669, 1686 (1984).

16. United States v. Curtiss-Wright Export Corp., 299 U.S. 304 (1936).

17. Chicago & Southern Air Lines, Inc. v. Waterman S.S. Corp., 333 U.S. 103 (1948).

18. See, e.g., Edward S. Corwin, *The President: Office and Powers,* 4th ed. (New York: New York University Press, 1957), 227–62. Remarking on the relationship between Congress and the president, Professor Corwin famously characterized the Constitution as an "invitation to struggle for the privilege of directing American foreign policy" (id. at 171).

19. See, e.g., Robert H. Jackson, *The Struggle for Judicial Supremacy: A Study of a Crisis in American Power Politics* (New York: Alfred A. Knopf, 1941), 175. ("The Court not merely challenged the policies of the New Deal but erected judicial barriers to the reasonable exercise of legislative powers, both state and national, to meet the urgent needs of a twentieth-century community.").

20. See Warner W. Gardner, "Government Attorney," 55 *Colum. L. Rev.* 438, 444 (1955) (footnote omitted) (The relevant opinion of the attorney general "is brilliantly executed, and marshals a number of debatable propositions into an array that is powerfully persuasive.").

21. 343 U.S. at 614. See also id. at 633–34 (Douglas, J., concurring).

22. Id. at 588. Justice Frankfurter penned a short addendum to Justice Black's opinion, indicating his agreement with the application of the principle of separation of powers to the case, while stating that "the considerations relevant to the legal enforcement of the principle of separation of powers [are] more complicated and flexible than may appear from what Justice Black has written."

23. Id. at 602 ("Congress could not more clearly and emphatically have withheld authority than it did in 1947."). Justice Frankfurter further noted: "Absence of authority in the President to deal with a crisis does not imply want of power in the Government. Conversely the fact that power exists in the Government does not vest it in the President. The need for new legislation does not enact it" (id. at 603–4).

24. Id. at 708.

25. See Matthew 7:29.

26. 343 U.S. at 634–35.

27. Id. at 635.

28. Id. at 640.

29. Id.

30. Id. at 641.

31. Id. at 641–42.

32. Id. at 643.

33. Id. at 646.

34. Id.

35. Id. at 646–47. He also noted (perhaps also based on personal experience), "The vagueness and generality of the clauses that set forth presidential powers afford a plausible basis for pressures within and without an administration for presi-

dential action beyond that supported by those whose responsibility is to defend his actions in court" (id. at 647).

36. Id.

37. See also Robert H. Jackson, *That Man: An Insider's Portrait of Franklin D. Roosevelt,* ed. John Q. Barrett (New York: Oxford University Press, 2003), xxi–xxii, 82–100. Following the oral argument in *Youngstown,* Justice Jackson wrote a letter to his son (which Professor Barrett quotes in his introduction), in which he noted that these were issues that he had "struggled with in several capacities" (id. at xxii). Justice Jackson also told his son that the solicitor general seemed to be "struggling and confused" at argument (id.). See also Robert H. Jackson, "A Presidential Legal Opinion," 66 *Harv. L. Rev.* 1353 (1953).

38. 343 U.S. at 647.

39. Philip B. Kurland and Gerhard Casper, eds., *Landmark Briefs and Arguments of the Supreme Court of the United States: Constitutional Law,* vol. 48 (Washington, DC: University Publications of America, 1975), 446–47 (Brief for the Plaintiff Companies at 27–28 (record reference omitted)). Ironically, one of the government's principal authorities was a case Davis had argued as solicitor general in the Wilson administration.

40. Id. at 895 (Transcript of Oral Argument).

41. Id. at 716 (Brief for the United States at 109 (footnote omitted)).

42. Id. at 109–10 (footnotes omitted).

43. Id. (Brief for the United States at 109 n. 11).

44. Justice Frankfurter methodically analyzed and refuted the government's reliance on these earlier instances. See 343 U.S. at 597–613 (Frankfurter, J., concurring).

45. *Landmark Briefs and Arguments,* at 919 (Transcript of Oral Argument).

46. Id.

47. Id. at 919–20. After noting that the North American case was "in essence a strike against the Government," Justice Jackson suggested another distinction: "The owners [in the North American case] all did acquiesce in the seizure, and there was never a contest of it, as far as I recall. They welcomed it, and went through with it to the end" (id. at 920).

48. Id.

49. Id. at 921.

50. Id.

51. 343 U.S. at 652.

52. Id. at 695.

53. See also id. at 594 (Frankfurter, J.) ("The accretion of dangerous power does not come in a day. It does come, however slowly, from the generative force of unchecked disregard of the restrictions that fence in even the most disinterested assertion of authority.")

54. Justice Jackson thought "it . . . relevant to note the gap that exists between the President's paper powers and his real powers" (id. at 653). That gap is attributable to several factors, including the greater relative power of the federal government over the states, the unanticipated prestige of the presidential office as an organ of government, and the unanticipated role of the president as party leader (id. at 653–54).

55. Id. at 644.

56. U.S. Const. article I, § 9, cl. 2. See also Ex Parte Merryman, 17 Fed. Cas. 144 (1861).

57. 343 U.S. at 650.

58. See Frankfurter, 55 *Colum. L. Rev.*, at 437 (describing Nuremberg's effect on Jackson). See generally Cindy Skach, *Borrowing Constitutional Designs: Constitutional Law in Weimar Germany and the French Fifth Republic* (Princeton: Princeton University Press, 2005), 32, 46–66, 98–107, 121.

59. 343 U.S. at 651.

60. Id. at 651.

61. Id. at 652.

62. Id. at 654–55.

63. Robert H. Jackson, *The Supreme Court in the American System of Government* (London: Oxford University Press, 1955), 24.

64. Id. at 25 (footnote omitted).

65. 323 U.S. 214 (1944).

66. Id. at 245–46 (Jackson, J., dissenting).

67. Id. at 244–46.

68. 323 U.S. at 248. Justice Jackson stated: "I should hold that a civil court cannot be made to enforce an order which violates constitutional limitations even if it is a reasonable exercise of military authority. The courts can exercise only the judicial power, can apply only law, and must abide by the Constitution, or they cease to be civil courts and become instruments of military policy" (id. at 247).

69. Id. See also *Supreme Court in the American System of Government,* at 59 ("But before we take the measure of the values the Court should and in some degree can protect, we must not overlook the things now practically beyond its control. Two of the greatest powers possessed by the political branches, which seem to me the disaster-potentials in our system, are utterly beyond judicial reach. These are the war power and the money, taxing, and spending power, which is the power of inflation. The improvident use of these powers can destroy the conditions for the existence of liberty, because either can set up great currents of strife within the population which might carry down constitutional forms and limitations before them.").

70. Perhaps the most significant decision on executive power between *Youngstown* and the "enemy combatant" cases was Dames & Moore v. Regan, 453 U.S. 654 (1981), which, according to Harold Hongju Koh, "marked a dramatic de facto expansion of Categories One and Two and a constriction of Category Three—the only category where the President might be overruled" ("Can The President Be Torturer in Chief?" 81 *Ind. L.J.* 1145, 1161 (2006) (footnote omitted)). Ironically, as Koh has noted, the opinion for the Court in Dames & Moore was written by Justice William H. Rehnquist, who had been Justice Jackson's law clerk during the term in which *Youngstown* was decided (id.). As Koh has also noted, Chief Justice John G. Roberts Jr., Justice Rehnquist's law clerk when Dames & Moore was decided, was partially responsible for preparing the opinion (id.).

71. 542 U.S. 507 (2004).

72. Justice O'Connor noted: "There is some debate as to the proper scope of this term, and the Government has never provided any court with the full criteria

that it uses in classifying individuals as such. It has made clear, however, that, for purposes of this case, the 'enemy combatant' that it is seeking to detain is an individual who, it alleges, was 'part of or supporting forces hostile to the United States or coalition partners' in Afghanistan and who 'engaged in an armed conflict against the United States.' . . . We therefore answer only the narrow question before us: whether the detention of citizens falling within that definition is authorized" (id. at 516 (internal quotations omitted)). Justice O'Connor did not consider the due process implications of the government's failure to define this term, which appears to have been adopted for the purpose of avoiding the established distinction between "lawful" and "unlawful" combatants. See Brief for American Bar Association as Amicus Curiae Supporting Petitioner at 9–11, Hamdi v. Rumsfeld, 542 U.S. 507 (2004) (no. 03-6696).

73. 542 U.S. at 508. Justices Souter and Ginsburg would have held that the detention was simply unlawful because it violated the Non-Detention Act (18 U.S.C. § 4001(a)), but they joined with the plurality on the narrow proposition that the cases should be remanded so Hamdi could contest the factual basis for his detention (542 U.S. at 553). Otherwise, there would have been no disposition that commanded a majority of the Court.

74. Id. at 524.

75. Id. at 527. See also Brief for Cato Institute as Amicus Curiae Supporting Petitioners at 2–3, Hamdi v. Rumsfeld, 542 U.S. 507 (2004) (no. 03-6696).

76. 542 U.S. at 527–28. The Mobbs Declaration was a declaration of nine paragraphs (one and a half pages) by Michael H. Mobbs, a special advisor to the undersecretary of defense. Mobbs reported that he was "head of the Under Secretary of Defense for Policy's Detainee Policy Group"; that he had reviewed "relevant records and reports" relating to Hamdi; and that, based on that review, he was "also familiar with the facts and circumstances related to the capture of Yaser Esam Hamdi and his detention by U.S. military forces." According to Mobbs, Hamdi went to Afghanistan to train with the Taliban in July or August 2001; continued to fight with them against the Northern Alliance after the United States began military operations against the Taliban and al-Qaeda on 7 October 2001; was captured by the Northern Alliance in "late 2001"; and was transferred at some point to U.S. custody. In January 2002, reported Mobbs, a detainee review and screening team "reviewed Hamdi's record and determined he met the criteria established by the Secretary of Defense for individuals over whom U.S. forces should take control and transfer to Guantanamo Bay." Finally, Mobbs wrote, a "subsequent interview of Hamdi has confirmed the fact that he surrendered and gave his firearm to Northern Alliance forces which supports his classification as an enemy combatant." The Mobbs Declaration comprised the entirety of the government's evidence.

77. Id. at 528.

78. Id. at 528–29.

79. Id. at 536.

80. Id. at 532.

81. Id.

82. Id. at 533.

83. Id. at 531.

84. Id. at 532.
85. Id. at 533.
86. Id. (citations omitted).
87. Id.
88. Id. at 533–34.
89. Id. at 535.
90. Id. at 536.
91. Id. at 538.
92. Id. At Nuremberg, Justice Jackson apparently supported the admissibility of affidavit evidence, on grounds of efficiency (given both the Nazis' meticulous record keeping and the enormous amount of work that the Tribunal was expected to accomplish in a relatively short period of time), but subject to certain conditions. Those conditions included affording the accused an opportunity to cross-examine the affiant. As Judge Patricia Wald has noted, "The Nuremberg Charter provided that to be admissible, evidence need only be probative to a reasonable person (this standard was of course considerably looser than our hearsay rules). Article 19 [of the Charter] freed the Tribunal from 'technical rules of evidence'—adjuring it to adopt 'expeditious and nontechnical procedures.'" Patricia M. Wald, "Running the Trial of the Century: The Nuremberg Legacy," 27 *Cardozo L. Rev.* 1559, 1580 (2006) (footnote omitted). "[T]he ultimate role that affidavit evidence played at Nuremberg was 'extensive and very important.'" Megan A. Fairlie, "Due Process Erosion: The Diminution of Live Testimony at the ICTY," 34 *Cal. Western Int'l L. J.* 47, 53 (2003) (footnote omitted). "The pattern that eventually developed at Nuremberg was one wherein the tribunal admitted affidavits, but admission was conditional on the right of cross-examination or, alternatively, written interrogatories." Id. (footnote omitted). A similar balance has sometimes been reached in the United States in civil and administrative cases decided under the Due Process Clause. See, e.g., Richardson v. Perales, 402 U.S. 389, 409 (1971); Wallace v. Bowen, 869 F.2d 187 (3rd Cir. 1989).
93. On 2 December 2003, the day before the government filed its brief in opposition to Hamdi's petition for certiorari, the Department of Defense announced that it would permit Hamdi to consult with his lawyer. See the Department of Defense news release at http://www.defenselink.mil/releases/release.aspx?releaseid=5831; Neil A. Lewis, "Sudden Shift on Detainee," *New York Times,* 4 December 2003, at A1. The Court granted certiorari on 9 January 2004.
94. 542 U.S. at 539.
95. To borrow a phrase from Auden, Justice Jackson's opinion is one that "respect[s] [its] elders but [is] not cowed by them, and [does] not tell fibs" (W. H. Auden, preface to *A Change of World,* by Adrienne Rich (New Haven: Yale University Press, 1951).
96. Brief for American Bar Association as Amicus Curiae Supporting Petitioner at 9–10, Hamdi v. Rumsfeld, 542 U.S. 507 (2004) (no. 03-6696).
97. In this case, of course, the prospect of even the limited review mandated by the Supreme Court resulted in the government's speedy release of Hamdi, subject only to his compliance with the government's demand that he renounce his U.S. citizenship and promise not to reenter the United States. See, e.g., Eric Lichtblau,

"U.S., Bowing to Court Ruling, Will Free 'Enemy Combatant,'" *New York Times,* 23 September 2004, at A1; Joel Brinkley, "Deportation Delayed for 'Enemy Combatant,'" *New York Times,* 1 October 2004, at A13; Joel Brinkley, "A Father Waits as the U.S. and the Saudis Discuss His Son's Release," *New York Times,* 10 October 2004, at A15; Joel Brinkley and Eric Lichtblau, "U.S. Releases Saudi-American It Had Captured in Afghanistan," *New York Times,* 12 October 2004, at A15; Joel Brinkley, "From Afghanistan to Saudi Arabia, via Guantanamo," *New York Times,* 16 October 2004, at A4.

98. Motor Vehicle Mfgrs. Assoc. v. State Farm Mut. Auto Ins. Co., 463 U.S. 29, 43 (1983) (citing Burlington Truck Lines v. United States, 371 U.S. 156, 168 (1962) (internal quotation marks omitted)).

99. Id. at 579.

100. See Aristotle, *Nicomachean Ethics,* book 1, chap. 7, § 1098a (Martin Oswald, ed.) (Indianapolis: Bobbs-Merrill, 1962) ("[O]ne should not require precision in all pursuits alike, but in each field precision varies with the matter under discussion and should be required only to the extent to which it is appropriate.").

101. Contemporaneous with Hamdi, the Court held in Rasul v. Bush (542 U.S. 466, 480 (2004)) that the grant of habeas jurisdiction in 28 U.S.C. § 2241 applied to alien detainees as well as citizens. However, Congress later retroactively stripped the federal courts of statutory habeas jurisdiction over aliens held at Guantanamo Bay. See Pub. L. No. 109-366 § 7, amending 28 U.S.C. § 2241. See also Boumediene v. Bush, 476 F.3d. 981, 987–88 (D.C. Cir.), 127 U.S., 1478, cert. granted, 127 S. Ct. 3078 (2007), which construed the Military Commissions Act of 2006 to strip statutory habeas jurisdiction with respect to alien detainees.

102. See Coffin v. United States, 156 U.S. 432, 453–54 (1895) (overruled on other grounds).

103. See Brady v. State of Maryland, 373 U.S. 83, 87 (1963) ("Society wins not only when the guilty are convicted but when criminal trials are fair; our system of the administration of justice suffers when any accused is treated unfairly. An inscription on the walls of the Department of Justice states the proposition candidly for the federal domain: 'The United States wins its point whenever justice is done its citizens in the courts.'"). See also id. at n. 2 ("[Former Solicitor General] Frederick William Lehmann [wrote] that the Government wins its point when justice is done in its courts.").

104. McCulloch v. Maryland, 4 Wheat. (17 U.S.) 316, 404–5 (1819).

105. Watts v. Indiana, 338 U.S. 49, 52 (1949).

106. See generally David Marquand, *Decline of the Public: The Hollowing Out of Citizenship* (Cambridge: Polity, 2004).

Privacy's End

Jed Rubenfeld

How adequate is the word "privacy" as a way to capture the essential meaning of the Fourth Amendment? Ever since Katz v. United States (concerned with the bugging of a telephone booth), the Supreme Court and commentators alike have conceived of the protections of the Fourth Amendment largely in privacy terms. This move was driven initially by the desire to escape from the limitations of an approach that spoke in property terms—ownership, possession, license to be present, and so on. This movement fit with the general culture as well.

As Jed Rubenfeld reminds us in this essay, the word "privacy" does not appear in the Fourth Amendment's text. Moreover, however helpful privacy may be in thinking about searches, it is almost useless in thinking about arrest or detainment—about "seizure" of the person. This is an intrusion that does much more than violate privacy in the usual sense: it is an interference with liberty and autonomy.

In place of privacy, Rubenfeld proposes another mode of analysis that promises to give the Fourth Amendment new legal and political life.

How fragile a thing, law. Constitutional principles that took root over centuries can wither and die in a few short years. Freedoms long prized—freedoms long distinguishing the United States from much of the rest of the world—can disappear in the blink of a firebomb.

Not long ago, the notion that police could seize Americans off the streets and throw them in prison without probable cause might have seemed laughable. "We allow our police to make arrests only on 'probable cause,'" we used to be told. "Arresting a person on suspicion, like arresting a person for investigation, is foreign to our system."[1] To call a particular confinement "nothing more or less than unadorned preventive detention"[2] was to condemn it, because unadorned preventive detention—once upon a time—did not exist in this country. The power to imprison on mere suspicion or "dangerousness" or executive say-so belonged to dictatorships. But the previous president of the United States had claimed the power to imprison any individual he declares an "enemy combatant"—including a U.S. citizen seized inside the United States—without probable cause, without criminal charge, with limited or no judicial review, and with preventive detention the explicit justification.[3]

Not long ago, it was possible to believe that the Fourth Amendment prohibited the government from tapping Americans' telephone calls except with probable cause and, absent exigent circumstances, judicial authorization. As late as 2004, the president declared:

> Now, by the way, any time you hear the United States Government talking about wiretap, it requires—a wiretap requires a court order. Nothing has changed, by the way. When we're talking about chasing down terrorists, we're talking about getting a court order before we do so. It's important for our fellow citizens to understand, when you think Patriot Act, constitutional guarantees are in place when it comes to doing what is necessary to protect our homeland, because we value the Constitution.[4]

These statements, it turned out, were not accurate. The president would later admit that, in 2002, he had personally but secretly authorized (and then repeatedly reauthorized) the National Security Agency to intercept hundreds, perhaps thousands, perhaps tens of thousands, of telephone calls and e-mail messages, without probable cause and without a court order.[5]

One cannot expect too much from judges in wartime. After all, the Constitution has been stretched before in times of war, real or perceived, hot or cold. But the weakness in Fourth Amendment law today—notice its strange and almost complete silence in the dispute over unlawful combatant detentions, despite the fact that arrests on less than probable cause were among the paradigmatic abuses that the Fourth Amendment was enacted to forbid—cannot be attributed solely to the winds of war.

To meet today's challenges,[6] Fourth Amendment law would need the strongest of anchors—the clearest understanding of what it stands for and against. But at the core of modern Fourth Amendment law, there is instead a kind of doctrinal black hole, known as the "reasonable expectation of privacy."[7] This concept, the supposed "touchstone of Fourth Amendment analysis,"[8] has never been able to do the work required of it.

Tempting as it is to employ the language of privacy in arguing against unwanted surveillance, I suggest here that it is time to bring an end to privacy's reign as the touchstone of Fourth Amendment law. Under expectations of privacy thinking, the Fourth Amendment has lost hold of its text, its paradigm cases, and its ability to stand firm against patently unconstitutional searches and seizures. I suggest that *personal life* is instead the Fourth Amendment's end.

I. The Rise of Privacy in Fourth Amendment Law

The term *privacy* cannot be found in the U.S. Constitution. This absence has been much remarked on,[9] but typically in connection with a different right of privacy, the one announced in *Roe v. Wade.*[10] It is as true of the Fourth Amendment as of the Fourteenth, however, that the text makes no mention of privacy—or reasonable expectations thereof. Instead, the Fourth Amendment guarantees a right of security. The first words of the Fourth Amendment set forth a right not to be private but "to be secure": "The right of the people to be *secure* in their persons, houses, papers, and effects against unreasonable searches and seizures shall not be violated."[11]

The term *secure* barely figures in modern doctrine. Current search and seizure thinking proceeds as if the first words of the Fourth Amendment were not there at all—as if the amendment simply read, "There shall be no unreasonable searches or seizures."[12] Perversely, when security is discussed in modern Fourth Amendment analysis, it is almost invariably pitted against Fourth Amendment rights: the nation's security, we are told, is what must be balanced against individuals' Fourth Amendment freedoms.[13]

This balancing idea completes the basic structure of modern Fourth Amendment law. In essence, in the great run of cases, current law has two elements. First, courts are asked to decide whether a challenged search or seizure violates the claimant's reasonable expectation of privacy; if so, courts are expected to balance this intrusion against the state interests served by the search or seizure. The idea of the claimant having a right to be secure in anything is simply absent.

With the elision of the word *secure,* another term in the Fourth Amendment vanishes as well: *the people.* In the Fifth Amendment, the holder of the enumerated rights is singular: "nor shall any *person* be . . . compelled in a criminal proceeding to be a witness against *himself.*"[14] Similarly, the Sixth Amendment's right holder is the singular "accused," who is granted, for example, the right "to be confronted with the witnesses against *him.*"[15] But the security right guaranteed by the Fourth Amendment is attributed to "the *people,*" who are "to be secure in *their* persons, houses, papers, and effects."[16] What is lost when modern doctrine passes over "the people" and "their" right to be "secure," replacing these terms with a suspect's "reasonable expectations of privacy"? That is the question I mean to raise in this essay.

It is not entirely clear when the Court first began to conceive of the Fourth Amendment as protecting a "right to privacy." Perhaps the decisive year was 1890, when Brandeis and Warren published their famous article under that title.[17] Prior to that year, there was not a single Supreme Court decision in which the terms *privacy* and *Fourth Amendment* both appeared.[18] By 1920, there were at least three occasions on which the Supreme Court had described Fourth Amendment violations as invasions of "privacy."[19] In 1928, Justice Brandeis wrote his celebrated *Olmstead* dissent,[20] and by 1946, with the great man dead five years, the Court could characterize the Fourth Amendment's central purpose in unmistakably Brandeisian terms, as "protection of the privacy of the individual, his *right to be let alone.*"[21]

Doctrinally speaking, however, the law and concept of trespass—rather than privacy—continued to provide the Fourth Amendment with its chief frame of reference until the 1960s. The great departure came in *Katz v. United States,*[22] which declared the wiretapping of a telephone booth unconstitutional. The Fourth Amendment, the *Katz* Court famously held, "protects people, not places."[23] Thus untethered from the law of trespass,[24] the Fourth Amendment required a new principle, and in a concurrence that eventually supplanted the majority opinion, Justice Harlan provided it. To state a valid Fourth Amendment claim, wrote Harlan, an individual must have "exhibited an actual (subjective) expectation of privacy," and that expectation must have been "reasonable."[25] The full Court soon adopted Justice Harlan's formulation,[26] and Fourth Amendment law has sought to protect "reasonable expectations of privacy" ever since.[27]

2. THE PROBLEMS WITH PRIVACY

The "expectations of privacy" analysis famously creates a potential circularity problem. This problem is real, but it has been much discussed—and much exaggerated—in prior commentary, and I am not interested in pursuing it here.[28] The real problem with privacy, I suggest, is more fundamental. Analysis based on expectations of privacy simply cannot come to grips with practices of detention and surveillance that ought to command the most serious Fourth Amendment attention.

When it comes to arrest, the simple truth is that expectations of privacy shed very little light. They do not speak to seizures of the *person*. Arrests *can* impinge on privacy, of course, but that is not what makes a paradigmatically unconstitutional arrest unconstitutional. It is the lack of proper cause that does so. The most arbitrary and baseless arrest could, at least in theory, be conducted with scrupulous regard for the arrestee's privacy. Hence, an oddity: although the Fourth Amendment was paradigmatically aimed at (among other things) arrests on mere suspicion, the "touchstone" of modern Fourth Amendment law fails to touch such arrests. This failure best explains why the Fourth Amendment has been relatively inconspicuous in the unlawful combatant debate; judges in such cases today tend to see a debatable due process issue, rather than a Fourth Amendment violation.[29]

But even with respect to surveillance, modern doctrine fails to stand against practices that seem to cry out for constitutional check. This is the third core problem with current Fourth Amendment analysis. It is only a single example—and it may not speak to everyone—but let me try to illustrate this point with a hypothetical.

Imagine a society in which undercover police officers are ubiquitous. Nearly every workplace has at least one, as does nearly every park, every store and restaurant, every Starbucks, every train and plane, every university classroom—and many families, too. These undercover agents wear hidden microphones and video cameras, recording everything they hear or see and transmitting it to governmental entities. Whenever you speak with anyone, you have to fear that this person may not be the person he claims to be. Your closest friends may be spies. Perhaps there is one in your own family.

Existing Fourth Amendment law would find nothing wrong with this picture. Far from forbidding the saturation of society with covert government agents, current doctrine would not even register it on the constitutional radar screen.[30] The Supreme Court has reasoned that whenever we speak with other persons, we inevitably assume the risk that they might report what we say to the police; hence no reasonable expectation of privacy is violated if our interlocutors do in fact transmit what we say to the police.[31] If no reasonable expectation of privacy is violated, no Fourth Amendment scrutiny applies.

Is that the right result? No answer is possible without invoking some conception of the Fourth Amendment's core purposes and principles. But if the Fourth Amendment stands against a certain kind of systematic state penetration of our personal lives—which we might call totalitarian—then modern doctrine has a serious problem. It is easy enough to say that the Fourth Amendment should prohibit totalitarian police practices. Many have said so before.[32] The difficulty lies in saying what exactly an antitotalitarian Fourth Amendment would look like and how it would differ from the law we have today.

3. THE PRIVATIZATION OF THE FOURTH AMENDMENT

A. The Depoliticization of the Fourth Amendment

When Fourth Amendment law took as its central term the Brandeisian "right to be let alone," it allied itself with an idea that in the twentieth century came not only to preoccupy constitutional law but also tort and statutory law.[33] The "right to privacy" captured the energies of judges and legislators throughout the last century at every level of American law—common,[34] regulatory,[35] and statutory.[36] By the end of the century, the Fourth Amendment could be seen as just one piece of a much more extensive network of privacy law. "Privacy" casebooks appeared in which the Fourth Amendment's "expectations of privacy," tort law's "right to privacy," and statutory privacy law are all brought together as if they were subdivisions of a single legal subject—which also includes, since the assumption is that any legal right named "privacy" must refer to the same object of concern, *Griswold,*[37] *Roe,*[38] and so on.[39]

Thus the Fourth Amendment came to be seen as protecting the same basic interests that other privacy laws protect. As a result, Fourth Amendment norms became increasingly understood to replicate against state actors the privacy norms that apply more generally throughout the private sphere.[40] So conceived, the Fourth Amendment loses any distinctive political valence—any specifically political meaning. It is, precisely, privatized.

To privatize the Fourth Amendment is to understand its purposes increasingly in terms of values that, instead of speaking to the distinctive dangers of state surveillance and detention, speak, rather, to an individual's comfort, dignity, respectability, or protection from embarrassment—the same interests that chiefly motivated Brandeis and Warren's seminal essay, which had nothing to do with the Fourth Amendment but dealt instead with invasions of privacy by gossip columnists and other private actors.[41] The problem with making privacy the central term of Fourth Amendment analysis is not that Fourth Amendment doctrine therefore favors "wealthy people."[42] The problem is that it has lost its moorings.

Conceptualized as a violation of the "right to be let alone," the police officer without probable cause or a warrant who breaks down your door in the nighttime, ransacks your home, and takes you to prison differs only in degree from the family member who walks in on you while you are in the bathroom or the salesman who calls you just as you sit down to dinner. Such, at least, is the conclusion reached by Richard Posner, who compares an unreasonable police search of one's house to an "unwanted telephone solicitation" or "the blare of a sound truck."[43] For Posner, the Fourth Amendment protects "solitude,"[44] and it "is valued because it enhances the quality of one's work or leisure."[45]

Here is the ultimate destination of a Fourth Amendment dedicated to privacy: it exists to enhance our leisure time. A Fourth Amendment so dedicated must eventually reduce itself to duplicating the privacy norms of the private sphere, and once it does that, it loses its political anchor. It becomes, in the words of one federal circuit court—yes, the Seventh Circuit—a guarantor of "peace and quiet" and "relaxation."[46]

There is nothing wrong with a Fourth Amendment so conceived, except that it will have no understanding of what it stands for. It will see its role inevitably shrinking as information technology expands. As long as the Fourth Amendment is parasitical on private sphere privacy, the former must die as its host dies, and this host is undoubtedly faltering today in the networked, monitored, and digitized world we are learning to call our own.

B. Repoliticizing the Fourth Amendment

What would it mean to repoliticize the Fourth Amendment? Suppose the goal of Fourth Amendment doctrine were not to make state actors obey generally applicable privacy norms. Suppose the goal were to lay down the law—a distinctive body of law—for those who enforce the law.

To state the obvious, the government's law enforcement power is unique. The difference is both quantitative and qualitative. The ability of government to intrude, monitor, punish, and regulate is greater than that of private actors by many orders of magnitude. But more than this, the state has a right and duty to intrude into people's lives that private parties do not.

As the nation's instrument for enforcing the law, the state does and should intrude into individuals' homes, papers, and effects more intensively and systematically than any private actor. With respect to private property, the police do and should take actions that would constitute trespass or theft if done by private parties. They do and should enter homes when no "sensible person" or reasonable stranger would.

But if it includes a license—to trespass, to search and seize, sometimes to kill—that no private person has, the state's power to enforce the law also poses to a free citizenry dangers that private persons do not. The Fourth Amendment must be responsive both to the distinctive needs of law enforcement and to its distinctive threats. Search and seizure law is the site of the delicate but critical constitutional balance between the use and abuse of the police power.

What is needed from Fourth Amendment law is a body of norms specifically directed to the special responsibilities of law enforcement and the special dangers it poses. Thus search and seizure law today needs to be repoliticized. It needs a new foundation, responsive to the amendment's essential concern with the use and abuse of police power.

It is not anachronistic to say so. Consider Francis Lieber's 1853 description of the Fourth Amendment's fundamental principles.[47] The law, said Lieber, commands a citizen to "be a man": "thou shalt be sovereign in thy house."[48] The Fourth Amendment, according to Lieber, expresses the "direct antagonism" of Anglo-American law to the "police government"[49] of the continental states, where the police force "enters at night or in the day any house or room, breaks open any drawer, seizes papers or anything it deems fit, without any other warrant than the police hat, coat and button."[50] Lieber, persecuted in his native Germany before fleeing to England

and then to Boston in 1827,[51] had the right starting point for the Fourth Amendment: the evils of "police government"—or what we today would call a *police state.*

Fourth Amendment law must enable police work in an increasingly perilous world while preventing the evils of a police state. That is the job, however difficult it might be. But what is wrong, exactly, with a police state? What, precisely, does a police state attack? The answer is personal life.

C. Personal Life ❧

It is a commonplace to observe that democracy requires a distinctive "public sphere" in which, for example, political opinion can be freely expressed and all citizens can in principle participate on equal legal terms.[52] But democracy requires more than a public sphere. It also requires personal life.

John Stuart Mill's *On Liberty* provides the classic statement of the importance of personal life to a free society. We remember that book today mostly for Mill's principle that society has no "jurisdiction" over "self-regarding" acts,[53] but *On Liberty* has a larger target: the evils of conformity. England, Mill writes, is in danger of falling prey to a stultifying conformity, which Mill captures, in a magnificent burst of ethnocentrism, through the example of China. "We have a warning example," he writes, "in China," where conformity is the "ideal"; where people are "all alike"; where all progress, all development, stopped millennia ago; and where society has remained "stationary" for "thousands of years."[54] Englishmen, says Mill, are already beginning to "resemble one another"[55] to a frightful degree. "Comparatively speaking," he writes, "they now read the same things, listen to the same things, see the same things, go to the same places," and "have their hopes and fears directed to the same objects."[56] If unchecked, Mill warns, this tendency to uniformity will crush England's "greatness" and maim the Englishman's greatest strength—his "Individuality."[57]

What does Mill argue is causing England to become "another China"?[58] It is a despotism—a modern, Occidental despotism, "the despotism of custom."[59] This despotism is new because of its relationship to democratic self-government. It is both caused by democracy and catastrophic for it. When democracy was "a thing only dreamed about,"[60] Mill writes, men imagined that it would mean the end of tyranny. But now that democracy is becoming "a great existing fact,"[61] a "concealed"[62] truth has emerged. "'Self-government'" turned out to mean "not the government of each by himself, but of each by all the rest."[63] Democracy gives supreme authority to public opinion and public sentiment. In turn, "the regime of public opinion" gives rise to a kind of "social tyranny," the "tyranny of the prevailing opinion and feeling"—"more formidable than many kinds of political oppression," because "society is itself the tyrant."[64] Completing his Chinese imagery, Mill writes that the defining feature of this "social tyranny" is to bind up and stunt all that "stands out": it seeks to "maim by compression, like a Chinese lady's foot, every part of human nature that stands out."[65]

It is worthwhile to recall the antidemocratic strains in Mill's liberalism, but *On Liberty* is not an antidemocratic book. Mill is not championing monarchy or aristocracy. Warning against an evil he sees as inherent in democracy, he is arguing for constitutional norms able to cure that evil—or at least cure its worst excesses. The most famous of these norms are the harm principle and freedom of speech. But the overriding theme of *On Liberty* is the demarcation and preservation of personal life.

Mill understands personal life (he uses the term *private life*)[66] to have one essential condition and one essential function. The condition is an escape from public scrutiny. The "eye" of public opinion, says Mill, is seemingly everywhere: "In our times, from the highest class . . . down to the lowest, everyone lives as under the eye of a dreaded and hostile censorship."[67] This "eye" and its judgment follow men everywhere, "leav[ing] fewer means of escape, penetrating much more deeply into the details of life, and enslaving the soul itself."[68] The necessary prerequisite for personal life is therefore an escape from the public "eye." The essential function of personal life is to enable resistance to the public demand for uniformity, thus promoting "individuality," "spontaneity," "non-conformity," and "humanity."[69] Without such resistance, society will be peopled by creatures of "weak feelings" and "weak energies."[70] Such persons may be fit to "subjects" and "dependents," but, claims Mill, "it was men of another stamp that made England what it has been; and men of another stamp will be needed to prevent its decline."[71]

To be sure, mid-nineteenth-century England is not exactly on all fours with twenty-first-century America. The English aversion to "sticking out" is not quite rampant in the United States. Here, it will be said, we already have the "manifold diversity" of taste, habit, and opinion at which Mill aims. In America, individualism is always in style, anything goes, counter-culture becomes money culture overnight, every opinion is met with equal and opposite force by its contrary, and the most "mainstream" news outlets are daily blasted by outlets every bit as mainstream as those they vilify. Yet despite all these truisms, Mill's fundamental point—when repositioned within a Fourth Amendment framework—continues to hold in the United States today. Indeed, it holds for every free society.

Imagine that the public "eye" of which Mill complained was not figurative but literal. Imagine that every word you spoke in your home or in personal conversations was audible to law enforcement agents, even in the absence of any special cause to believe you were a criminal. Imagine that every image you see on your computer was recorded and compiled by the police, who also added to their file every purchase you made, every movie you watched, every person you met or communicated with, and so forth. It is not to be believed that this scrutiny would fail to change people's behavior. The freedom to defy prevailing norms depends on the existence of robust domains of personal life that proceed under one or another type of informational opacity.

A society in which people do not feel entirely free to express their true opinions in public will be a democratically challenged society. Such is American society, now and always. But a society in which people do not feel free to express their true opinions even in personal life is democratically lost.

D. The Antitotalitarian Imperative

I am now in a position to lay out the basic principles of an antitotalitarian Fourth Amendment. The aim of a totalitarian state is to obliterate personal life. In a totalitarian state, conformity with public norms obtains in principle at all times and in all places. To bring this about, a totalitarian government engages in systematic, often covert surveillance of its populace, "penetrating," in Mill's words, ever "more deeply into the details of life," with the object of "enslaving the soul."[72] At the same time, a totalitarian government engages in detentions—preventive detentions—of "suspicious" individuals, meaning individuals whose norm-defying behavior has led the authorities to perceive them as potentially "subversive" or "dangerous," even though they have not yet committed a crime in the standard sense of that term. These practices of surveillance and detention define a police state, and they define the chief targets of an antitotalitarian Fourth Amendment, which prohibits every form of search and seizure that threatens the existence, the conditions, or the basic functioning of personal life.

The purpose of personal life, for constitutional purposes, is not to free people to engage in acts society has criminalized. Unlike the First Amendment or the "right of privacy" protected by *Roe v. Wade,*[73] the Fourth Amendment does not insulate any particular activity from punishment. The freedom of personal life is radical but not anarchic. It is a freedom designed for a self-governing people—a people that makes its own law. The freedom of personal life is, in other words, a law-abiding freedom: the freedom to defy noncriminal public norms or not, as one chooses.

4. PARADIGM CASES AND SECURITY

A theory of the Fourth Amendment—or any other constitutional right—is of little interest if it cannot do justice to the Constitution's text and its paradigm cases. Let me try, therefore, briefly to show how a Fourth Amendment committed to personal life would capture the amendment's text and paradigm cases far better than current doctrine does. At the same time, I will clarify the critical doctrinal shift that would follow if Fourth Amendment law were organized around personal life, rather than privacy.

Why does the Fourth Amendment guarantee a right "to be secure"? Why is this security a "right of the people," rather than an individual's right, as in the Fifth and Sixth Amendments? And why is the Fourth Amendment paradigmatically violated by arbitrary arrests? Current doctrine cannot answer these questions; a Fourth Amendment organized around personal life can.

A. Paradigmatic Sites of Personal Life

The original paradigm case for the Fourth Amendment involved the indiscriminate search of a house on a general warrant.[74] The modern paradigm case, *Katz,* involved the tapping of a personal conversation without probable cause.[75] It is in our homes and our personal conversations that most of us most characteristically and most powerfully experience the freedom to do and say as we would. Indeed, if we do not experience this freedom in our homes or in personal conversations, we are unlikely to have it or to exercise it anywhere else. In other words, our homes and our personal conversations are the central sites of our personal lives, the distinctive experience of which is the freedom to speak or act as we wish, defying public norms if we choose. Thus reconceiving the Fourth Amendment to protect personal life would fully capture that amendment's paradigm cases.

Ironically, although it was in *Katz* that reasonable expectations of privacy made their first appearance in Fourth Amendment jurisprudence, conversations—that which *Katz* held to be protected—are not paradigmatic sites of privacy. In conversation, we expose our thoughts or beliefs to someone else. And if we happen to be speaking to someone we hardly know, then what we expose is arguably no longer private at all. This simple argument creates the logical problem that opens up cracks in current doctrine. A conversation is not only a site of hoped-for privacy within the logic of current case law; it is also a breach in one's privacy, a surrender of it, and hence less worthy of Fourth Amendment protection under a privacy rationale. This contradiction within modern doctrine is what produces, on the one hand, *Katz,* which flatly bars the state from listening in on our personal conversations unless there is probable cause, and, on the other hand, cases involving undercover agents, which freely permit the state to listen in on our personal conversations.

While personal conversations are equivocal with respect to privacy, they are unequivocally a site of personal life. Privacy is necessarily in tension with relationships or interactions in which one individual shares his thoughts or desires with others. Personal life is not; it consists, in important part, of such relationships and interactions.

Equally fundamental, the securing of personal life explains why arrests are paradigmatic objects of Fourth Amendment concern. It is, as suggested previously in this essay, unnatural to think of privacy as the reason behind the Fourth Amendment's prohibition of unreasonable seizures. In fact, far from protecting against a loss of privacy, the Fourth Amendment's prohibition of unreasonable seizures requires a loss of privacy. Say the police have evidence linking an individual to known terrorists—evidence sufficient to generate suspicion but not probable cause. The Fourth Amendment requires the police (or at least used to require them) to obtain much more information about this individual before they could lawfully seize him. In the standard case, the police would track, follow and record his movements. They would question persons familiar with him and his doings. To be sure, these measures would all be deemed not to violate the man's privacy, for otherwise they could not be done (constitutionally) unless the police already had probable cause. But equally obviously, all this prying, tracking, watching, photographing, and information gathering would have significantly eroded the man's privacy—making his personal affairs increasingly visible to the state.

In short, the Fourth Amendment does not require that seizures be reasonable in order to ensure privacy. It requires an erosion of privacy in order to ensure that seizures be reasonable. This conclusion will seem surprising or paradoxical only as long as Fourth Amendment law takes privacy as its beginning and end. Fourth Amendment law so conceived can barely understand the problem of unreasonable seizures. It can understand obliquely, if at all, the constitutional danger they pose—or how to meet that danger.

Invasions of privacy are intrusions. Seizures are *seclusions.* They do not pry into the detainee's private relationships or things, as searches do. They *extract* him from those relationships and things. They *take him away from his own life.* Every seizure has this effect to one degree or another. The more complete the victim's seclusion, the more complete his severance from the places and people he knew, the more complete the destruction of his personal life. An imprisoned man loses his liberty, of course, but he also loses his life—the life he used to lead.

Obviously a seized man is not dead, so he has not been deprived of life as such. Moreover, a man in prison remains in an ongoing, determinate relationship with the state, so in this sense, he still has a public life (consisting of his being the state's prisoner). The life he has been deprived of is, in short, his personal life—the life that belonged to him.

To have a personal life is to have a part of one's life that does not belong to the public or to the state. In this regard, the critical feature of incarcerations is not their deprivation of liberty: it is that they deprive the arrested individual of the life that belonged to him. An imprisoned man belongs to the state. His movements are not his own. His time is not his own. His occupations will be directed by his custodians. Seizures of the person attack the very existence of personal life.

B. Security and the Test of Generalizability

The right to privacy embedded in modern Fourth Amendment thinking is an individualized, depoliticized right—the right to be let alone—the purpose of which seems to be, basically, to protect individuals against embarrassment, indignity, and interruptions that degrade the quality of their work and leisure time. The protection of personal life in an antitotalitarian

Fourth Amendment has a different end: to secure the freedom to defy public norms. The word *secure* is not fortuitous here. Security is critical to the freedom of personal life, and the security that is required must, both conceptually and practically, belong to the people as a whole.

One way to see this point is by contrast. A primary aim of the arbitrary detentions, the surprise police entries into the home, and the covert surveillance definitive of a police state is to create a certain kind of insecurity. Such practices are designed to establish so pervasive an insecurity throughout society that people are cowed into conformity. In a state where people cannot speak without fear of being overheard by public authorities, where they cannot come to the attention of the state without incurring the threat of arrest, the freedom to defy public norms is not likely to thrive.

In other words, a democratic society cannot have a functioning personal life—in which people possess the freedom to speak and act as they would—unless people enjoy a certain security. Specifically, they must justifiably believe (1) that their personal lives can and will be kept distinct from their public lives—that what they do or say in personal life is not known or reported to public authorities; and (2) that, so long as they have not given the state cause to believe they have actually violated the law, their personal lives cannot be taken away from them should their defiance of public norms become known or suspected.

This security needs to be socially widespread. It is precisely not an individual right: it is not like physical liberty or the right to cross-examine witnesses, which one individual can in principle enjoy even if everyone else in his circumstances is denied it. Personal life is a public good, but not only a public good: it is a good that one cannot enjoy unless others enjoy it as well (because personal life consists largely of interaction among individuals). If personal life is to serve its constitutional function, people in general need to be secure in their persons, homes, conversations, papers, and effects.

As straightforward as these observations may seem, they impose a fundamental requirement on Fourth Amendment analysis—a requirement that current doctrine does not meet. Every search and seizure has potential adverse effects, not only on the individuals whose persons or things are searched or seized, but on the people as a whole. Every search and seizure asserts a governmental power: the power to search or seize in the particular kind of circumstances presented. If the judiciary upholds the search or seizure, it upholds the power. It announces that individuals are without constitutional protection against such searches or seizures, and it authorizes the government to exercise this same power in the future. If that power is acted on, it will have implications not only for the privacy interests of the targeted individuals but for the security of every single person subject to it. The only way for judges to vindicate the security the Fourth Amendment protects is to take account of this potential widespread effect on the populace of the search or seizure power they are called on to assess. In other words, judges must ask what the effect would be on the right of the people to be secure in their persons and things if the surveillance or detention power the government has asserted were to be systematically implemented.

By "systematically implemented" I do not mean that the judiciary must imagine the government searching or seizing every single person or thing to which the power at issue could potentially apply. It is enough to imagine the challenged surveillance or detentions generalized into regular, routine practices—implemented on a scale broad enough to become part of people's common knowledge and everyday life. The doctrinal test demanded here is a distant cousin of Kant's most famous formulation of the categorical imperative.[76] A search or seizure is unconstitutional if the "maxim" that would uphold it cannot be generalized—if the surveillance or detention power the government asserts cannot systematically be implemented without undermining the popular security the Fourth Amendment guarantees. For lack of a better word, I will refer to this test as the test of "generalizability."

C. Applying the Test: Undercover Agents

It is this test that current doctrine utterly fails in dealing with undercover police agents. In *White,* a plurality of the Court reasoned that the use of a wired informant violates no reasonable expectations of privacy because individuals who reveal plans of wrongdoing to others assume the risk that their interlocutors will report those plans to the authorities.[77] Accordingly, in *White* and subsequent cases, the Court has held that the use of undercover agents triggers no Fourth Amendment scrutiny at all.[78] As a result, in principle, current doctrine grants the government an unchecked power to implant undercover agents ubiquitously. Yet the Court has never considered the generalized effect of such a state of affairs, its effect not only on "wrongdoers"[79] but on law-abiding people as well.

Were covert informants and police agents to become ubiquitous, a great deal more than a loss of privacy would ensue. The true loss would be borne by everyone, including those who were never spied on (therefore suffering no actual governmental invasion of their privacy) and those who stopped saying anything personal to anyone else (therefore never suffering an exposure of anything private).[80] A society with ubiquitous undercover agents is a secret police state.[81] It is a state that deliberately seeks to destroy the security that people enjoy in their personal lives—the confidence that what one does in pesonal life belongs to personal life and will not generally be known to public authorities.

In such a society, personal life would not die altogether, but it would subsist in anemic or solipsistic forms. State action that causes personal life to be lived under a cloud of fear—fear that the state is omnipresent, fear of retaliation for saying or doing the wrong things—violates the security the Fourth Amendment centrally protects. Thus it cannot be the law that undercover agents trigger no Fourth Amendment scrutiny of any kind.

This is not to say that the Fourth Amendment bars covert police operations as such. Under the test of generalizability, the appropriate Fourth Amendment rules for undercover agents would vary according to context. For example, the Fourth Amendment would call for no strictures whatsoever on undercover agents offering to buy or sell narcotics on the street. This practice, even if generalized, would create no significant threats to personal life, which could flourish in perfect health even if one had to regard every stranger who solicited a narcotics deal as a potential police spy. However, because the home is so central to personal life, undercover entries into the home might properly be subjected to the standard announced in *Terry:* a reasonable, articulable suspicion of past or imminent criminal activity.[82] Under this rule, police officers would not be permitted to obtain entry into everyone's home by posing as private actors (utility employees, Jehovah's Witnesses, strangers in need of assistance); the threat of ubiquitous entries would thereby be forestalled. But they would be permitted to enter an individual's home where they had an articulable suspicion of criminality reasonably directed at that specific home.

By contrast, the most exacting Fourth Amendment safeguards—probable cause and a warrant—could be required where the state attempts to infiltrate into the heart of an individual's personal life. For example, the probable cause standard might apply where the government turned an individual's spouse into a wired informant inside his house or used an undercover agent to seduce an individual not just on a single occasion but repeatedly and over time, that individual becoming his intimate. Although current doctrine apparently has no objection to it,[83] this practice works a profound corruption of personal life. If implemented on a widespread scale, it would utterly undermine—in a fashion current doctrine has no tools to grasp—people's security in their homes and personal conversations.

CONCLUSION

This essay is intended merely to chart a course, the end point of which is meant to be a Fourth Amendment revitalized with the strength and clarity it would need to stand up against the extraordinary, unconstitutional practices of surveillance and imprisonment deployed by the United States government in recent years. I have no space to complete that story here. I must leave its details to future work.

I know my strategy must seem curious. The best way to arm judges to take a constitutional stand against executive overreaching probably is not to begin by reconceptualizing the constitutional terrain on which the judges are supposed to take their stand. But my aim here is not so much reconceptualizing terrain as recapturing it. The concepts I have described—the right of security, the test of generalizability, the liberty and necessity of personal life—are not meant to be new. They are meant to be the essential components of a Fourth Amendment that, I hope, will strike readers as familiar, even if it is not the Fourth Amendment we have today.

NOTES

This essay appears in expanded form as "The End of Privacy," 61 *Stan. L. Rev.* 101 (2008).

Special thanks to Jefferson Powell, James Boyd White, Bruce Ackerman, Akhil Amar, Eric Citron, Hannah Jacobs, Matt Splitek, Lucy Wang, Sam Wiseman, and Steven Winter.

1. Papachristo v. City of Jacksonville, 405 U.S. 156, 169 (1972).
2. United States v. Alexander, 471 F.2d 923, 964 (D.C. Cir. 1973) (per curiam).
3. See infra part 4.
4. "President Bush: Information Sharing, Patriot Act Vital to Homeland Security; Remarks by the President in a Conversation on the USA Patriot Act, Kleinshans Music Hall, Buffalo, New York," http://www.whitehouse.gov/news/releases/2004/04/20040420-2.html.

5. See James Risen and Eric Lichtblau, "Bush Lets U.S. Spy on Callers without Courts," *New York Times,* 16 December 2005, at A16. See infra part 5B.

6. In addition to eavesdropping without probable cause, federal law enforcement officers have in recent years sought to obtain data on the Internet search histories of millions of people not individually suspected of crimes (see Gonzales v. Google, 234 F.R.D. 674 (N.D. Cal. 2006)), have amassed "pen register" data (e.g., numbers dialed) on millions of people (see Leslie Cauley, "NSA Has Massive Database of Americans' Phone Calls," *USA Today,* 11 May 2006, at A1), and have perhaps been opening hard-mail correspondence, too (see Dan Eggen, "Bush Warned about Mail-Opening Authority," *Washington Post,* 5 January 2007, at A3).

7. Katz v. United States, 389 U.S. 347, 360 (1967) (Harlan, J., concurring).

8. California v. Ciraolo, 476 U.S. 207, 211 (1986).

9. See, e.g., Sarah Weddington, "Reflections on the Twenty-fifth Anniversary of *Roe v. Wade,*" 62 *Alb. L. Rev.* 811, 824 (1999) ("The word 'privacy' does not appear in the Constitution.").

10. 410 U.S. 113 (1973).

11. U.S. Const. amend. IV (emphasis added).

12. See, e.g., Florida v. Bostick, 501 U.S. 429, 439 (1991) (stating that the "Fourth Amendment proscribes unreasonable searches and seizures"). See infra part 3 for more discussion on the role of security in the Fourth Amendment.

13. See, e.g., National Treasury Employees Union v. Von Raab, 489 U.S. 656, 657, 665–66 (1989) (holding that "national security hazards" must be "balance[d] [against] the individual's expectation of privacy").

14. U.S. Const. amend. V (emphasis added).

15. U.S. Const. amend. VI (emphasis added).

16. U.S. Const. amend. IV (emphasis added).

17. See Samuel Warren and Louis D. Brandeis, "The Right to Privacy," 4 *Harv. L. Rev.* 193 (1890).

18. The Court did, however, use the word *privacies* when discussing the Fourth Amendment in Boyd v. United States, 116 U.S. 616, 630 (1886).

19. Perlman v. United States, 247 U.S. 7, 14 (1918); Weeks v. United States, 232 U.S. 383, 389–90 (1914); Flynt v. Stone Tracy Co., 220 U.S. 107, 174–75 (1911).

20. Olmstead v. United States, 277 U.S. 438, 471–85 (1928) (Brandeis, J., dissenting).

21. Davis v. United States, 328 U.S. 582, 587 (1946); Oklahoma Press Pub. Co. v. Walling, 327 U.S. 186, 204 n. 30 (1946).

22. 389 U.S. 347 (1967).

23. Id. at 351.

24. See id. at 353 (affirming that the Fourth Amendment may be violated "without any 'technical trespass under local property law'") (quoting Silverman v. United States, 365 U.S. 505, 511 (1961)).

25. Id. at 361 (Harlan, J., concurring) ("My understanding of the rule that has emerged from prior decisions is that there is a twofold requirement, first that a person have exhibited an actual (subjective) expectation of privacy and, second, that the expectation be one that society is prepared to recognize as 'reasonable.'").

26. One year after *Katz,* the Court declared that "wherever an individual may

harbor a reasonable 'expectation of privacy,' *id.,* at 361 (MR. JUSTICE HARLAN, concurring), he is entitled to be free from unreasonable governmental intrusion" (Terry v. Ohio, 392 U.S. 1, 9 (1968)).

27. See, e.g., Kyllo v. United States, 533 U.S. 27, 32 (2001); Bond v. United States, 529 U.S. 334, 338 (2000); Minnesota v. Olsen, 495 U.S. 91, 95 (1990); California v. Greenwood, 486 U.S. 35, 38 (1988); Maryland v. Garrison, 480 U.S. 79, 90–91 (1987); Smith v. Maryland, 442 U.S. 735, 740 (1979). See also California v. Ciraolo, 476 U.S. 207, 211 (1986) ("The touchstone of Fourth Amendment analysis is whether a person has a 'constitutionally protected reasonable expectation of privacy.'") (quoting *Katz,* 389 U.S. at 360 (Harlan, J., concurring)).

28. For more on this circularity problem, interested readers may wish to consult my more thorough treatment of the topics discussed in this essay. See Jed Rubenfeld, *The End of Privacy,* 61 *Stan. L. Rev.* 101 (2008).

29. See, e.g., Hamdi v. Rumfeld, 542 U.S. 507 (2004); Al-Marri v. Wright, 487 F.3d 160 (4th Cir. 2007).

30. See, e.g., United States v. Lee, 359 F.3d 194, 199 (3d Cir. 2004) (rejecting defendant's challenge to video and audio recording by an informant); United States v. Davis, 326 F.3d 361, 362 (2d Cir. 2003) ("It is firmly established that audio recordings, obtained without a warrant and through hidden recording devices by an invited guest, do not violate the Fourth Amendment.").

31. United States v. White, 401 U.S. 745, 749 (1971) (plurality opinion) (holding that a defendant has no "justifiable and constitutionally protected expectation that a person with whom he is conversing will not then or later reveal the conversation to the police"). See United States v. Karo, 468 U.S. 705, 716 n. 4 (1984) (treating the use of wired informants as constitutionally unproblematic); United States v. Caceres, 440 U.S. 741, 750 (1979).

32. See, e.g., White, 401 U.S. at 765 (Douglas, J., dissenting) (counseling the majority to "spend some time in totalitarian countries [to] learn firsthand the kind of regime they are creating" by allowing warrantless wired police informants); Daniel J. Solove, "Digital Dossiers and the Dissipation of Fourth Amendment Privacy," 75 *S. Cal. L. Rev.* 1083, 1086 (2002).

33. See generally Warren Freedman, *The Right of Privacy in the Computer Age* 1–31 (1986); Anita L. Allen, "Privacy in American Law," in *Privacies: Philosophical Evaluations* 19–30 (Beate Rössler, ed., 2004).

34. See, e.g., William Prosser, "Privacy," 48 *Cal. L. Rev.* 383, 389 (1960) (observing a complex of four distinct common law privacy torts that had developed since the Warren and Brandeis article). This complex of four privacy torts is summarized in the Restatement (Second) of Torts §§ 652B–E (1977).

35. See, e.g., Federal Education Rights and Privacy Act (FERPA) Regulations, 34 C.F.R. §§ 99.01–99.35 (2006); Children's On-Line Privacy Protection Rule, 16 C.F.R. §§ 312.1–312.5 (2006).

36. See, e.g., Electronic Communications Privacy Act of 1986, Tit. I–III, 18 U.S.C. §§ 2510–21, 2710–11, 3121–27 (2000 & Supp. 2002); Federal Privacy Act of 1974, 5 U.S.C. § 552A (2000); Children's On-Line Privacy Protection Act of 1998, 18 U.S.C. §§ 6501–6506 (2000); Family Education Rights and Privacy Act (FERPA), 20 U.S.C. § 1232g (2000); Health Insurance Portability and Accountability Act, 42.

37. Griswold v. Connecticut, 381 U.S. 479 (1965).

38. Roe v. Wade, 410 U.S. 113 (1973).

39. See, e.g., Daniel J. Solove and Marc Rotenberg, *Information and Privacy Law* xi–xxii (2003); Madeleine Schachter, *Informational and Decisional Privacy* vii–xv (2003); Richard C. Turkington and Anita L. Allen, *Privacy Law* xiii–xxxi (2d ed., 2002).

40. See, e.g., Minnesota v. Olson, 495 U.S. 91, 98–99 (1990) ("To hold that an overnight guest has a legitimate expectation of privacy in his host's home merely recognizes the every day expectations of privacy that we all share. Staying overnight in another's home is a longstanding social custom that serves functions recognized as valuable by society. . . . From the overnight guest's perspective, he seeks shelter in another's home precisely because it provides him with privacy."); California v. Greenwood, 486 U.S. 35, 43 ("Fourth Amendment analysis must turn on . . . our '*societal* understanding that certain areas deserve the most scrupulous protection from government invasion.'") (quoting Oliver v. United States, 466 U.S. 170, 178 (1984)); Robbins v. California, 453 U.S. 420, 428 (1981) (plurality opinion) ("Expectations of privacy are established by general social norms."); James A. Bush and Rece Bly, "Expectation of P.rivacy Analysis and Warrantless Trash Reconnaissance after *Katz v. United States*," 23 *Ariz. L. Rev.* 283, 293 (1981) ("[S]ocial custom . . . serves as the most basic foundation of a great many legitimate privacy expectations") (citation omitted).

41. See Warren and Brandeis, supra n. 17, at 196 ("To satisfy a prurient taste, the details of sexual relations are spread broadcast in the columns of the daily papers. To occupy the indolent, column upon column is filled with idle gossip which can only be procured by intrusion upon the domestic circle.").

42. William Stuntz, "Race, Class, and Drugs," 98 *Colum. L. Rev.* 1795, 1824 (1998).

43. Richard S. Posner, "The Uncertain Protection of Privacy by the Supreme Court," 1979 *Sup. Ct. Rev.* 173, 190.

44. Id.

45. Id. at 193.

46. United States v. Kramer, 711 F.2d 789, 793 (7th Cir. 1983). Judge Posner did not deliver the opinion in *Kramer,* but he was on the panel. See id. at 789.

47. 1 Francis Lieber, *On Civil Liberty and Self-Government* 76–84 (1853).

48. Id. at 78.

49. Id.

50. Id. at 78–79.

51. Frank Friedel, *Francis Lieber: Nineteenth-Century Liberal* vii, 27–62 (1947; photo. reprint, 2003).

52. See, e.g., Jürgen Habermas, "Civil Society and the Political Public Sphere," in *Between Facts and Norms: Contributions to a Discourse Theory of Law and Democracy* 329–87 (William Rehg, trans., 1996); see also Iris Marion Young, *Inclusion and Democracy* 164 (2002) ("[P]ublic spheres . . . deepen democracy by multiplying fora and aspects in which people are represented in public discussion, and by activities that make public officials and powerful private actors accountable."). Ingeborg Maus has observed: "In current theories of democracy, the principle of a critical public sphere, which at the time of the Enlightenment was still treated as an inde-

pendent complement of popular sovereignty, tends to take the place of popular sovereignty. The public judgments of the citizens are euphemistically referred to as self-government, whereas political action is left to professional government" ("Liberties and Popular Sovereignty: On Jürgen Habermas's Reconstruction of the System of Rights," 17 *Cardozo L. Rev.* 825, 877 (1996)).

53. John Stuart Mill, *On Liberty,* 135–36 (1859; photo. reprint, 2002).

54. Id. at 128–30.

55. Id. at 130–31.

56. Id. at 131.

57. Id. at 1269.

58. Id. at 130.

59. Id. at 126.

60. Id. at 11.

61. Id. at 12.

62. Id. at 11.

63. Id. at 12.

64. Id. at 13, 129.

65. Id. at 13, 129.

66. Id. at 21, 28, 158.

67. Id. at 21.

68. Id. at 13.

69. Id. at 102, 132.

70. Id. at 125.

71. Id. at 126.

72. Id. at 13.

73. 410 U.S. 113 (1973).

74. Akhil Reed Amar, "Fourth Amendment First Principles," 107 *Harv. L. Rev.* 757, 772 (1994) (describing Wilkes v. Wood, 19 How. St. Tr. 1153 (C.P. 1763), 98 Eng. Rep. 489, and calling it "*the* paradigm search and seizure case for Americans").

75. Katz v. United States, 389 U.S. 347 (1967).

76. Immanuel Kant, *Groundwork for the Metaphysics of Morals* 37 (Allen W. Wood, ed. and trans., 2002) (1785) ("Act only in accordance with that maxim through which you can at the same time will that it become a universal law.").

77. United States v. White, 401 U.S. 745, 752 (1971) (plurality opinion).

78. Id. at 750.

79. Id. at 749, 752.

80. Justice Douglas said in his dissent in *White,* "Must everyone live in fear that every word he speaks may be transmitted or recorded and later repeated to the entire world? I can imagine nothing that has a more chilling effect on people speaking their minds and expressing their views on important matters. The advocates of that regime should spend some time in totalitarian countries and learn firsthand the kind of regime they are creating here" (401 U.S. 745, 764–65 (1971) (citations omitted)).

81. See, e.g., Maria Łoś and Andrzej Zybertowicz, *Privatizing the Police-State: The Case of Poland* 31–32 (2000) (describing the ubiquitous use of covert agents as part of the "anatomy" of a police state).

82. Illinois v. Wardlow, 528 U.S. 119, 123 (2000) ("In *Terry,* we held that an officer may, consistent with the Fourth Amendment, conduct a brief, investigatory stop when the officer has a reasonable, articulable suspicion that criminal activity is afoot."); Terry v. Ohio, 392 U.S. 1, 20 (1968).

83. Cf. United States v. Squillacote, 221 F.3d 542, 551 (4th Cir. 2000) (suggesting that the FBI's use of a "mature male undercover agent" to "capitalize on [the defendant Squillacote's] fantasies and intrigue" did not require a warrant or even implicate the Fourth Amendment).

Anti-Social Behaviour Orders in the United Kingdom

A. W. Brian Simpson

For centuries the common law, in Great Britain and America and elsewhere in the world, has elaborated bit by bit a complex procedure for the trial of criminal cases, including certain features thought essential to elementary fairness: clear notice of the rule one is supposed to have violated, notice of charges, opportunity to be heard and to confront witnesses, assistance of counsel, proof beyond a reasonable doubt, the right of appeal, and so on. The process of the investigation of offenses has likewise been subject to regulation, perhaps most dramatically as a matter of constitutional law under the Fourth, Fifth, and Sixth Amendments.

As A. W. Brian Simpson explains in this essay, in recent years the United Kingdom has established quite a different system for dealing with disturbing, offensive, or generally anti-social behavior, especially by young people, called the Anti-Social Behaviour Order. Under this program, a person can be subjected to what amounts to an injunction to refrain from certain conduct specified in the order, with virtually none of the protections of traditional common law. This system converts courts into administrators of a program of social control. In this essay Simpson describes this development, which he sees as presenting the question: Is this the end of criminal law?

In this essay, I shall talk about what are known as ASBOs, Anti-Social Behaviour Orders, a legal innovation brought into UK law by the Blair government in 1998. For many years, there has been a recognition that law enforcement agencies have not been very successful in dealing with groups of badly behaved young people, sometimes called feral youths, who create disorder and a sense of insecurity, mainly in relatively deprived urban residential areas, but also in city centers late at night and on public transport. The sort of behavior involved varies but may include shouting and swearing, personal abuse directed at bystanders, public drinking, vomiting and urinating, various forms of damage to property (including paint spraying, smashing bottles, and throwing beer cans around), and so on. Everyone agrees there is a problem. Just before writing up this discussion, I was on a train to London from my home when a group of such youths, mainly male, but including some young women, boarded the train. None had bought tickets, and the ticket collector was so intimidated by their noisy and aggressive behavior that he let this pass. One seized my newspaper, not to read it, but simply to annoy me. Various passengers moved to other parts of the train. Mercifully, the youths all left at an intermediate station, and peace descended again. They provided a very mild example of the problem.

In 1995, the Labour Party issued a consultation paper entitled *A Quiet Life: Tough Action on Criminal Neighbours*[1] that discussed the problem and its possible solution, and in the Crime and Disorder Act of 1998, the Blair government introduced the ASBO as one remedy. The rules governing ASBOs have been modified since then by legislation in 2002 and 2003,[2] and my account has to somewhat simplify a complex body of law. So I will not mention all the safeguards built into the system. In essence, an ASBO is a court order, in effect an injunction, usually made by a magistrate's court,[3] requiring a person to abstain from specified anti-social behavior, prohibiting him or her from certain specified conduct, or both. Applications must be made by local government authorities, by the police, or by registered social landlords and housing trusts and county councils; members of the public cannot directly make applications. Orders cannot be made against children under the age of ten, but otherwise anyone can be made subject to one, and there is no upper age limit. People of my age are not immune, but most orders are made against young persons. Originally they only had local force within a local government area, but today ASBOs made anywhere in England and Wales can apply throughout that area.[4] Violation of such an order is a criminal offense, which therefore incurs a liability to suffer criminal penalties. These may include imprisonment for up to five years for those over seventeen. Those between twelve and seventeen can be made subject to a detention and training order—that is to say, they can be locked up—but those aged ten and eleven cannot be, though they may be ordered to perform some community service. Violation of an order is also an arrestable offense—that is, arrestable by a police officer without warrant.

Acting in an anti-social manner, which has to be proved before an order can be made, is not defined in the legislation except as acting in "a manner that has caused or was likely to cause harassment, alarm or distress to one or more persons not of the same household as [the subject or the order]."[5] The responsible government department, the Home Office, has issued *A Guide to Anti-Social Behaviour Orders and Acceptable Behaviour Contracts* and various other documents explaining ASBOs and the related Acceptable Behaviour Contracts (ABCs).[6] The latter are agreements that can be entered into between local governmental agencies and troublesome people, mainly young people; the procedure is inevitably somewhat coercive. Violation of such a contract can lead to the imposition of an ASBO or to a possession order related to residential accommodation.[7] Official guidance on what is to count as anti-social behavior lists harassment of residents or passersby, verbal abuse, criminal damage, vandalism, noise nuisance, writing graffiti, engaging in threatening behavior in large groups, racial abuse, smoking or drinking in public while under age, substance abuse, joyriding, begging, prostitution, curb crawling, throwing missiles, assault, and vehicle crime. Another official guidance document includes rowdy and nuisance behavior, yobbish behavior and intimidating groups taking over public spaces, fly-posting, dealing and buying drugs on the streets, dumping rubbish and abandoning cars, anti-social drinking, and the misuse of fireworks. The English yob, or lout,[8] shades into the English hooligan and, like elephants, is hard to define but supposedly easy to recognize. What needs to be noticed is that the concept is not limited to cover only conduct that is criminal, though, in fact, most of these examples involve conduct that could, depending on the circumstances, be criminal. Furthermore, conduct that may be forbidden under an ASBO is in no way confined to criminal conduct. For example, a person might be forbidden to be in a town center at night.

The United Kingdom has long since signed up to the European Convention on Human Rights, and under the Human Rights Act of 1998, the convention is partly assimilated into UK domestic law. Article 6 of the convention specifies certain requirements that must be satisfied in criminal proceedings.[9] In English law, proceedings in applications for ASBOs count as civil proceedings, not criminal proceedings.[10] The policy of characterizing the proceedings as civil has all sorts of consequences. For example, the criminal burden of proof does not apply to the requirement, specified in the legislation, that the order must be thought necessary, though it does apply to the proof of the alleged previous anti-social acts. There are important consequences in the law of evidence, in that hearsay evidence and professional evidence can be relied on without a right of confrontation; an order may be made on the basis of anonymous complaints. It also has consequences for legal aid, which is more generously provided in criminal proceedings than in civil proceedings. Thus it is more difficult to appeal against an ASBO. ASBOs may also fall foul of other provisions of the convention.

Plainly, the introduction of the ASBO is based on disquiet over the "stable door" principle that underlies regular criminal law. Under this principle, we shut the door after the horse has left—after a murder has been committed, a robbery carried out, or whatever.[11] ASBOs express the concept of taking preventative measures; the point of an ASBO is not to punish for past misconduct but to prevent future misconduct. ASBOs also reflect other departures from the underlying presuppositions of traditional criminal law. Traditionally we have tried to specify with as much precision as possible what conduct violates the criminal law and which applies to everyone of the age of responsibility. We use the notions of actus reus and mens rea, which express the analysis of human action mocked by Gilbert Ryle in his *The Concept of Mind* as that of the ghost in the machine. Under the ASBO system, all this goes by the board, and since the court imposing the order can specify what conduct is to be forbidden for the future[12] under threat of criminal penalties, the court is given the power to make criminal law ad hominem. Another important departure from tradition arises because traditional criminal law is episodic; typically it deals with one act or a list of discreet acts, not with the concept of a course of conduct. The problem of the English yob is not conceived to be this or that individual yobbish action—one noisy act of swearing, or vomiting, or discarding of one piece of litter, or one menacing look—but, rather, a threatening or harassing course of conduct. It is to this course of conduct, rather than to its individual components, that the ASBO is directed. All this was set out quite clearly when ASBOs were introduced.

ASBOs also form but one part in a general policy of addressing social problems caused by bad behavior through elaborate administrative mechanisms. I have already briefly mentioned ABCs. In 2007, the Blair government also launched what it calls its Respect Programme, details of which are set out in *The Respect Handbook: A Guide for Local Services.*[13] Briefly, the idea is to establish areas in which, because they are troubled by bad behavior, governmental agencies will adopt integrated plans to establish what is thought to be the root of the problem—the absence of a culture of respect.

> The Respect programme is a cross governmental and wide ranging response to anti-social behaviour and its causes. It means promoting good behaviour—for example in work with young people. It means councils, police, social landlords and others tackling anti-social behaviour head on. . . . It means mainstreaming those changes across all local services through Local Area Agreements (LAAs). Ultimately it means a broad approach to help build a modern culture of respect.[14]

Thus the old mechanisms for promoting social order are to be in part at least replaced by proactive and preventative action, which can, for example, include action that targets what are known as problem families. All this is to be coordinated by administrative arrangements—for example, the appointment in governmental organizations, typically local authorities, of what is called "a key worker to 'grip' the problem."[15] You will be reminded, no doubt, of the love affair with czars—drug czars or whatever. In Britain today whenever the press draws attention to a social problem in no time at all there are calls for the appointment of a "Czar" to sort the problem out. Why "czar" is beyond me.

Lurking behind the introduction of the ASBO and the Respect Programme is, I suspect, another problem, which is not made very explicit. It is the sense that regular policing has in some degree lost control of the streets and of public places. An endless refrain in England is that you never see a police officer on the beat anymore and that the public wants a change. Government endlessly claims that it has this matter in hand, but the complaints continue. The ASBO and related initiatives seem to rest on the idea that the way forward is not more police on the streets but, rather, a targeted approach to yobs and problem families. But this is not normally said.

English law has indeed long embodied a peculiar preventative institution, the bind over to keep the peace and be of good behavior, which in my time was occasionally used by magistrates in an attempt to prevent future bad behavior. I recall a case in an Oxfordshire village where two elderly men were before us on cross charges of assault arising from their habit of hurling abuse at each other in the local pub. We threw out the charges, but it was clear that they were something of a continuing nuisance, so we bound them over in a sum of five pounds to keep the peace and be of good behavior. It seemed to work, as they never came back. The power to bind over is still widely used. But the status of bind overs is currently in some doubt because of possible problems with the European Convention, highlighted in the case of *Hasman and Harrap v. United Kingdom*[16] Briefly, what happened was that the applicants had blown a hunting horn and engaged in hallooing in order to disrupt the activities of the Portman fox hunt. This arose before foxhunting with hounds was made illegal by legislation (which seems to have so far had minimal effect on the practice of foxhunting). The criminal court that dealt with the matter found that they had not committed any breach of the peace but that they were hunt saboteurs (which is not a criminal offense) who intended to continue to disrupt hunts and that their conduct was, believe it or not, *contra bonos mores.* The European Court of Human Rights held that their right to freedom of expression under Article 10 had been violated, and the reasoning raises problems for bind overs generally. To date, the UK government still has not said what it proposes to do to conform with the European Convention, but bind overs currently exist under something of a cloud.[17] In a resolution of 5 July 2005, the Committee of Ministers of the Council of Europe urged the United Kingdom to take necessary measures and report back; the matter will be reviewed at six-month intervals until this is done.[18]

ASBOs have, naturally enough, excited much criticism from civil libertarians,[19] and John Mortimer is writing a new book, *The Antisocial Behaviour of Horace Rumpole,* in protest.[20] Some criticism has centered on the uncertainty surrounding the basic concept, and there have been some bizarre examples of their use. One individual, aged eighty-seven, was forbidden from making sarcastic remarks about his neighbor. Another, who operated a pirate radio station, was forbidden from entering buildings more than four stories high.[21] ASBOs have been seriously considered against persons who feed gulls in city centers, where they can be a nuisance, and one person was threatened with one for proposing to publish an advertisement for the job of pope after the death of John Paul II. An ASBO was issued against a farmer for letting his pigs and geese escape. An autistic child was given an ASBO for noisy use of his trampoline, and one was used to prohibit a suicidal woman from jumping into rivers or canals or onto railway lines. ASBOs have been used to prevent prostitutes plying for hire in streets and against nonaggressive beggars.[22] ASBOs have also been criticized because they bring with them the risk of even more use of imprisonment; the procedures may be labeled civil, but the end of the road with ASBOs is loss of liberty. The daily average prison population has risen from around forty thousand in 1993 to over seventy-four thousand in 2003 and is still rising. As for the effectiveness of ASBOs, the jury is out, and it is, methodologically, difficult to see how this can be measured, given the obscurity surrounding the social evil against which they are directed. It is known that among badly behaved young persons, some prestige is attached to being subject to an ASBO, as, from experience with football hooligans, one might expect to be the case.

Because the ASBO simply leaves to administrative bodies and so-called courts (who do not simply apply the law but make it up) the job of deciding what counts as anti-social behavior and what to do about it, I cannot help but wonder whether the ASBO might be the first step in a process that ends up with a general bypassing of traditional criminal law. The latter no doubt has its imperfections, but it also reflects a commitment to the idea of individual responsibility and to the ideals associated with the rule of law. There was a time, long ago, when what I call "traditional criminal law" did not exist; society relied instead on the feud. In the end, it became attenuated and ultimately passed away, and at the time, nobody anticipated this. Are we at the start of a new revolution, in which preventative control replaces regular trial and punishment? In the world of the ongoing "war against terror"—as it is ludicrously called, meaning nonstate terror—there are calls for preventative detention, and to some extent, it already exists. Is this all part of a pattern? These are thoughts I leave to you to ponder. I am afraid it all has the air, to me, of 1984, and 1984 is now some years back.

NOTES

1. London Labour Party, 1995.

2. The relevant acts are the Police Reform Act in 2002 and the Anti-Social Behaviour Act in 2003.

3. They can be made by county courts, the civil courts for small claims, or any criminal court.

4. The order may be local. I do not here discuss the position in Scotland or Northern Ireland or in the Crown Dependencies, the Isle of Man and the Channel Islands.

5. Crime and Disorder Act of 1898 § 1(1) (a).

6. The documents are available online at http://www.homeoffice.gov.uk/anti-social-behaviour/.

7. I do not further discuss ABCs here.

8. These labels are not usually applied to badly behaved young women, for whom more offensive terms are more normally used.

9. The article also deals with the determination of civil rights and obligations, but the requirements for criminal proceedings are more stringent.

10. This view, on which the government insisted, was accepted by the House of

Lords in a test case, *Clingham v. Royal Borough of Kensington and Chelsea, Regina v. Crown Court at Manchester ex parte McCann and Others* (October 2002).

11. To be sure there are exceptions in regular criminal law—for example, crimes of attempt and possession and victimless crimes generally.

12. ASBOs must be made for two years, though they can be discharged; they may extend for longer periods without any specified maximum.

13. The *Respect Handbook* (January 2007) is available at http://www.respect.gov.uk/members/article.aspx?id=12070 (last visited 4 August 2008), together with references to other sources of information and an action line.

14. *Respect Handbook,* 5.

15. Ibid., 32.

16. European Court of Human Rights, application no. 25594/94 (24 November 1999).

17. The United Kingdom is obliged to report to the Committee of Ministers of the Council of Europe what action it proposes to take in response to the judgment. It has initiated a consultation document on the matter, *Bind Overs: A Power for the 21st Century* (London: Home Office, 2003), but that, to date, is all.

18. RecDH (2005) 59.

19. For excellent discussions, see A. Ashworth, "Social Control and Anti-Social Behaviour: The Subversion of Human Rights?" 120 *L.Q.R.* 263 (2004); S. Bright and C. Bakalis, "Anti-Social Behaviour: Local Authority Responsibility and the Voice of the Victim," 2003 *Camb. L.J.* 305; S. MacDonald, "A Suicidal Woman, Roaming Pigs, and a Noisy Trampolinist: Refining the ASBO's Definition of Anti-Social Behaviour" 69 *M.L.R.* 182 (2006) (and see also the same author in "The Nature of the Anti-Social Behaviour Order—*R (McCann & Others) v. Crown Court at Manchester.* 66 *M.L.R.* 630 (2003)). There are also valuable pieces in the *Criminal Law Review* for 2001 (at 873) and 2004 (at 908—P. Ramsay, "What Is Anti-Social Behaviour?").

20. *The Independent,* 28 December 2006.

21. Pirate stations abound in London and interfere with normal reception; to operate with maximum effect, they need access to a high building for transmissions.

22. All these examples are from S. MacDonald's 2003 article cited supra n. 19.

Conscience and the Constitution

John T. Noonan Jr.

We all have to live with the reality of unjust laws, both as citizens and as voters. But the judge is in a special position, for his office and role may require him to support something he regards as deeply wrong. What is the judge to do about the tensions that arise between his conscience and the Constitution under which he acts?

This is the question Judge John Noonan addresses in this essay, focusing on three especially difficult and repeated situations.

What is it right for a judge to do when confronted with a criminal conviction that was valid when obtained but would be invalid under constitutional principles more recently announced and said by the Supreme Court to be prospective only? Surely in one sense it is unjust to affirm the prior conviction.

What attitude should the judge, or the courts more generally, take towards congressional efforts not only to determine the jurisdiction of the courts, and to establish rules of decision for them, but to tell the courts what precedents they are to take as authorities in making the judgment required of them? (Congress did this in the Anti-terrorist and Effective Death Penalty Act.)

What is a judge to do who believes that the death penalty itself is a deep moral wrong, or, worse, that it is an assumption by the state of what belongs to God alone, for in inflicting death the state becomes the lord of life?

In elaborating the elements of the conflicts that these situations present Judge Noonan is exploring a crucial question at the heart of all legal responsibility: When and how do I demonstrate that I understand the empire of force and know how not to respect it? When am I acting as its servant or agent?

We know we have a constitution, although what that means, as we shall see, becomes a matter of dispute. We also have consciences, whose character and source of authority are clearly matters of dispute. I do not understand the authority attributed to conscience unless in some way it is responsive to God; but obviously there are persons who would identify themselves at least as agnostic who do not disavow the special place of conscience as interior guide, different from law or from animal instinct, in enjoining a moral goal or moral obligation.

I do not believe that we could have either democracy or law without the guidance of conscience. We would be lost in the field of force. As a witness, let me quote Winston Churchill, speaking in tribute to a man he had often opposed but recognized as a man of conscience:

> The only guide to a man is his conscience, the only shield to his memory is the rectitude and sincerity of his actions. It is very imprudent to walk through life without this shield. . . .[1]

How do conscience and the Constitution relate to each other? I propose to examine three main areas of particular importance to a judge: (1) The unfairnesses created by constitutional change; (2) Trespass by Congress affecting the mental process by which a judge decides a case; and (3) The effect of role on responsibility in the unique context created by the death penalty.

The first two matters are also affected or controlled by the role of role. Granted that an opinion, like a poem, should be a communication from a person to other persons, unlike a poem, an opinion brings force to bear upon the persons who are the parties to the case. Restricted by his or her role, the judge cannot fully respond to these persons as persons. Does role put the judge in the empire of force or in the countervailing world of words by which humanity rises above brute force?

CONSTITUTIONAL CHANGE AND ITS POSSIBLE UNFAIRNESSES

Justices have referred to "our unchanging constitution."[2] This position, prominently advocated by Justice Scalia, was recently adopted by seven justices in *Danforth v. Minnesota.* Operatively, they all act with awareness that change is possible and even likely. Chief Justice Roberts, dissenting, has noted the "ebbing and flowing decisions" of the Supreme Court on the death penalty. A minority becomes a majority and so alters the Supreme Court's reading of the Constitution, so the chief justice concludes that his present minority will become the majority. He is "encouraged by [today's] majority's determinations that the future can change the past."[3] That encouragement exists for everyone unsatisfied with a constitutional ruling. Reinterpretation of constitutional doctrine means that what was once said to be the Constitution is abandoned. The ancient document now means what the majority says it means.

Suppose a man is accused of sexually abusing a six-year-old girl. At his trial the girl's mother testifies to what the girl reported to her. After the mother's words are heard, the man is not allowed to examine or cross-examine the child. The man is convicted. He is sentenced to forty-five years in prison.[4] Two years later the Supreme Court of the United States rules that the Constitution guarantees every accused person the right to confront his accuser, child though she may be. Under this rule the man was tried and convicted in violation of the Constitution. But the Supreme Court's interpretation of the confrontation clause is new. The court's reading is not retroactive unless the new interpretation can be called a "watershed." The Supreme Court declines to call the change in the meaning of the Constitution a watershed.[5] The prisoner remains in prison, convicted under a form of trial now recognized to be unconstitutional.

Or take the multitude of cases of unconstitutional sentencing created by the Supreme Court in 2005 ruling that the Sentencing Guidelines, which had controlled federal judges since 1987, violated a defendant's right to have a jury determine every fact increasing his punishment beyond the statutory range.[6] At a time when the Guidelines were thought to be constitutional, a man is convicted of drug dealing, and the judge determines that the amount the man sold was in excess of five hundred grams of cocaine. According to the Guidelines, the judge must sentence him to thirty-seven years of imprisonment. The judge thinks that the Guidelines if treated as mandatory are unconstitutional and the sentence that they prescribe too heavy, but he believes he must follow them and does. Fifteen years later, the Supreme Court takes another look at the Constitution and reaches the conclusion that the Guidelines, if treated as mandatory, are unconstitutional. The judge is petitioned by the prisoner to follow the new reading of the Constitution and the judge's own conscience and reduce the sentence. The judge reads in the Supreme Court opinion that the new reading is not retroactive. The sentence stands.[7]

A cost of change is anomaly in the law as indicated by the confrontation clause case and the sentencing cases: persons are currently punished under laws that are currently understood to be unconstitutional. Can a judge conscientiously uphold a penalty now understood to be contrary to law? Does not the injustice cry to heaven when a person has been deprived of liberty by an error of constitutional magnitude, an error made in the first place by those charged with the responsibility of interpretation? If the *Danforth* view is adopted that the Constitution always read as the Court now reads it, is not the conflict with conscience intolerable?

The answer is made that "the system"—the prosecutors, the judges, the prison wardens—relied on the interpretation in force when the conviction was made, the sentence imposed, and the defendant incarcerated. Is their work to be treated as wrong, are their efforts, exerted in good faith to enforce the law as it existed, to be retroactively disparaged and destroyed? Their justified reliance on the Constitution once in force should not, it is argued, be jostled out of place by the new Constitution that has come into being. If this kind of subversion of justified reliance were the regular result of change, the interpretation of the Constitution should never change. Frozen in time, the Constitution should mean today what it meant yesterday and what it meant in 1789.

The jurisprudential problem is diminished by open recognition that constitutional change is a necessity if the Constitution is to live.[8] The imperative to change cannot be stifled by fear of the repercussions of retroactivity. The system requires responsiveness to change if the system is to be human at all, but the system can't change all at once or too suddenly; hence, no retroactivity.

That conclusion leaves the problem of conscience: the problem of incarcerating someone imprisoned under an invalid law. The problem may be seen as presenting a conflict of conscience with itself. By oath, a judge is bound to obey the Constitution, and by unchallenged custom that means the Constitution as currently read by the Supreme Court, even when that court refuses to read it retroactively. Against that duty to obey the current Constitution is the duty not to hold in prison a person who has been unlawfully convicted. The old interpretation of the law has been contradicted by the new; conscience confronts a dilemma; the empire of force needs enlightenment.

CONGRESSIONAL LAWMAKING TO DETERMINE THE DECISIONS OF A COURT

Congress possesses great constitutional power to determine what happens in the federal courts. Most fundamentally, under Article III of the Constitution, it creates, and so can abolish or limit, the jurisdiction of any federal court other than the Supreme Court. Congress, therefore, for all practical purposes, can decide what controversies deserve federal judicial consideration.

Those who trust in linear logic as an appropriate guide to life may say, "The greater power includes the less. If Congress may abolish the jurisdiction of courts, Congress may prescribe how the courts shall decide. Q.E.D." But such logic is deficient in gauging the limits set by the Constitution. The Constitution gives the government the power to kill. But the grant of this greater power is not a grant of the lesser power to torture. The limit set on the powers of Congress over the judiciary arises from the judiciary being constitutionally recognized as a separate branch of government. Congress may not destroy the distinction by intruding into the judicial sphere and masking congressional policy as judicial decision-making.

Congress appears to have effected that intrusion by the enactment of the Anti-terrorist and Effective Death Penalty Act (AEDPA).[9] The act determines the decisions of the federal courts exercising jurisdiction in habeas corpus suits by state prisoners. AEDPA instructs the courts that they may only grant habeas relief if a state court has rendered a decision contrary to an express holding of the Supreme Court in force at the time of the state court's decision. Under this limitation, neither subsequent decisions of the Supreme Court nor its dicta may be taken into account, and none of the decisions of circuit courts or district courts may be considered at all.[10] Law that counts for habeas has been shrunk to explicit holdings of the Supreme Court. If *In re Neagle* had arisen in 2000, instead of 1890, Justice Field's marshal could have been hung by California.[11]

Under AEDPA, the Constitution for habeas purposes is frozen in time—the time of the state decision under challenge. Not only is it frozen in time, it is curtailed in its interpretation. The act goes as far as possible to embody the belief that the Constitution does not change. The belief is not perfectly enshrined. Grudgingly, as it were, AEDPA admits that the Supreme Court may have emitted an interpretation that a state court missed when it was deciding the case. Otherwise the reliance of the state judges on their own jurisprudence is not to be disturbed. Such is the heavy cost of comity.

Even when the law to be applied is limited to "clearly established law," the Supreme Court itself is not always able to state convincingly what the Court had clearly established. Chief Justice Roberts, dissenting, observed that the majority took more than a dozen pages in close analysis of plurality, concurring, and even dissenting opinions to explain what the relevant "clearly established" law was. In the chief justice's view what the state court had had to apply was not clearly established law; it was, instead, "a dog's breakfast of divided, conflicting, and ever-changing analyses."[12] The apparent simplicity of the statutory phrase has disintegrated. The federal judge reviewing the state court decision may often encounter a dog's breakfast when seeking to reach the narrow rule that AEDPA says is the only relevant rule.

Dog's breakfasts are not apt to be edible for humans. But the fundamental difficulty with AEDPA's restrictions is that they touch the thinking process of the federal judge. Normally the district judge looks at the practice of other district judges, at the binding precedents set by the circuit and suggested by the opinions of other circuits or by other state courts, and at the current opinions of the Supreme Court, including both holdings and dicta. No need to mention that more than once a brilliant article or note in a law review or the considered judgment of a learned treatise writer may be found to state with exactness what is current constitutional law. Even if the academy's productions are understood as only advice and the district court decisions discounted as nonbinding along with out-of-circuit opinions, there remains the likelihood of indisputably relevant law expressed in binding circuit authority and in recent decisions of the Supreme Court that are now off-limits for the federal judges ruling on habeas. In the normal course of judging, a district or circuit court would pay attention to dicta, as well as to holdings, of the Supreme Court. Sometimes they are not easy to distinguish. Normally it would be a rash judge who ignored emanations from an opinion of the Supreme Court. Now, the current law that in other circumstances would guide or control a judge thinking about the case must be removed from his mind and discarded.

That result makes sense if one believes that the Constitution never changes. It makes little sense if the Constitution is applied, as it normally is applied, in the terms given it by its most recent authoritative interpreters. Congress, it would seem, has intruded into the judicial sphere, making the judges spokesmen for congressional policy in favor of the ante quo. AEDPA embodies a blinkered concept of law. Constitutional law is treated as what once was the law. The development of doctrine is despised. That despisal is a direct legislative interference in the independence of the judiciary.

Nonetheless, several circuits have ruled that AEDPA is constitutional, and the Supreme Court, assuming that it is, has repeatedly enforced it.[13] A federal judge has sworn to adhere to the Constitution—but to which Constitution, that document as generally understood to speak as currently developed, or that document as it now appears to be successfully reinterpreted by Congress to allow Congress a role in judicial decision-making? Either way he decides, a judge will be observing his oath and following his conscience. But which conscience is correct? Confronting the empire of force with the rule of law conscientiously applied, the judge sees the difficulty and not the solution.

The unfairnesses of nonretroactivity, already noted, recur in this context. But here nonretroactivity results not from the Supreme Court's denial of retroactivity to one of its own decisions but from the trespass of Congress upon judicial territory. The restraint put upon the judge's mind by nonjudicial force is palpable.

How is this second dilemma different from the first? One may at least partially resolve the first by holding that the Constitution is what the Supreme Court says it is—if retroactive, retroactive; if not retroactive, not retroactive. In the second case, a legislative body has taken on itself to interfere with judicial minds—a considerably greater strain on the understanding of the Constitution, even if one could accept it simply because the Supreme Court has accepted the intrusion as that court's new understanding of the Constitution.

As a practical matter if the judge refuses to follow AEDPA because he believes that it is contrary to the Constitution, he will be reversed; his judgment will have held out false hope to the prisoner, wasted the time of the lawyers and other judges, and accomplished nothing good. But are practical considerations the way to decide a matter of conscience?

What then of the restraint placed by role? No question of responsibility can be explored without recognition of the role of role. Roles create and assign responsibility, create and limit power. Stepping beyond his assigned role or robe, the judge becomes an ordinary citizen without responsibility for injustice in the case before him and without power to effect a different result. Does recognition of his role relieve his conscience?

THE CONSTITUTIONAL LIMIT ON PUNISHMENT

The Eighth Amendment to the Constitution bans cruel and unusual punishment. But what is cruel and what is unusual? What about sentencing a man to fifteen years imprisonment wearing a chain about his body, when he has embezzled less than $1,000? Do we look to what was done by virtue of common law in the seventeenth century, as Justice White and Justice Holmes once opined, or do we look to the sanctions against criminal conduct current in 1789, as an originalist might argue, or do we measure "cruel and unusual" by the standard set by an evolving civilization?

In a landmark case in 1910, *Weems v. United States,* improbably decided by a vote of four to two (the two being White and Holmes), the Supreme Court opted for an evolving standard, assuming, as we often optimistically do, that our civilization is changing for the better.[14]

Here, as in my earlier examples, constitutional change has been in the direction of greater recognition of humanity. Over objections from within the Court, the Supreme Court has continued on that course set by conscience. But not as to the death penalty, so long established as acceptable in the moral tradition guiding Europe and the American offshoots of Europe. The Hebrew Bible prescribed death for adultery, blasphemy, sodomy, and witchcraft, to give a few examples of what was stated to be God's law. St. Paul wrote in a Roman variation of the tradition when he advised the Christians of Rome to obey the authorities:

> . . . for the authority does not bear the sword in vain! It is the servant of God to execute wrath on the wrongdoer. (Romans 13:4)[15]

Given such biblical antecedents, the moral respectability of the death penalty has had a long life. As a punishment for murder, who could challenge the fit—a life for a life? The status of the penalty changed with recognition of its uniqueness. No doubt there are objections to it based on the inevitability of error in some cases in which it is applied beyond any correction. That is not the fundamental objection.

For the secular humanist, I perhaps unwarrantedly assume, the objection is that death is the extinction of the person. Like a hapless bug, the person is wiped out and is no more. To inflict such a fate not on a bug but on a living human being seems to constitute cruelty and, in light of changes that are worldwide, even unusual cruelty. In conscience and in constitutional argument the secular humanist may conclude that he should not be the agent of death.

A theist, believing in the existence of the soul, has a different basis for objection. For him the fundamental point is that in imposing death, the state becomes the lord of life. The state asserts its supremacy over the individual human being and terminates his earthly pursuit of a destiny that is not earthly. The lordship of life lies with God alone. It is not for any human being, clothed with brief human authority, to decide that this human life must end now. To say that God has delegated the authority to kill seems to be a species of legal fiction no longer sustainable.

Three kinds of judges may be involved in a death penalty case that results in an application for federal habeas: the trial judge who imposes the sentence; the member of an appellate court affirming the sentence; and a federal judge reviewing the case on habeas.

The trial judge. A trial judge imposing a sentence of death is a direct cause of the prisoner's execution. He does not himself make the fatal injection. He is responsible for the death. If the trial judge has conscientious objections to taking a human life in this way and yet the law requires it, the judge should recuse himself. I do not believe that the judge's unwillingness to follow the law in this relatively rare kind of case disqualifies the judge from being a judge. A comparable conclusion would be that all judges who believe abortion to be immoral should resign their office.

The state appellate judges. On appeal, typically sitting with several other appellate judges, a judge may face a criminal case where death has been imposed. If the issues on appeal go to questions as to the process or as to the prisoner's guilt, I do not see a conscientious objection to the appellate judge participating in the decision, even though the decision may result in affirmance and so in application of the sentence. If the challenge on appeal is to the sentence itself, a more difficult question is posed. Ratifying the sentence, the appellate judge puts himself in a position close to that of the trial judge. The conflict of Constitution and conscience for him appears to be the same, even though the appellate judge may be only one of three or five or nine. The course for the conscientious objector should be the same as for the trial judge.

The habeas judge. In the usual case, this kind of judge is being asked to relieve from capital punishment a person who has been convicted of a crime and sentenced in a state court. The person has exhausted all appeals offered by the state system and has turned to the federal forum, seeking a writ of habeas corpus. He alleges that the state conviction was secured by means, or ended in a judgment, contrary to the Constitution of the United States. A federal judge is not, then, imposing death upon him. A federal judge is determining if the process or its result violated federal law. If a federal judge finds no constitutional violation, the federal judge is without power to intervene and protect the prisoner on the brink of death. The federal judge in this not uncommon case is not "a death penalty judge."

True, the federal judge's denial of the habeas petition will be understood by many uninformed people as a kind of approval of the state's proposed action. The federal judge cannot be held accountable for such misinterpretation. True, a justice of the Supreme Court could state his or her belief that the death penalty itself was unconstitutional and that view might become the law of the land. A Supreme Court justice is in the difficult position, perhaps, of reconciling conscience with the Constitution.

Take, for example, Justice Blackmun's announced reason for not participating in death penalty appeals to the Supreme Court—that he did not want "to tinker" any longer with "the machinery of death?"[16] In *Callins v. Collins,* Justice Scalia pitted the text of the Constitution, which he followed, against the moral and intellectual scruples of Justice Blackmun after more than twenty years' experience of trying to ensure fairness in capital cases. Justice Scalia found it unnecessary to state that the text of the Constitution never changed: that was the given of his reproach of Justice Blackmun. The latter argued that experience required a changed reading of the unchanged text.[17]

A justice of the Supreme Court has the ability to dissent from any ratification of the death penalty because a justice enjoys a role in which he can conclude that the death penalty is contrary both to the Constitution and his conscience. If that were Justice Blackmun's position, it seems that he should have continued to dissent. A dissent is often the seedbed of change in our evolving Constitution. If Justice Blackmun meant that he no longer wanted to deal with the numerous procedural errors that may infect a death penalty case, it is still difficult to see why he should have taken himself out of the review of the process. Did he not have an objection in both conscience and Constitution to performing his duty?

Other federal judges, lacking the power to override Supreme Court precedent, are bound by law and, I would add, in conscience to comply with the Supreme Court's construction of the Constitution. Under this construction, habeas judges, other than Supreme Court justices, do not cooperate in a state's infliction of death. The role again relieves the judge of responsibility.

The Constitution, Lloyd Garrison famously said, as he fanned the fire at Framingham, is "a covenant with hell."[18] He was, of course, speaking of the constitutional support of the institution of slavery. That dilemma of conscience or Constitution was resolved by war and constitutional amendment. I do not count on these ways of resolving the lesser difficulties of the criminal justice system: too few are affected by them or see them. Our age is not afflicted by a depersonalization as deep and as destructive as slavery. Nonetheless, the dilemmas I point to are real, require recognition, and await resolution. I will sketch the tentative resolution I have reached after twenty years' experience.

Not all our responsibility as human beings comes from law, but all our power as judges comes from law establishing our role. Unless we act within that role, we are merely bystanders on a busy street trying to direct traffic. Our role requires us to discern and follow the law. If the Supreme Court has decided that the Constitution changes but not retroactively, no federal judge has the power to make the change retroactive. When power depends upon role, role is not a device for denying responsibility; rather, responsibility cannot exceed the role.

Role is constitutive of judicial power. Responsibility accompanies the exercise of this power. First, in carrying out his role the judge must be aware that his action or inaction, attentiveness or negligence, courtesy or boorishness impact other people. He is not interacting with anonymous Ps and Ds. He is affecting actual lives. Second, the judge should not become an automaton applying black letter law in a machinelike way. If machines could do the job, we wouldn't need judges. Empathy, a quality machines do not possess, is needed to understand testimony, to reach a fair result, to pronounce and review a sentence. Third, the judge must be aware that his role does not dispense him from moral responsibility that exists apart from his role. Concretely, if the role requires him to perform a wicked or unjust act, he should recuse himself from the case or resign from the bench. If, for example, what the role requires puts him in the position where he must impose a sentence of death, he could in good conscience recuse himself or, if the situation arose repeatedly, resign.

I have tried to put these conclusions into practice. They aren't necessarily right or beyond revision. They are meant to make the judge a person unswallowed by the empire of force.

NOTES

1. Winston Churchill, tribute to Neville Chamberlain, 12 November 1940, House of Commons, *Parl. Deb. H.C.* (5th Series) 1940.
2. E.g., Georgia v. Randolph, 121 S. Ct. 1525, 1539–40 (2005) (Scalia, J., dissenting).
3. Brewer v. Quaterman, 127 S. Ct. 1706–23 (2007) (Roberts, C. J., dissenting).
4. Bockting v. Bayer, 408 F.3d 1127 (9th Cir. 2005).
5. Whorton v. Bockting, 127 S. Ct. 1173 (2007).
6. United States v. Booker, 543 U.S. 220 (2005).
7. E.g., Carrington v. United States, 470 F.3d 920, 921 (2006).
8. See Burnet v. Coronado Oil & Gas Co., 285 U.S. 393, 405–14 (1932) (Brandeis, J., dissenting and giving at least fifteen examples of the Supreme Court changing its mind as to the meaning of the Constitution.)
9. 28 U.S.C. § 2254(d)(1)(1996).
10. Williams v. Taylor, 520 U.S. 362, 412 (2000).
11. See In re Neagle, 135 U.S. 1 (1890).
12. Brewer v. Quaterman, supra n. 3, at 1715 (Roberts, C. J., dissenting).
13. E.g., Hughes v. Johnson, 191 F.3d 607, 612 (5th Cir. 1999); Duhaime v. Ducharme, 200 F.3d 597 (9th Cir. 2000); Moton v. Utah, 28 Fed. Appx. 854 (10th Cir. 2001).
14. Weems v. United States, 217 U.S. 349 (1910).
15. The quotation from Romans 13:4 is from the New Revised Standard Version.
16. Callins v. Collins, 510 U.S. 1141, 1145 (1994) (Blackmun, J., dissenting).
17. Id. at 1141 (Scalia, J., concurring).
18. Francis Jackson Garrison, *William Lloyd Garrison (1805–1879): The Story of His Life Told By His Children,* 3:44 (1889).

Law as a Tool

H. Jefferson Powell

What is the proper attitude for the president to take toward a judgment of the Supreme Court on a constitutional issue with which he disagrees? Toward a duly enacted act of the national legislature which he thinks is beyond its constitutional powers? H. Jefferson Powell examines these questions in this essay, beginning with a decision by President Madison to follow such a judgment by the Court and obey the act of Congress requiring him to do so. Madison thus established a practice of respect for the judgment of the other branches that has had continued life in the executive branch until almost the present day. The lawyer for the president and the president himself have been obliged, in the course of their daily work, repeatedly to confront, as an ethical and not merely political matter, the nature and force of the obligation to respect the judgments of the other branches, at least where they were rationally defensible. In this sense there has long been in the executive branch an internalized ethic of obedience to the law.

There are many signs that this attitude is changing for the worse. Lawyers for the executive branch are coming to regard acts of Congress simply as obstacles to be overcome through specious reasoning, or tools to be employed by similarly insincere argument to confirm whatever the executive branch wants to achieve. As Powell argues, this movement toward the view of law merely as a tool or instrument subverts an essential ingredient in the idea of free government.

The intuition that brought the contributors to this volume together was—and I quote eloquent words that no one will be surprised to know were crafted by Jim White—a shared sense that "our public world has been changing under our feet faster than we can see or understand it, especially with respect to the fundamental character of law and democracy," and that the changes, "some of them distressing, show up everywhere." In my own area of teaching, scholarship, and public service—American public law—I have that sense very strongly, but when I began preparing this discussion, I found it surprisingly difficult to say what, in my own experience as teacher, scholar, and executive branch lawyer, actually justifies me in claiming to feel a sea change going on in public life. Much of what seems amiss in the public life of the United States—and perhaps in the Western world more generally—is hardly new.

Members of Congress engaging in partisan bickering and petty self-aggrandizement while neglecting the business of the Republic—this is a good account of Congress during the Gilded Age of the late nineteenth century. Supreme Court justices suspected of ideological bias or personal animus—you may recall that Thomas Jefferson described the opinions of John Marshall's Court as "huddled up in conclave . . . delivered . . . with the silent acquiescence of lazy or timid associates, by a crafty chief judge, who sophisticates the law to his own mind, by the turn of his own reasoning."[1] Obfuscation or dishonesty on the part of the executive branch—in the early 1920s, Justice Department corruption reached such depths that a House of his own party considered the impeachment of Attorney General Henry Daugherty. Rank and rampant partisanship—the Jacksonians' attacks on President John Quincy Adams and the anti-Jacksonian onslaught against Old Hickory himself cannot be topped for vulgar, defamatory content. The public sphere in any reasonably free and open society is going to seem, much and perhaps most of the time, in rather bad shape, on the brink of some disaster or the other. There has never been a golden age, for law or democracy, and nostalgia for what never existed may not be a useful tool in social criticism.

So, if the intuitive premise of the present collection has any validity, we must be able to trace it not only to the surface pathologies of our society, important as they unquestionably are, but beneath them. Or to put it bluntly and personally, if I have anything useful to say in this setting, it cannot simply be to retail my personal views on recent and current events, views that, I am sorry to say, often seem even to me distressingly predictable. In preparing this analysis, therefore, I have asked myself, again and again, what about American public law in the present day seems different to me at a fundamental level from my perceptions of American law in the past eras that I study and teach. I think I may have an answer, but to explain it, I need to start quite some time ago, with a date I have long thought deeply important, at least as a symbol, in American constitutional history: April 13, 1809.

On that date, James Madison, president for just over one month at that point, wrote a letter. Madison was responding to a letter he had received from Simon Snyder, governor of Pennsylvania and a major figure in Madison's Republican Party, a letter that has to have caused Madison some heartburn. Snyder, along with a great many other Pennsylvania Republicans, was up in arms—literally, in the case of some state militiamen—over a decision of the federal Supreme Court styled *United States v. Peters.* The details of the case need not detain us; what is important for present purposes is Snyder's request. The governor and the Republican majority in the state legislature were of the view that the Supreme Court's decision was not only erroneous but unconstitutional, "a usurpation of power and jurisdiction," in the legislature's words—indeed, just the sort of federal overreaching that the Republican Party had come to national power by resisting. A decade before, James Madison had been a leader in the fight against Federalist usurpation in Congress and the executive; it was a "pleasing idea," Snyder purred, that the executive branch of the national government was now in the hands of a chief magistrate who would uphold the Constitution's limits on federal authority with respect to the judiciary and Congress. Unmistakably, if tactfully, Governor Snyder was urging President Madison to nullify the Supreme Court's decision by refusing to enforce it.

I want us to be clear about how plausible Snyder's request was. First, Madison emphatically believed in the legitimacy and the duty of constitutional interpretation by actors besides the federal courts. On the national stage, he was perhaps the most prominent defender of the role of Congress and of the state legislatures in addressing constitutional issues, while almost his last act as president, in March 1817, was to veto a bill simply because he thought it unconstitutional, though he strongly approved of its policy. For Madison, the president was independently responsible for interpreting the Constitution and for upholding the instrument in its true or best interpretation.[2] Second, Madison was no stranger to the idea of the executive ignoring Supreme Court process: as secretary of state, Madison had snubbed the Court in *Marbury v. Madison,* disdaining even to have counsel put in an appearance on his behalf; more recently, Attorney General Caesar Rodney had publicly rejected an opinion by Justice William Johnson in which Johnson insisted that the executive was obliged to enforce judicial orders.[3] Rodney made his statement in the waning days of the previous administration, to be sure, but he remained as attorney general under Madison. Third, Snyder's constitutional argument was, at a minimum, substantial by Republican standards. And finally, Madison had powerful political reasons to avoid angering Snyder or the Republicans in the Pennsylvania legislature. Quiet instructions to the U.S. marshal to desist from his efforts to evade the state militia and enforce the Supreme Court's order could hardly do Madison any political harm, while spurning his fellow Republicans risked significant damage to the political coalition on which Madison's success as president depended. The newspapers, indeed, were already speculating that President Jefferson would have left the Supreme Court swinging in the wind. Madison, then, had good reasons, based in both principle and expediency, for acceding to Snyder's request or, at the very least, appearing to give Snyder's views careful consideration. But this Madison declined, politely but emphatically, to do.

"It would be unnecessary, if not improper," the president informed the governor, virtually by return post, "to enter into any examination" of the constitutional issues Snyder had raised. He continued, "It is sufficient, in the actual posture of the case, to remark that the Executive of the [United] States is not only unauthorized to prevent the execution of a Decree sanctioned by the Supreme Court of the [United] States, but is expressly enjoined by Statute, to carry into effect any such decree, where opposition may be made to it." Madison's opinion about whether John Marshall and his colleagues were right on the law, even if he thought them not only wrong but guilty of unconstitutional usurpation, was simply irrelevant. Congress had given him no discretion to second-guess the Court but, instead, had directed him to enforce its decrees: as a result, Madison concluded, "no legal discretion lies with the Executive of the [United] States to decline steps which might lead to a very painful issue." In other words, if the state authorities resisted, Madison would be compelled to exercise federal executive power to carry out the decision of the federal judiciary and the will of the federal Congress, through force if necessary.[4]

This was, I believe, a tremendously important moment in American history. As I have suggested, it would not have been very costly for Madison to take a different course, and he could have justified doing so on intellectually defensible grounds. Madison had real alternatives in deciding how to respond to Snyder, and I believe that he chose as he did for reasons that I will suggest briefly. But let us pause first to take stock of the practical consequences of that letter in April 1809. By choosing to respond to Snyder as he did, Madison inaugurated what has largely been a consistent course of conduct on the part of the executive branch, a course of conduct that is now an axiom of the American legal system, one on which the high Court itself sometimes relies expressly, as when it declined to concern itself about the danger of executive resistance to its decision in the case of the Watergate tapes.[5] If Madison had done what Snyder wanted—disobeyed an act of Congress and ignored a decision of the Court—and if that had become the settled practice of our system, many things in our constitutional history might have been different indeed.

So why did President Madison choose as he did? I suspect many (perhaps most) contemporary constitutional scholars would agree with his decision and rest its propriety on respect for the role of the Supreme Court in our system. But that is not how Madison explained his rejection of Snyder's request. It seems, instead, that for Madison, it was Congress's action, Congress's will, that determined the president's legal discretion (or, rather, lack of discretion) on the matter. He wrote that the president was "unauthorized"—in context, clearly meaning that he had no statutory authority—to pick and choose which decisions of the Court to enforce. On the contrary, he informed Snyder, the president was "expressly enjoined by Statute" to enforce them all. Even if some constitutional judgment about the role of the judiciary is lurking in the background of the letter, Madison thought it sufficient to rest his decision to enforce the Court's order on his duty to execute faithfully Congress's law.

But what about the president's duty and power to execute the Constitution according to the president's independent judgment about its meaning? Madison certainly was not implying that the Constitution means whatever Congress or the Court happens to think it means or that the president has to pretend that it does. Recall the 1817 veto I mentioned. The bill's constitutionality had been thoroughly examined in Congress, and its Republican defenders included some of the best constitutional lawyers in the country; there was good reason, furthermore, to believe that the justices of the high court would agree. Madison, who very much favored the bill's objectives, could sign it into law with the happy reflection that no one he need care about would criticize him on constitutional grounds. Henry Clay later claimed that "no circumstance, not even an earthquake that should swallow up one half of [Washington], could have excited more surprise" than the news that "Mr. Madison had rejected his own bill—I say his own bill."[6] In 1809, Madison had acquiesced in the judgments of others without even being willing to address the constitutional questions at issue. In 1817, it was Madison *contra mundum* (against the world) on the constitutional issue, and the likely convergence of the legislative and judicial branches on a view at odds with his own did not matter. The 1817 veto exemplifies independent presidential interpretation of the Constitution with a vengeance.

You will already have seen where I am headed. I do not think Madison was muddled or inconsistent or that his 1817 veto contradicted his 1809 letter. Quite to the contrary, Madison was acting out of a vision of the role of the executive branch in the American legal order—a vision that, for most of our history and up until quite recently, has been dominant, in part because of Madison's seminal role. Madison faced the question of whether the 1817 bill was within Congress's powers straight up, as it were. He was faced with no constitutional obligation that conflicted with his duty to preserve, protect, and defend the Constitution as he best understood it. Since he thought the bill beyond Congress's authority, he could—no doubt, he thought he should—veto it. But 1809 presented a very different question, because it involved a statute, a law already duly enacted by Congress. Where obedience to an act of Congress is at issue, the president fulfills his independent obligation to preserve, protect, and defend the Constitution by recognizing and acting on his Article II duty to take care that the laws be faithfully executed. With respect to such laws, the president's constitutional judgment is (or ought to be) a resolution to carry them out. What Governor Snyder wanted him to do, whether Snyder realized it or not, was to ignore a clear constitutional obligation. By law, Congress had expressly enjoined the president to enforce the Court's decisions, without exception; if Madison read an exception into the statute—stipulating that the executive should enforce the Court's decisions unless they are constitutionally wrong—he would be rewriting the laws, not ensuring their execution. As Justice Holmes wrote many years later, "The duty of the President to see that the laws be executed is a duty that does not go beyond the laws."[7] There was for Madison, therefore, no conflict between the president's duty to the Constitution and his duty to federal statutes—the latter was simply a subset of the former.

I said earlier that Madison's vision of the executive's role has been dominant through most of American history, but that was a little inaccurate. Eventually, by the middle of the nineteenth century at the latest, lawyers raised a question that complicated Madison's binary logic: what should happen if an act of Congress was so patently unconstitutional on its face that the president's judgment to that effect is as certain as the judgment that he must generally see to the faithful execution of the laws? It is hardly surprising that once this question was raised, the executive branch took the position that in such an unfortunate circumstance, the president should follow his clear and specific judgment on the particular law's invalidity rather than his clear but general judgment on his duty to execute statutes. In an 1860 opinion, for example, Attorney General Jeremiah Black advised President Buchanan that he was not obliged to select a particular military officer to carry out a given mission even if an act of Congress appeared to impose such an obligation: decisions about "what officer shall perform any particular duty," Black reasoned, were unmistakably within the discretion of the president as commander in chief, not Congress as the creator of the army.[8] If the statutory language had to be construed to conflict with that constitutional principle, it could simply be ignored. From the era of Black and Buchanan until quite recently, officers of the executive branch and their legal advisors adhered—or at least claimed to adhere—both to the general principle that the executive's duty is to enforce federal statutes and to the exceptional proviso that it is possible for a statute to be so unmistakably unconstitutional, at least when it attempts to deprive the president of his own constitutional role, that the president is justified in declining to acquiesce in Congress's will.

You will not have missed the fact that I included a waffle phrase in what I just said—perhaps executive officials have only claimed to adhere to the general principle and the exceptional proviso both. After all, a skeptic might say, the principle and the proviso really are not consistent. The principle speaks in Madison's voice, arguing for enforcing statutory language without picking and choosing what parts are valid, but the proviso is Black's and says something very different—that one should enforce statutes only so far as one thinks they are valid. A skeptic would surely say that Black endorsed precisely what Madison told Snyder the president lacked, discretion about which laws are to be faithfully executed; that Black's exception would inevitably swallow Madison's rule; that talk about how the executive is ordinarily required to enforce statutes or can refuse to do so only if Congress's constitutional error is unmistakable is nothing but a smoke screen or, more benignly, a public rhetoric or convention that cannot be taken seriously as a determinant of action.

A skeptic can say all that. But as the theologian John Howard Yoder once pointed out, "moral rhetoric has a kind of sacramental effect." "The hard-nosed political realist can always say that [it] is not binding or convincing," Yoder explained, but to most people, "it still tends to have some power of conviction."[9] "Convictions are a badly libelled lot," a Chaucer scholar once wrote, and on subjects free of undue skepticism, they are mostly used "to say what [the writer] meant rather than to say the exact opposite of what he meant."[10]

Madison and Attorney General Black were not skeptics about the law.[11] Of course, they realized that dishonest lawyers can manipulate legal reasoning, just as they knew that bad lawyers can get it wrong. But they also believed that upright and intelligent lawyers can use legal reasoning not as a mere tool to get to extralegal ends but as a means to the honest—the faithful—interpretation of the law. They had internalized the processes of legal reasoning as a kind of ethic or even a faith. Working within such an ethic, lawyers like Black experienced no practical dissonance between their felt obligation as executive officials to enforce Congress's will as expressed in statute, on the one hand, and the existence of an outer limit to the scope of that obligation, on the other. Madison's rule was not subverted by Black's exception because it was not really a rule but an expression of the executive branch lawyer's understanding of his duty. The rhetoric or convention of talking about a general obligation to execute in good faith whatever laws Congress may have enacted was a signal pointing to the ethical substance of that duty. The existence of boundaries to that duty in no way overthrew or even lightened the duty's ethical weight: it merely defined it in one dimension. In this context, good faith is no guarantee of freedom from error, but it does prevent the enterprise from becoming empty. One of Black's immediate successors, Amos T. Akerman, expressly rejected the cynical conclusion that it is meaningless to ask if a given statutory restriction on the president is clearly invalid: "In constitutional and legal inquiries, right or wrong is often a question of degree." But despite the fact that it is often "impossible to tell precisely where in the scale right ceases and wrong begins," argued Akerman, the internalized ethic of faithful interpretation and execution opened the possibility of meaningful legal reasoning.[12]

The norm among executive branch officials from Black's time until quite recently was as I have just described it. A norm is not a description, of course, and there have doubtless been many, many cases of corruption and sheer incompetence. At the same time, even the corrupt and the incompetent did their misdeeds in a world in which the claims of the law to rationality and meaningfulness were generally accepted. This is not the time or place to attempt anything like a proof of that claim, so let me instead briefly point out two examples of this internalized ethic of law at work. President Theodore Roosevelt is generally remembered for his stewardship theory of the president, which he explained with typical color: "While President . . . I have used every ounce of power there was in the office and I have not cared a rap for the criticisms of those who spoke of my 'usurpation of power.' . . . [T]he efficiency of this Government depends upon it possessing a strong central executive." What is less often remembered is that Roosevelt's flamboyant statements about the president's duty to act fearlessly "for the public welfare, whenever and in whatever manner [is] necessary," regularly included the caveat "unless such action [is] forbidden by the Constitution or by the laws" or the caveat "unless prevented by direct constitutional or legislative prohibition." In practice, as Roosevelt's secretary of war and successor William Howard Taft pointed out, it was the caveat, not the flamboyant claim, that often controlled President Roosevelt's actions.[13]

The best-known opinion of Justice Robert Jackson is his concurrence in the Steel Seizure Case. Jackson concluded that opinion with an eloquent statement of Madison's 1809 principle.

> With all its defect, delays and inconveniences, men have discovered no technique for long preserving free government except that the Executive be under the law, and that the law be made by parliamentary deliberations.

When one reads the opinion preceding this conclusion as whole—not in snippets, as I fear we often do—one may notice the balance Jackson struck between his zealous adherence to Madison's principle and his sympathy for executive officials tempted to circumvent it out of honest concern for the public welfare. (He was, you will recall, attorney general before he went onto the Court.) Jackson accepted Black's proviso, so he was not willing to rule out the possibility that there are circumstances in which the executive may rightfully ignore a legislative command. But Jackson made it clear that within this logical and legal possibility lie "grave dangers for the country," not from the corrupt and incompetent (who are with us always), but from the sincere and intelligent. It is the latter, the honest president or executive branch lawyer acting out of a genuine concern for the public welfare, who poses the real danger to "the balanced power structure of our Republic," precisely because of his or her honesty. Dishonesty and error may work great harms, but those harms are particular; the honest official, seeking to justify his or her evasion of the laws, can undermine the very ethic of executive respect for the laws made by parliamentary deliberations.[14]

Jackson did not spare himself in stating this problem—famously, his opinion rejected the executive's reliance on his own public statements as attorney general as "self-serving press statements of the attorney for one of the interested parties."[15] But the most significant bit of legal advice he gave President Franklin D. Roosevelt as attorney general shows Jackson's careful adherence as an executive officer to Madison's principle. In the summer of 1940, when FDR decided to accede to a request by Britain, virtually under a maritime siege by Nazi Germany after the fall of France, to transfer surplus warships to the Royal Navy, he asked Attorney General Jackson to address the legal question of presidential authority. It would have been child's play to give President Roosevelt an opinion that simply asserted his authority as commander in chief in a context of grave national danger, and FDR's resolve to effect the transfer in return for U.S. access to bases on British territory in the Western Hemisphere left Jackson little room to maneuver. Nevertheless, Jackson signed a formal opinion that carefully circumscribed the implications of his (mostly) affirmative response. Only four years earlier, the Supreme Court had described the president's authority over foreign relations as "delicate, plenary, and exclusive"[16]—a phrase tailored to support a claim that legislation in the area is of dubious relevance at best. Jackson rejected the temptation: notwithstanding the Court's language, he wrote that the president's authority, even in this area, "is not unlimited," and he devoted most of his legal analysis to a careful parsing of the relevant statutes, concluding that it was lawful to transfer some of the warships but not others. Even in a context where the executive policymakers had made up their minds already, Jackson strove to maintain Madison's principle that the executive is under the laws.[17]

For the remainder of this analysis, I would like to presuppose, for the purposes of argument, that my historical claim is correct—that an internalized ethic of obedience to the laws was the norm within the executive branch until relatively recently. In what sense, then, accepting this presupposition, has there been a change? My answer is that the idea of executive enforcement of the laws that Congress has passed, what I am calling "Madison's 1809 principle," has been transformed. Though not rejected as a formal matter—smart officials in the executive branch continue to pay lip service to something that has become a mere convention—the principle is no longer internalized, no longer an ethic imposing a personal and even moral duty. The faithful execution of the laws, which Article II enjoins and which Madison envisioned as the central role of the executive branch, is now something very different. Far from being the premise of executive action, the laws are an obstacle and a tool—an obstacle in that Congress's words are seen as potential roadblocks in the path of serving the public, rather than the public's structured means of stating what will serve it; a tool in that an executive branch lawyer should treat Congress's words as an opportunity to justify what the executive policymakers already are intent on doing, not (as with Jackson in 1940) as the basis for confining any long-term damage to the balanced power structure of our Republic resulting from executive decisions.

The transition from Madison's principle as an internalized ethic to its present status—I will say what exactly I think its present status is shortly—can be seen most clearly in the various and sincere efforts to preserve its objective that the executive carry out Congress's will. When the law is not an internal ethic but, rather, an external demand, ensuring that it is obeyed must be external, worked either through its administration by a distinct enforcer or through endlessly detailed specification of rules of compliance. The federal Internal Revenue Code becomes the paradigm. No taxpayer is expected to accept for himself or herself the code's main objective, the raising of revenue. Quite to the contrary, taxpayers are expected and allowed to attempt to minimize the code's success, and that attempt is regulated by an external enforcer and by the multiplication of rules of compliance that have to be tweaked unceasingly in response to taxpayers' endless efforts at circumvention. The law is, brazenly, a tool by which the Internal Revenue Service tries to lay hands on taxpayers' money while they use it to evade that result.

What has happened in American public law is that we have assimilated the relationship between the executive branch and Congress's laws to the relationship between taxpayers and the tax code. Executive branch officials no longer understand the execution of Congress's objectives as the fundamental purpose of their part of the government. Statutes are obstacles or opportunities and, in either case, a factor external to the executive's own agenda.

In saying this, I do not mean to succumb to an undue cynicism. Indeed, I think the clearest evidence of the decline of Madison's principle as an ethic lies in what men and women of good faith and intelligence in the executive branch have tried to put in its place. As the laws become merely external to the executive's own self-understanding, respect for Congress leads to a search for external means of compelling the executive to obey Congress. The obvious first thought, at least to litigation-minded Americans, is to enable more and more people to sue the executive on more and more issues, so that the courts can play the role of external enforcer. I am not going to dwell on that move, important as it is, because it is not generally one that executive branch lawyers, with their professional orientation toward defending the client's interests, can endorse. Interesting, however, is the intraexecutive analogue: to identify some bit of the executive itself as the enforcer—perhaps the Justice Department, vis-à-vis the White House, or (as Lincoln Caplan argued in the late 1980s in a widely praised book)[18] the office of the solicitor general within the Justice Department—and expect it to act in a quasi-judicial fashion, setting aside the president's concerns. This produces quite bizarre notions—for example, that it is proper for the position the executive takes in litigation to be determined, in effect, by essentially anonymous career attorneys rather than by politically accountable officials. For our purposes, however, it chiefly shows the disappearance of the Madisonian perspective, which assumed that a politically motivated and politically accountable executive was at the same time capable of good faith in enforcement of the laws.

Another, very common approach to squaring this circle is the attempt by executive branch lawyers to create their own rules governing the executive's dealing with acts of Congress. We did a lot of that in the Clinton years, when I served in various capacities in the Justice Department. We articulated principles about what the president should and should not do with signing statements, we came up with rules to determine when the executive could act on Attorney General Black's proviso and decline to enforce a statute, we told the president what he needed to consider in deciding whether he could deploy troops into hostilities in the absence of congressional authorization, and on and on. I think most of what we said made good sense, and I know we approached the issues in good faith. But the whole enterprise was fatally flawed, at least as a solution to the problem of how to compel the executive to respect Congress. If the law is not internalized, if it is not an ethic, any rules, including the rules the executive itself devises, are necessarily external—once again, obstacles or opportunities to be circumvented or used as necessary in the pursuit of the executive's own objectives. The externalization of the law cannot be cabined, and it controls how executive officials view their own rules, in the same way it controls their approach to Congress's.

It is only a short step (and probably an inevitable one) from this futile search for external constraints to the wholesale adoption by the executive of an entirely adversarial view of Congress. Such a view turns Madison's position in 1809 upside down: the purpose of statutory construction is not to ascertain what Congress willed so that the executive can enforce that will but, rather, to ensure the executive's discretion to do whatever it wishes, limited only by what it is politically feasible to claim. I believe that this effective repudiation of Justice Jackson's ideal that "the Executive be under the law" made by the legislature is visible in the endless invocation by executive branch lawyers of the so-called avoidance canon—the belief that statutes should be construed so as to avoid constitutional problems. In a world in which Madison's principle is an internalized ethic, the avoidance canon could serve as a means of avoiding the need to invoke Black's proviso, by giving as much scope to Congress's purposes as possible within our constitutional framework. In a world in which the laws are merely external, the avoidance canon functions as a means of denying any force to Congress's purposes without shouldering the burden of actually invoking Black's proviso and declaring a statutory provision unconstitutional. Where the law is no longer an ethic, it can only be a tool.

The consequences are serious. Think about Jackson's 1940 opinion on the deal with Britain involving warships for bases. Jackson actually invoked a form of the avoidance canon at one point in his opinion, reasoning that a statutory provision apparently requiring the president to obtain the concurrence of one of his military subordinates before disposing of military hardware could hardly have such a meaning in light of the chain of command that, as a constitutional matter, gives the civilian president plenary authority over the actions of uniformed personnel. The statutory scheme should be read, therefore, to vest in the president final authority over the issue, while structuring his decision-making process just as any sensible president would order it. A contemporary executive branch lawyer, in contrast, would be likely simply to invoke the president's power as commander in chief and his responsibility for national security and to announce that the statutes Jackson worried over would raise "grave constitutional problems" if construed to apply to the deal. Therefore, he or she would continue, the executive should construe the statutes not to constrain the executive's discretion to make and execute such a deal. In this scenario, the statutes (which Jackson found to have precisely the effect of partially invalidating the deal) would effectively be dead letters even as the executive claimed that it was applying them. The difference is not one of legal doctrine but one of fundamental vision.

If I am right in my claim that executive branch officers and lawyers bring to their tasks this change in the underlying understanding of their role, what is to be said and done? It is not clear to me that the change can be reversed. Cultural ideals can die—and perhaps Madison's vision is dead. A great deal of contemporary legal, political, and philosophical scholarship seems implicitly devoted to the proposition that law can only be a tool in anyone's hands. The patently political treatment of constitutional issues in many Supreme Court opinions reenforces that assumption in the most powerful manner, both in American political life at large and on the ground in law schools, where I and my colleagues teach those opinions to our students. Perhaps it is too late, but I choose not to accept that despairing conclusion. President Madison and Attorney General Black and President Roosevelt and Justice Jackson—if I read them rightly—are witnesses to the existence of a better way. Perhaps one part of a hopeful response to this change, one to which academics can contribute, is to remind ourselves, our students, and our political culture that the cynical view of the law as invariably a tool is not the only view that men and women of intelligence can hold. This might be seen as hero worship, but I am undeterred. Maybe some heroes and heroines are just what we need now.

If it is true, as Justice Jackson said—and I believe it is—that "men have discovered no technique for long preserving free government except that the Executive be under the law, and that the law be made by parliamentary deliberations," the law cannot become a mere tool without the idea of free government becoming a bitter joke. The struggle to find alternatives to the fashionable—and politically potent—reduction of law to a mere tool is not academic in the invidious sense: it is a struggle to maintain the possibility of free and decent government. If freedom and decency are to prevail, we must find a way for Jackson's and Madison's principle once again to be an ethic we share in our hearts.

NOTES

1. Letter from Thomas Jefferson to Thomas Ritchie, 25 December 1820, in 10 *The Writings of Thomas Jefferson, 1816–1826,* at 169, 171 (Paul Leicester Ford, ed., 1899).

2. 8 *The Writings of James Madison* 386–88 (Gaillard Hunt, ed., 1908).

3. On this affair, see Jefferson Powell, *Languages of Power,* at 230–39 (1991).

4. For the texts of Snyder's and Madison's letters, see ibid., at 253–54.

5. During the oral argument in the tapes case (United States v. Nixon, 418 U.S. 683 (1974)), President Nixon's lawyer was somewhat equivocal about whether Nixon would obey a negative ruling. The Court nevertheless decided the case against Nixon's claims, and a few hours after it announced the decision, the president publicly stated that he would obey the Court. For a discussion, see Larry Alexander and Frederick Schauer, "On Extrajudicial Constitutional Interpretation," 110 *Harv. L. Rev.* 1359, 1364–65 (1997).

6. 32 *Annals of the Congress of the United States* 1371 (Joseph Gales and William Seaton, ed., 1854ff.).

7. Myers v. United States, 272 U.S. 52, 295 (1926) (dissenting opinion).

8. Black's opinion is reported as "Memorial of Captain Meigs," 9 *Op. Att'y Gen.* 462 (1860).

9. Yoder, *The Priestly Kingdom: Social Ethics as Gospel,* at 97–98 (1985).

10. Sister Madeleva, *A Lost Language,* at 17 (1951).

11. See the exquisitely unskeptical discussion of the president's statutory powers to address South Carolina's secession in Black's November 1860 opinion entitled "Power of the President in Executing the Laws," 9 *Op. Att'y Gen.* 516.

12. Akerman's opinion is reported as "Civil-Service Commission," 13 *Op. Att'y Gen.* 516 (1871).

13. The quotations of Roosevelt and Taft's comment on Roosevelt's practice can be found in Taft, *Our Chief Magistrate and His Powers,* at xxii, xlviii (H. Jefferson Powell, ed., 2002).

14. Youngstown Sheet & Tube Co. v. Sawyer, 343 U.S. 579, 655, 634 (1952) (Jackson, J., concurring).

15. Id. at 647.

16. United States v. Curtis-Wright Export Corp., 299 U.S. 304, 320 (1936).

17. See "Acquisition of Naval and Air Bases in Exchange for Over-Age Destroyers," 39 *Op. Att'y Gen.* 484 (1940).

18. Caplan, *The Tenth Justice: The Solicitor General and the Rule of Law* (1987).

Law, Economics, and Torture

James Boyd White

It is common to observe that in the past decade or so there has been a massive transfer of wealth from ordinary people and the poor to the rich. But it is plain that there has been very little effective resistance to this transfer by the majority who are disadvantaged by it and who presumably constitute the ultimate power in a democracy. Why is this so?

This is the first question James Boyd White addresses in this essay.

The second question, seemingly unrelated, has to do with a deep change in the understanding of law and its practice, both in the courts, where judicial opinions now tend to be written in a dead and mechanical way, and in law schools, where there seems to be little interest in or excitement about what lawyers and judges actually do and, instead, a focus on questions of policy. Why has this change occurred and what does it mean?

The third question in a sense bridges the other two: why is it that there has been so little public outrage and outcry at the efforts by the administration to make the torture of suspects or captives a normal and legalized part of our government's business?

In this essay White's aim is to suggest at least preliminary answers to these questions, and to a fourth as well: What are we to do about the situation in which we find ourselves?

In our invitation to them as speakers at this conference Jeff and I encouraged the contributors to this volume to talk in whatever way seemed best to them, whether or not it happened to comport with usual academic styles of thought or expression. I here take advantage of our own invitation and talk a little differently from the way I usually do, about what I take our culture of politics and law to be like at the moment. What I say will necessarily be impressionistic and personal, and of course I do not ask you to accept any of it on my say-so.

Take these reflections, rather, as a question, which is how far your own experience, or your own thinking, is like or unlike my own. Perhaps I may say that, in the terms suggested by Cathleen Kaveny, I am speaking in something of a prophetic voice, not a casuistical one, and it is a fair question for you to ask whether this is justified and, if so, how.

As I think about the way things are changing under our feet, a series of phenomena come to my mind. Maybe they are connected, maybe not. That is one of my questions.

MAKING THE RICH RICHER

The first of these is the response—or more properly nonresponse—of the public and the media to the remarkable transfer of national wealth to the very rich that has taken place in our lives. I grew up under Eisenhower, when there was a 90 percent tax on incomes over one hundred thousand dollars (a million dollars in our terms) and a general sense that our country was committed to fundamental equality. This was perhaps in part the result of World War II, of which people at every economic level bore the cost, even unto death. It was clear to almost everyone that we were somehow all in this together. The sense of solidarity I mean was expressed both in Truman's desegregation of the military and in his proposed civil rights bill, and perhaps it underlies *Brown v. Board of Education* as well.

The transfer of wealth to a class of super-rich began modestly under Kennedy and has taken off in the past decade. It has been I think a deliberate goal of the Bush administration, but its roots are much deeper in our world than that. What concerns me is that in recent years, aside from a few harmless op-ed pieces, and a few more substantial articles in progressive journals, there has been little real concern about this transfer of wealth—certainly not the mass outrage one might have expected. I include law school faculties and students among those unconcerned.

The Consumer Dream and the Ideology of the Market

My question is this: why has this transfer not been instantly and unanimously resisted by the enormous majority of people at whose expense the rich are multiplying their wealth—a majority most of whom are not doing well economically, some of whom are doing very badly?

This is a matter of mass psychology, and of course I am no expert, but I sense here a feeling of helplessness in the face of overwhelming force. I think that the concentration of wealth is not in the eyes of most people a good thing; they feel rather that nothing can be done about it and that, in a world like this, one had better simply look to his or her own welfare, not large questions of law and democracy.

The rules of the game have somehow shifted over the past twenty years or so: it seems that one is not to expect equality, or fairness, or compassion, from our society or its government; one is not to expect decent social and medical services, or clean air, or a mature response to the immense problems of global warming; one is not to expect lawyers and judges to talk in an earnest and serious way about what justice requires. These things are not going to happen, so don't waste your energy complaining. It is a kind of learned helplessness.

Obviously I cannot wholly explain this shift, but one factor seems to me to lie in the way we have come to talk about the nature and purpose of our country, and of human life itself, which is largely in economic terms. For the society as a whole the dominant motive is assumed to be the powerful but empty desire for wealth, without regard to what good or evil that wealth might do; for the individual, felicity is defined largely in terms of ownership and consumption. The "American Dream" is no longer a dream of escape from totalitarian rule and lawless government, as it once was, but a dream of expansive, seemingly unlimited, getting what you want. Of course this way of talking has no place for democratic government—for that requires action, judgment, responsibility, not mere consumption.

This way of imagining life is not only an empty and trivializing image of human experience; it hides the crucial truth that what the consuming economy in fact creates is not just more opportunity for consumption but power, power in the form of wealth. And great wealth gives great power. As the government withdraws from the regulation of the economy, which it has been doing for decades now, its place is taken by private individuals or private organizations which have immense power over the lives of all of us.

The rhetoric supporting this movement speaks of government as the enemy, and of the market as freedom for us all. But the power that is created by the disparity of wealth is real power, and unlike governmental power, it is for the most part not shaped or guided by law and democracy. The owners and managers are not elected by the people, not subject to the

Constitution, not supposed—or sometimes even allowed—to be motivated by any ideal other than the acquisition of wealth and power, and usually not responsive to argument or complaint.[1]

This arrangement is implicitly—and sometimes explicitly—defended by the argument that this power actually is subject to the control of the people, not through government, but through what is called the discipline of the market, which, the argument runs, is both more efficient and fairer than regulation through law. But the market cannot be a substitute for democratic government: it has no place or role for any of the institutions through which government works, or for the kind of public deliberation, thought, and argument by which those institutions live; it works not by the principle of "one person, one vote" but by the very different principle of "one dollar, one vote"; and it simultaneously generates and obscures immense imbalances in wealth and power. The market contains no check on the drive to unlimited economic expansion, a drive that is proving to be suicidal, threatening the living planet upon which everything we are and do depends.

Those who argue for "getting the government off our backs" are really arguing for the transfer of power from a democratically responsible government to a regime without any democratic legitimacy at all, indeed without any governing rationality.

The consumer dream of our culture teaches us that we have no responsibility, no capacity for action, no right to demand meaning in our work and lives, and no obligation for the welfare of others. It induces the sense of learned helplessness I referred to earlier—which is exactly the opposite of the kind of vigorous independence and competence upon which democracy depends.

Advertising and Propaganda

One particularly strong feature of the culture of consumption is an immense and relentless campaign, so pervasive and so normalized as to have become invisible, to persuade the public to accept and act on its premises. I refer here to the world of consumer advertising, especially to its apotheosis in television. This kind of advertising persuades people not only to buy this or that item but more importantly, to accept and live by the whole infantile dream of the consumer economy. It is only in a narrow sense that advertisements compete with each other; in a deeper way they reinforce one another constantly.[2]

Even more disturbingly, this kind of advertising has a direct analogue in the way in which national politics proceeds, for it has become accepted that a political campaign is run like an advertising campaign—though a better word for this cultural form, given its connection with state power, would be *propaganda*.

Both propaganda and advertising are marked by the desire to manipulate others through the use of slogans and clichés and images, sound bites and buzzwords. As they become widespread—active and present in our minds and speech—both forms of speech tend to destroy in us the capacity for independent thought and expression upon which self-government depends.

One characteristic of both forms is that nothing is meant, everything is said for the moment, all on the assumption that the people who make up the audience have no memory, no capacity for critical thought. We are invited to join a world where thought is not possible.[3] In neither domain—the consumer economy or the world of politics and government—are we defined as responsible participants in a world of shared life and action. Rather, we are manipulated objects of an empire.

The Fact of Empire ☙

So here is my rather glum conclusion: My intuition is that the reason we do not rebel at the immense and unfair transfer of wealth, and all that is associated with it—from golden parachutes for failed CEOs to sixty-millon-dollar bonuses for successful investment bankers—is that in some sense we do not believe that we really have democracy at all any more, at least in the sense in which we once thought we did.[4] Democracy and its law are based on a vision of fundamental equality among human beings, and neither can survive in a world in which equality is systematically denied by such disparities of wealth and power. Under these conditions the best we can have is a series of contests among the powerful resolved by plebiscites.

I believe we have become to a large degree the subjects of an oligarchy, an internal empire. By *empire* here I do not mean just the cultural forces, strong as they are, that make up what Simone Weil calls an "empire of force," but an actual political reality in which unelected people rule much of our lives. Their object is to extract as much economic value as possible from the earth and the oceans and the air, and from the labor—and unemployment—of billions of people.

This empire has co-opted many of us—perhaps all of us—who might be its critics, because we to a large degree benefit, though in a relatively small way, by the same policies that enrich the super-rich. We eat at expensive restaurants, and take trips to Europe, and buy expensive suits. So do the reporters for the *Washington Post* and the *New York Times.* There is in our world almost no voice for the poor, which is perhaps a third of our nation. The *New York Times* does of course take positions of concern for the poor on its editorial pages. But its "Arts," "Style," "Escapes," and "Travel" sections, and the advertising in its Sunday magazine, all with one voice affirm the value of wealth and consumption and the world of radical inequality they create.

Democracy at Work

Having painted this distressing picture, I want to affirm that in my experience there is a remarkable force of another and opposed kind in American life—not much seen in the media or in the world of national politics—which I would call a natural readiness for self-government. We see it in local politics all the time, in elections for the school board, say, and in homeowner associations and other private groups. This is the world where we know how to create an organization—with president, vice president, treasurer, secretary—which is subject to bylaws and a statement of purpose, and whose meetings follow *Robert's Rules of Order.* We know how to live in the space it defines: how to hold meetings and reach decisions and live with them even when we disagree; how to define our common values and purposes and try to live by them.

But this capacity for self-government—perhaps our greatest national treasure—is simply not much visible either in the ways I see the nation described in the media or in the ways politicians and officials talk about it or in the way I see the national government functioning. Congress, for example, does not seem to work as I describe the school board working, in a real way, with real debates and real decisions: all too often it seems to be only an image or phantasm of itself, a pretense of government, in which almost nothing is ever said that anyone means. What one hears is almost always calculated and shaped, as a piece of advertising is shaped, by asking what will work with the audience one is simultaneously flattering and manipulating. This is sometimes even true of judicial opinions.

THE ABANDONMENT OF LAW

My second phenomenon—perhaps you perceive it too—is the experience of reading certain Supreme Court opinions which seem evidently written by clerks and not much rewritten by the justices.[5] These opinions seem to speak in no one's voice, without seriousness, without a sense of responsibility for what is done or said, as though deciding the case and explaining the decision were empty exercises.

The Courts and the Law Schools

Such opinions do not seem to me in any way to reflect, as I was taught an opinion should, a deep struggle to determine the meaning of the relevant legal authorities—and in the process to find one's own mind growing and learning—but rather express a largely unexamined judgment one way or the other as to the result of the case, often based on rather crude previous commitments of a political kind, which are not tested in the crucible of thought and argument.[6] This kind of formulaic jurisprudence does not expose the true reasons and thinking of the Court, and subject it to criticism; and it does not produce texts that can be read with the kind of care and attention we are used to giving texts in the law.

For a comparison, let me suggest you look through a volume of Supreme Court reports from forty or fifty years ago. The difference is striking: here we have distinctive voices, distinctive minds working seriously, responding to each other, trying to say the truth as they see it. Of course they are subject to frailty, as we all are, but at their best they are engaged in a process of self-education, and the education of the public as well. Just to list the names is to invoke a different world. (In 1962, for example, when I was in law school, the justices were Black, Frankfurter, Douglas, Clark, Warren, Harlan, Brennan, Stewart, and White. These are respectable people by any measure.)

I also see a turning away from the law in law schools themselves, which have in some ways become closer to "think tanks" or public policy institutes than the schools of professional training I once knew. In casebooks the cases are often reduced to paradigms meant to facilitate argument about theory, rather than seen, as they occur in practice, as complex challenges to the mind, in which law interacts with facts, facts with law, different laws with different laws, and all these things with our developing sense of justice. Rather, the main interest seems to be in questions of policy and theory abstracted from the life of the lawyer or judge.

I was taught that the central legal questions, for lawyer and judge alike, are these: What texts should count as authoritative, and why? What do they mean, and why? What weight should be given to the judgment a text reflects, and why? How in the light of all these things, and in the context of the present, should the case be decided? Of course lawyers will disagree on the merits of all these questions, but they will agree in affirming a world in which power is distributed, regulated, reviewed.

The tendency I mean is manifest perhaps particularly in what is called "law and economics," but not only there. It runs through the ways in which scholarship is evaluated and it shows up in our almost total silence about law teaching. When I went into law teaching it was with great doubt about whether I would ever write anything, but with great confidence that the teaching of law was itself an activity—an art with a meaning—that could occupy a mind and justify a life. I wonder if anyone thinks that today.

A system of policy critique of the kind that is at work in our law schools may make useful discoveries, but such a system cannot perform the functions of law itself. Neither economics nor sociology nor psychology nor any other field can address, let alone resolve, the distinctive legal questions about the identity and meaning of authoritative texts and about the degree of deference due the judgments of others.[7] Taking economics as my example—though the same point could be made about any other field—I would say: One cannot do law in the language of economics, or economics in the language of the law. To try to do either would be as ludicrous as trying to do science in the language of religion, or religion in the language of science.[8]

Cost-Benefit Analysis

My sense of what has been happening is well exemplified in two brief passages by Judge Richard A. Posner. In the first, discussed in another context by Jed Rubenfeld, Posner is writing in favor of what he calls "pragmatism," meaning the decision of legal cases by a judicial balancing of costs and benefits. The only reason for attending to prior legal texts, in his view, is that to disregard them would have social costs, and these costs should be taken into account by the person with power.

> The point is not that the judge has some kind of moral or even political duty to abide by constitutional or statutory text, or by precedent; that would be formalism. It is merely that continuity and restraint in the judicial function are important social goods, and any judge proposing to innovate must consider not only the benefits of the innovation but also the costs in injury to those goods.[9]

To me this misunderstands the nature of both law and democracy, including the obligation—moral, political, and legal—to respect the authority of legal texts and the fundamental principle of separation of powers. In the world called into being by this passage law would lose its essential meaning.

More recently, in a letter to the *New York Review of Books,* responding to a critical review by Professor David Cole of his book *Not A Suicide Pact,* Judge Posner said that Cole must realize that his civil libertarian principles "are not the product of 'text, tradition, and reason' since equally capable legal thinkers hold opposite views." Posner continues:

> This is possible because there is no consensus on what methodology to use to resolve constitutional disputes and because text, tradition, precedent, and reason so often tug in different directions. . . . Realism requires recognition that constitutional decision-making at the highest level (The US Supreme Court) in the most difficult cases is driven in the main by policy judgments based usually on just the kind of balancing that Cole deplores. Or pretends to deplore; for I imagine *au fond* the reason he dislikes the administration's counterterrorism measures is that he thinks they impose greater costs, in harm to civil liberties, than the benefits they confer in reducing the risk of further terrorist attacks. The rest is rhetoric.[10]

This passage adds to the misunderstanding expressed in the first. Together they represent with great clarity the state of affairs I am trying to define. Of course the meaning of the authoritative texts of the law is often highly arguable in a range of cases. But that does not mean that we can dismiss them as useless, or that in the zone of disagreement we are free to apply whatever version of cost-benefit analysis, or other method or theory, happens to appeal to us. What Posner contemptuously dismisses as "rhetoric" is nothing less than the entire world of law: its structure of authority, its democratic basis, its creation of a constituted government based upon separation of powers. In its place he proposes a view that all that matters is power, a view in which not only is there no need to respect the opinion of another, there is no way in which this can be done.

Indeed there is something deeply incoherent in Posner's view, for how is the question to be answered, Whose calculation of costs and benefits is to count? Apparently the judge's; but the position that the judge occupies, and upon which Posner relies, does not reflect some present judgment of costs and benefits, but rests upon law in the sense in which I have been describing it: the democratic allocation of function to decide, within limits and subject to guidance and review. To say that some judgment of better and worse lies behind this legal structure—including the obligation to respect the judgments of others and to engage in good-faith legal debate when, as often, the meaning of the texts is arguable—is to say nothing at all.

What Law Can Be

I have a sense, then, that law itself is being eroded and transformed, just as I said earlier democracy is being eroded and transformed, and in both cases in the service of what I have called the empire. This fact has a tragic quality for me because the law by its nature should be a strong force of resistance to the principles of empire, a strong force of defense for democracy.

For the law is built at its foundations upon the principle of separation of powers, not their merger into a single force. In this, it is the opposite of empire. In our law every institutional actor must acknowledge and respect judgments made by others: the legislature must respect the judgments expressed in the constitution, the courts the judgments of the legislature, lower courts the judgment of higher courts, and so on. This means that the lawyer never addresses a person who has all the power. Both lawyer and judge constantly turn to other texts, composed by other persons, who have made judgments on the questions in the case which they are bound to respect.

It is crucial that the texts that our law invokes as authoritative, and to which the judges and lawyers pay respect or deference, all rest in some way upon the authority of democratic institutions. They are statutes passed by elected legislatures, or opinions issued by judges appointed by elected governors, or contracts written by the parties themselves, and so on. In affirming the value and validity of its own processes the law is thus always affirming democracy.[11]

The law is not a closed system, operating behind locked doors, but is connected in hundreds of ways to our democratic culture. To disregard this structure of authority and to replace it with a theory—whether philosophical, political, or economic in kind—is to erode our democracy at the root. For in the world of theory the rightness of the result depends upon its congruence with the theory in question, necessarily a theory without any basis in democratic authority but resting solely upon the commitments of those who are persuaded by it: the community of believers.

At the simplest level, what the law teaches is that we live in a world in which different people can have different, decent, and reasonable views; that we need a way to respect these views and judge among them fairly, that is, openly and honestly; that the world constructed by the law is one that distributes the power to decide such questions differentially to various public and private agents—so that even if we lose this case, or this issue, we have a residue of autonomy and freedom; and that, all this being true, we cannot fairly and rightly decide disputes by reference to theory, or to our own estimate of costs and benefits, or to the sorts of clichés and buzzwords and slogans that characterize much political talk. The law, at its best, improves our thought and our language. What has been happening to law, however, is that it is becoming an instrument of empire, and in the process losing its essential character.

TORTURE

My third phenomenon is the public response—or once more, the nonresponse—to the recent efforts of the administration to legalize what any sensible person would call torture—certainly if he or she were subjected to it—and the related effort to remove from all protections of the law a class of human beings selected by officials as "enemy combatants." Of course, there are honorable exceptions in the bar and in the public world, but there has not been what there should have been, a universal public outcry of a sort that would have driven the beast of torture off the field of our shared life.

This has haunted me more than anything else. Not so much because American soldiers have on occasion beaten, abused, tortured, and killed people they have captured. Those are terrible things, but war always includes them, just as it includes the incineration of little children, the rape of women, the purposive destruction of life itself. What is new here are the efforts to make torture part of the approved business of government, claiming for it the authority of law, and to establish the existence of a class of persons under the control of the government who are completely beyond any protection of law.

To connect this image with what I said about the state of legal thinking, I think we hear an all-too-familiar voice in the famous "torture memorandum" composed by Jay Bybee, now a federal judge:[12] it is written in mechanical and conclusory terms, as though a routine legal analysis of a rather empty kind could simply be used without thought and without question to justify human torture. There is no sense of a person in the prose, no one making judgments for which he is responsible. It troubles me to think, as I do, that this is a voice for which we who teach in law schools may be especially responsible.

The Propaganda of Torture

Part of the reason for our supine lack of response is our habituation to the sort of advertising and propaganda I have mentioned, for which the fears generated by the events of 9/11, and unceasingly stimulated since, provide strong nourishment. According to this thin and inadequate form of thinking, there is an ineradicable line between "us"—the good people of America under unjustified and aggressive threat—and "them," those others whose torture or "severe interrogation" is in question. Why should we care about what happens to them? They are the enemy, or at least irredeemably "other."

But of course they are not these things in fact: they are fellow human beings, some of them citizens of our country. They are selected for torture or abuse not by some foolproof process that will identify without error the "bad," whoever they are, but by who knows whom, acting on who knows what information, and with who knows what motives, with all this happening behind a deliberate screen of secrecy.

The central principle of democratic government is official responsibility, and here that is entirely erased. No one stands up as the one who has made the crucial decisions; no one in the public even knows that most of them have been made.

The fate of Guantanamo prisoners who were returned to their own countries is instructive. Almost all of them were released after investigation by their home governments, it turning out that many of them had been seized without any justification at all by persons seeking a bounty offered for the identification of "terrorists." Only a handful were tried in their home countries and at the time of this writing none of those had been convicted of any crime.[13]

Even if someone is in fact an "enemy," that of course does not justify his torture. Maybe he has to be killed, if he is shooting at you, but when captured, he should be treated humanely and with dignity, as we hope our soldiers will be treated when they are captured.

The "Need for Information"

It is sometimes argued that torture is justified by the need for "information." This argument works by another specious form of thought, which, when added to the first, seeks to establish a sense of necessity that will remove torture from the moral sphere almost completely. The form of thought I mean is captured in this question, repeated endlessly in the media and even in classrooms: if you knew that there was an atom bomb somewhere downtown with a timer ticking wouldn't you torture the people who knew about it to make them tell you where it was, or how to disarm it?

The question seems to pose a serious problem of moral thought, but, like many such hypotheticals, it is not real. You can never "know" there is an atom bomb, or a timer ticking; and you can never "know" that you have one of the "people who know about it." The facts assumed by the hypothetical never exist in any individual case. And even if there were one such case that would do nothing to justify the hundreds or thousands or tens of thousands of cases in which we have engaged in torture. The question about the ticking bomb invites us to live in a false world—the world ultimately of advertising and propaganda—not the real world.

The unreal hypothetical is used not to support the proposition that it might possibly support, namely, that in a wildly rare and dramatic case one would use torture, but something very different, namely, that torture itself should be evaluated simply by weighing the costs and benefits of the practice. "You believe in torture in one case in a million," we are being told, "therefore you can have no objection to our regular use of torture as an instrument of policy, under whatever procedures and standards we choose."

The logic of cost-benefit analysis is epitomized in the ticking-bomb case, but it runs far more widely and deeply in our culture than that hypothetical. All of the practices of abuse and inhumanity rest upon the same claim, that "national security" or the "safety of the nation" require it, an invocation of "cost-benefit analysis" that typically reflects no analysis whatever.

Irrationality

Despite its claims to a high degree of rationality, the kind of cost-benefit analysis that is so often offered as an alternative to legal thought in fact tends not to the rational but to the irrational.[14] It is a long-standing truism in the critique of "balancing," for example, that the outcome is often determined by the way in which the interests are articulated. Are we to define the question as the "safety of the nation" versus "this person's desire to keep this piece of information to himself"? Or as "the value of this piece of information" versus "our system of government under law"? The outcome-shaping characterization is of course often driven by desire, perhaps unconscious desire, for a certain result. In this sense the designation of costs and benefits, seemingly so rational, is often in the end not that at all.

And who is to quantify the danger that terrorism presents? The incantation of the phrase "national security" is offered as a universal acid that will erase everything except the fear that it stimulates. This talk about overwhelming necessity fails to address the obvious questions—obvious to a lawyer, that is: Who shall determine whether such a necessity exists? Under what procedures and standards? Subject to what review? These are the core questions of legal thought, and they are by this logic erased. For to take those questions seriously would be to invoke the whole apparatus of law as we know it. This cannot be allowed to happen, if one agrees that the importance of national security—as defined by whom?—is of infinite importance, because it would limit the power of the government to "protect us."

It cannot be allowed for another reason, I think: namely, that torture cannot in the end be legalized. It cannot bear the light of day, but must go on behind locked doors in unmarked buildings, in mysterious and unknown places reached by darkened airplanes, and carried out by anonymous interrogators and their anonymous assistants. The cost-benefit analysis must not include, because it cannot do so, the reality of the torture itself, the evil it does to the tortured and to the torturers alike.

The corrosive effect of "cost-benefit analysis" here is even worse than I have said. The question presented by the ticking-bomb case is whether the "known" existence of the ticking bomb would justify torture. But of course such a bomb may in fact exist though unsuspected by us; if so, it presents exactly the same real-world danger as if it were known; does that not justify the use of what is euphemistically called "extreme measures" to find out? Indeed anyone may know something that is of comparable value, perhaps without even knowing how important it is. The true need for information is just as great in those cases as in the ticking-bomb case itself. To think in terms of a single value that trumps all others, here "national security," is a form not of rationality but irrationality, ultimately a kind of insanity.[15]

The logic at work here leads to universal spying, universal wiretapping, universal torture, limited only by whatever costs are perceived by the perpetrator—or, more accurately, by the superior officer who in the comfort of his or her own office orders the perpetrator to torture. And this line of thinking not only justifies torture; it would justify anything. It erases not only protective legal rules, but the inherent protections of legal thought itself.

Once you start on a process of interest balancing in which one of the items is of potentially infinite value you have committed yourself to an impossible world of paranoia, not law—a world like the world of human slavery—in which one value cancels all others, in which appetite, as Shakespeare says, becomes a universal wolf and at last eats up itself.[16]

Democracy and Empire

The spring from which I think all these evils flow, including our incapacity to resist them, is the fact that at some level we know that we in this country are running an empire—an external one as well as the internal one I described earlier. And we know, I think rightly, that it is not possible to run an empire on the assumptions and aspirations of democracy under law. The very idea and existence of the empire depends upon a line between "us" and "them"—we, the rulers who have the power, and they, including our own citizens, the ruled, who are subject to it. In the eyes of the empire the ordinary people of this country have no different status from foreign nationals: all are subject to the same imperial regime. Our nation is on its way to becoming a third-world country politically as well as economically.

But the fact that we have become an imperial nation, internally and externally, is something no one can bear to admit, for it contradicts our deepest principles. It is I think at bottom our need to deny this fact that makes us so ready to submit ourselves and our judgments to slogans, clichés, and falsehoods—to live in the false world of advertising and propaganda.

This perception about empire, if I am right, connects my three themes: the concentration of wealth in the hands of the few, the transformations in what we mean by law, and the acceptance of torture. The antidemocratic principles necessary to the functioning of the empire with respect to the outer world also become the principles by which it functions internally, and if these are inconsistent with law, we are implicitly told or shown, law itself must change its character. To try to be democratic at home and function as an empire abroad would make a mockery of the principles of equality and justice under law that are essential to what we mean by democracy. An empire by its nature denies the fundamental principle of human equality and requires dominance and subjugation, wherever it reaches.

Although this is not often said explicitly, I think that in both its forms the subjugating power of the empire is supported by the same implicit argument, namely, that the simple fact of immense power imbalance not only justifies empire but requires it. As a nation we are so powerful, the argument runs, that we are simply not subject to the constraints of law and justice; likewise the rich and the super-rich—individuals and corporations alike—are so powerful that we cannot imagine demanding fairness from them or insisting upon equality with them. In both cases the fact of gross disparity overwhelms the hope of equality by declaring it impossible.

This is a modern version of a very old argument, seen (and rejected) in both Plato and Thucydides, namely, that justice is a proper topic of thought and argument only among equals. Where there is disparity of power those who have it will do what they want, the Athenians tell their victims in the famous Melian Dialogue; the rest must submit or die, and there is no point in pretending otherwise. The Athenians in this way seek to justify their refusal to recognize any constraint upon their power to kill and enslave all those who have rebelled against them. They claim to be beyond the reach of justice or its language.

I see in our own empire a similar claim—externally, on behalf of the nation with respect to other nations; internally, on behalf of the rich with respect to the people. The very fact of power of this scale and magnitude is implicitly said to make law and democracy impossible; and, as I have been arguing in this essay, we tend to believe the claim, without quite knowing that we do so.

In this context what Thucydides himself shows and says is of real interest. He demonstrates that the world of city-states in fifth-century Greece is regulated by a genuine international law, seen not as the command of some supranational sovereign but as the product of convention and agreement among the relevant states. He shows us how this system works in a real way, without any sovereign power; how it can be destroyed by a state (Athens) that has amassed so much power that it believes it can disregard the law and justice itself; and how this destruction leads eventually to the destruction of the superpower in question—which without law and justice cannot think rationally or sensibly about its own character, its own interest, even its own ambitions.[17]

As Thucydides tells the story it is a true tragedy, for Athens has no real alternative. The international legal system of that day presumed the equality of the states, which the power of Athens itself destroyed. For us, however, there is a solution, for in the intervening centuries humanity has invented the rule of law—equality under law, equality as an achievement of law. Instead of claiming immunity to law, the strong in our world should make every effort to affirm their allegiance to law, and to the fundamental equality that law and democracy together assert. To make the affirmation meaningful, they should accede to law especially where they have the economic or military power to repudiate it. For it is ultimately upon law and justice—both among nations and within our nation—that our strength, our very identity, depends.

This history teaches us that where there are immense imbalances of power the powerful should not reject with contempt the claims of law and justice, as the Athenians do, but quite the reverse. It is precisely at the point where one nation or group has the power to disregard such claims that it is most important, for the powerful themselves and for the rest of the world, that they cheerfully submit to them. In the end, it is not just the weak who need the rule of law and the claims of justice; all of us do.

NOTES

1. For discussion of the debate at the American Law Institute on corporate purposes in the 1980s, see my "How Should We Talk about Corporations?" in *From Expectation to Experience* 111–23 (2001).

2. It is worse even than that. As I was preparing this essay, I saw references in the newspaper to the fact, if it is a fact, that virtually all the ads in the broadcast of the Super Bowl contained violence against human beings. To connect this theme with my next, the torture of human beings, I am told that the number of incidents of torture on mainline television programs has escalated enormously since our government began its campaign to legalize torture.

3. Here I think of President Bush's to me astonishing remark when he was challenged about Guantanamo on a trip to Europe. He said that "he would like to close the camp and put the prisoners on trial"—as though there were some other person, say the president of the United States, who had created Guantanamo in the first place and was now keeping him from closing it (*New York Times,* 8 May 2006, A17). A similar effect is achieved by the arguments of government lawyers that such practices as the repeated suffocation known as "waterboarding," electrical shocks, deafening noise, sleep deprivation, threatened attack with dogs on naked prisoners, and so on are not "torture" but only "cruel, inhuman, and degrading," which enables

them to say, with all apparent sincerity, and as if we could possibly believe such a thing, that they are opposed to torture too.

4. I think here of the response of the public and the media to the 2000 election and the Supreme Court case *Bush v. Gore.* Whatever one's view of the merits of the election and of the judicial case, there was at stake here the integrity of the electoral process itself, raising the question whether, and in what sense, we live in a democracy. I would have thought nothing would have engendered more alarm and criticism and conversation than such a crisis, especially among lawyers. (Compare the popular resistance seen recently in Mexico to a challenged national election.) But we seemed simply to accept what we were told, as if it did not matter much to us. I include most law schools and law teachers in that "we." Of course there were some articles on the subject, but I hardly heard the matter discussed, and certainly not as an important matter on which we as lawyers and law teachers had a special responsibility to speak. Why was this? Was it because in a deep sense we did not think we had a democracy any longer?

5. I should say that I do not include all opinions or all justices in this criticism. Justice Souter in particular seems to me to adhere to high standards of legal thinking and judging. Likewise, I do not mean to criticize the clerks by what I say: they are not deciding the cases and cannot be expected to explain with any authenticity why someone else is doing so. All they can do is what they do, which is to produce a set of canned arguments, like those in a typical law review note, in such a way as to tilt the balance in the direction their justice has ordered.

6. For one example, see the opinion of the Court in *Free Speech Coalition v. United States* (535 U.S. 234 (2002)), discussed in my *Living Speech: Resisting the Empire of Force* 143–60 (2006). This opinion, by Justice Kennedy, seems to me very poor; but some of his other work is distinguished, especially the joint opinion in *Planned Parenthood v. Casey* (505 U.S. 833 (1992)), analyzed in my *Acts of Hope: Creating Authority in Literature, Law, and Politics* 153–86 (1994). I would also include the bombastic and bullying tone of some opinions, full of self-certain contempt for those who think differently. Both kinds of opinions seem to me to move in the direction of abandoning a central principle of law, the principle of responsibility.

7. My colleague Philip Soper has built a whole ethical theory on what he has learned from the law's practices of deference. See his *An Ethics of Deference* (2002).

8. Not to say that there is no place for economics, or other disciplines, in the law. Of course there is, whenever the discipline has something to teach the law, which is very often indeed, from the use of expert testimony on questions of engineering, for example, or matters of historical fact, to the way in which psychology can illuminate anti-social conduct or the nature of insanity, to the way in which sociology can demonstrate the existence of social conditions that call for our response. But in no case can the language of the external discipline substitute for that of the law; it must be translated into it, an activity that requires its own complex art.

What economics should do is to accept and welcome its place as one language among many, one way of thinking among many, each of which has its own contribution to make. A central task in addressing any serious problem is that of assessing the resources and limits of each available method. In the law, it is the law that has this task, just as in history, it is history, in psychology, psychology, and so on. The problem of economics as practiced in law schools is in this sense a problem of writing and translation. For elaboration of this point, see my *Justice as Translation* 76–79 (1990).

9. Richard A. Posner, "Pragmatism versus Purposivism in First Amendment Analysis," 54 *Stanford Law Review* 737, 739 (2002). See Rubenfeld's response in id. at 753.

10. Richard A Posner, letter to the editor, *New York Review of Books,* 11 January 2007, 63.

11. The law is a system of thought and language that is open to others—in principle to all others—and is in this way as well deeply democratic in nature. In any legal case a whole field of knowledge and expertise may become relevant, from engineering to sociology or psychology to history or medicine. The law is committed to learning what it can from these systems of knowledge. Likewise, especially under our jury system, our law has a commitment to the validity and value of ordinary language, the language of the citizen as such, for it must always be ready to be translated into that language, particularly in jury instructions and in closing arguments. The awareness that at some time the law will have to make sense to ordinary people is a discipline that erodes what might otherwise be the hermetically sealed overconfidence in the specialized language of the law and undermines the tendency to professional hierarchy.

12. Jay S. Bybee, Memorandum for Alberto R. Gonzales, Counsel to the President, Re: Standards of Conduct for Interrogation under 18 U.S.C. Sections 2340–2340A, 1 August 2002, in Mark Danner, *Torture and Truth: America, Abu Graib, and the War on Terror* (2004). For a fine analysis of the legal issues addressed, and not addressed, in this memorandum, see Jose Alvarez, "Torturing the Law," 37 *Case Western Reserve Journal of International Law* 175 (2006).

13. See the Associated Press story by Andrew O. Skelsky in the *Detroit Free Press,* 16 December 2006, 6A.

14. In this context I would like to call attention to one of the most systematic and extensive efforts to use cost-benefit analysis to decide what to do about a social problem, namely, the *Report of the Commission on the Third London Airport* (1971). The question at issue was where the third major airport near London should be located, and the matter was subject to exhaustive analysis of social costs and benefits. To the extent possible these were determined not by fiat but by market transactions, which were used to establish the cost of travel time to the West End, the value of green spaces to a local community, and so on. The Commission concluded that the airport should be located in the only green area between London and Birmingham. This result depended, as the dissenter pointed out, upon a particular calculation of the value of travel time, which if modified only slightly would have sent the airport to estuary lands east of London.

So which calculation was right? And how do you determine the value of green land to a neighboring community or of a Norman church to be destroyed by the bulldozers? The study was defective in another way, the dissent argued, for it failed entirely to address the social benefits of locating the airport to the east that would arise from investment and expenditure in this relatively poor area, and contribute at least in some measure to the righting of the imbalance between East London and West London. What the majority said in response amounted to an expression of fear, that the longer travel time to the eastern location might lead American travel agents to skip England altogether and pour their customers, and their money, into Germany or France—a fear that was not given a number, as could not rationally have been done. The final fillip is that it was finally decided that there was no need for such an airport at all. (Actually in recent years the airport at Stansted, one of the original candidates, has been more widely used, mainly for European travel.)

In the context of what faces us today, this kind of analysis may lead, as perhaps it has, not only to conduct that is immoral and wrong, as in the torture carried out by our government or with its consent, but to conduct that actually has the opposite of the intended effect, as our torture and abuse may indeed also have done. All this is done in the name of national security, but it may well be that our lawlessness is making us less secure—as well as having the "social cost" of turning us into a nation that tortures. (Unless the real reason for the program of torture is not to get information at all, but to define us as a lawless and torturing nation in the hopes that this will make people fear us.)

15. *Dennis v. United States* (341 U.S. 494 (1951)) shows this process at work, as does *Barenblatt v. United States* (360 U.S. 109 (1959)).

16. I mention slavery because something similar is at work in the logic of the torture cases, including a repudiation of the essential principle that our law is neutral as to persons. We now have a class of persons who are not persons under the law, without a right to lawyers, judges, or appearances in court, without a right to any regular proceeding, presided over by a neutral judge, in which they can see and question the evidence against them. They may be tortured or killed, in the government's view, without any recourse other than that which happens to be afforded, or not, by the administration in its mercy. This is an image of power that is profoundly imperial, restoring at a stroke a vision of a king beyond law that precedes the Magna Carta, a vision that may have no formal antecedents in European or American history except those of the totalitarian states of the twentieth century. These people are "enemy combatants" because some unnamed person, on the basis of unrevealed evidence or rumor, has decided they are. They are the juridical equivalent of slaves, but without even the few protections granted by the law of Mississippi or Alabama in the early nineteenth century.

17. For fuller discussion, see my *When Words Lose Their Meaning* 59–92 (1984).

Contributors

Martin Böhmer, Dean of the Law School of the Universidad de San Andres, Buenos Aires, Argentina

M. Cathleen Kaveny, John P. Murphy Foundation Professor of Law and Professor of Theology, University of Notre Dame

Howard Lesnick, Jefferson Fordham Professor of Law, University of Pennsylvania

The Honorable John T. Noonan Jr., Ninth Circuit Court of Appeals

H. Jefferson Powell, Professor of Law, Duke University

Jedediah Purdy, Professor of Law, Duke University

Jed Rubenfeld, Robert R. Slaughter Professor of Law, Yale University

A.W. Brian Simpson, Charles F. and Edith J. Clyne Professor of Law, University of Michigan

Barry Sullivan, Jenner & Block LLP, Chicago

Joseph Vining, Hutchins Professor of Law, University of Michigan

Robin West, Professor of Law, Georgetown University

James Boyd White, Hart Wright Professor of Law emeritus and Professor of English emeritus, University of Michigan